Beyond Chicken Soup

A Collection of Contemporary and Traditional Food Favorites

Jewish Home Auxiliary
Rochester, New York

B E Y O N D C H I C K E N S O U P

We want to thank everyone who made **Beyond Chicken Soup** possible. The contributors, cooks, and tasters set the stage. Our dedicated steering committee and copy writers, all volunteers, with support from the Jewish Home staff, devoted countless hours to compile a cookbook that will warrant applause for your efforts. A special thank you to our families for their patience and help.

Throughout **Beyond Chicken Soup** you will find many helpful hints to incorporate into your cooking repertoire. Suggested variations enable you to adapt recipes to your own taste. You can tell at a glance if a recipe needs extra time for marinating or chilling, or if a special pan is required. Our explicit instructions take the guesswork out of knowing when a recipe is done. Ingredients stand out in the directions; all ingredients are kosher. Following Jewish dietary laws, recipes are designated dairy, meat, or Parve (neutral). Recipes have been designated Parve if cheese or other dairy products are listed as optional ingredients. We've done all this to make **Beyond Chicken Soup** a book you will reach for often.

Enjoy,

Annette L. Shapiro   *Lois Mae E. Kuh*

Copyright © 1996
Jewish Home Auxiliary, Rochester, New York
Library of Congress Catalog Card Number: 96-075097
ISBN 0-9651374-0-6
First Printing 1996   10,000 copies

Printed in the USA by
WIMMER
The Wimmer Companies, Inc.
Memphis

WHO WE ARE

The Jewish Home of Rochester

The spirit of the Jewish Home of Rochester is embodied in our nursing facility and our adult day health services building, the Atkin Center, in Rochester, New York. This modern facility affirms the tradition of quality care for the aging that began in 1920, when the first Jewish Home of Rochester was founded by a group of local women in a frame house that could only accommodate 10 residents. Since then, the Home has outgrown two facilities, opening its present home in 1985. The Summit at Brighton retirement community and expanded geriatric medical services are planned for the near future as we continue to grow and to meet the changing needs of our Jewish community.

Our mission is to improve the health, well-being, and quality of life of our Jewish community's elderly, as well as that of our general community, being mindful of the values implicit in our heritage. From its humble beginnings as a haven for those in need, to today's state-of-the-art health-care facility serving 362 residents and 175 adult day participants, the Home has sustained an unwavering commitment to provide seniors with a fulfilling, quality lifestyle while meeting their special needs.

The Jewish Home Auxiliary

Since 1920, the Jewish Home Auxiliary has been a major component of the Jewish Home of Rochester, serving the Home in whatever capacity was needed. In its early years the Auxiliary was the Home's primary source of volunteers. Called the Daughter's Club, this 300-member group performed care giving and rehabilitative services for residents.

Today, more than ever, as the Jewish Home of Rochester faces new cost-consciousness in health care and managed care, the goal of the 1100-member Auxiliary is to enrich the lives of residents through service projects and the funding of special programs. The proceeds from **Beyond Chicken Soup** go toward these endeavors.

Chicken Soup. Its appeal is universal. No matter where it is cooked, no matter what goes into the pot – it could be ginger and shredded lettuce, lemon and mint, even lily buds and cloud ears – it is still called chicken soup. However, the most satisfying, the most fulfilling, is the recipe our forebears brought with them to America. It is the recipe that is served to celebrate the Sabbath and every other special day. It is Jewish chicken soup. . . THE chicken soup!

It is a magic potion that delights the senses, an elixir that gratifies hunger. Its curative powers have been extolled by Maimonides, the Mayo clinic and every mother who has had a child with the sniffles. We could not have grown up without it. And, without chicken soup there would be no need for matzoh balls or kreplach, and what a pity that would be!

Our Jewish culinary tradition goes far beyond chicken soup. Jews have lived in many lands, and have spoken many languages. In every country recipes were borrowed and adapted. This includes America's current emphasis on light, healthy ingredients and time-saving cooking methods.

This is what **Beyond Chicken Soup** is all about.

Beyond Chicken Soup takes you on a culinary adventure beyond the time-honored classics of our Jewish heritage. Don't be surprised to find a contemporary version alongside a traditional dish whose roots go back to biblical times. Since our shelves are now laden with ingredients with strange names and exciting tastes, we have included recipes that evoke exotic images. Clever cooks contributed recipes that turn fat-laden favorites into heart-healthy alternatives every bit as good as the originals. Busy schedules demand "quick and easy" recipes that take advantage of new convenience foods and new tools for preparation. And, we have not forgotten the extravagant recipes reserved for special occasions and indulgences. All these and more await you in the pages ahead.

The 350 recipes in this book are all winners! They were selected from over 1,300 recipes submitted from near and far. Every one was tested time and time again. Our criteria: great taste and appearance, clear directions, and, of course, the ready availability of the kosher ingredients.

We hope every recipe you use from this cookbook brings you lavish praise from family and friends. Unvoiced, but sincere none-the-less, is the praise that will be directed your way from the 362 residents of the Jewish Home of Rochester. **Beyond Chicken Soup** benefits them, too. The Auxiliary

INTRODUCTION

of the Jewish Home supports a wide variety of programs designed to help the residents preserve individual dignity, promote self-worth, continue old interests and stimulate new ones. That's the real reason ***Beyond Chicken Soup*** came into being. That's why so many volunteers of the Auxiliary have devoted so many hours to its realization. The book you are holding is the result. Use it in good health.

BENEFACTORS

The Jewish Home Auxiliary acknowledges the generosity of the following friends:

WEGMANS

Etta K. Atkin	Eva Kaufman Family
Miriam Atkin	Fran and Michael C. Kaufman
Lil Atkins	Kessler Group, Inc.
Janice S. Birnbaum	Fanny Kessler and Family
Donna and Bruce Cohen	Carol and Wilfred Kolko
Shaney and Art Cohen	William and Mildred Levine
Louise and Henry Epstein	Jean and Ruben Natapow
Dolly and Harold Fishman	Selkowitz, Inc.
Audrey and Burt Gordon	Martin and Barbara Slater
Sally Calderon Family	Eli and Mildred Sokol

S TEERING C OMMITTEE

H O L I D A Y / F O O D   C O N N E C T I O N

The dining table is the center of the family, particularly on the Sabbath and the many Jewish holidays. At holiday time, there is a great deal of discussion of food and preparation of the various dishes. It is a time when family and friends come from near and far. Mealtime is a time of sharing events and of breaking bread.

The **Sabbath** is considered the most sacred day of the Jewish year, thus each week brings ultimate sanctity into the Jewish home. While any festive meal is appropriate for the Sabbath, each community developed its own customs concerning traditional Sabbath foods. For some communities, fish was considered a Sabbath delicacy, e.g., Cayman Island Fillets, page 144. The two required foods for the Sabbath are Challah and wine. Traditionally, two loaves of Challah are placed on the table, e.g., Challah, page 77. Wine is necessary for the kiddush, or sanctification, which occurs at the beginning of every sacred Jewish event.

Apples and honey are the only ritual foods associated with **Rosh Hashanah**, the Jewish New Year. They are accompanied with the words: "May it be God's will to renew for us a good and sweet New Year," e.g., I Love You Honey Cake, page 240.

Once **Yom Kippur**, the holiest day of the Jewish religious calendar, begins, no food is consumed. Some suggest, in order to observe the fast properly, one should consume a heavy, sumptuous meal beforehand. Others believe that a light meal enables one to fast more comfortably. In either case, fish is appropriate for breaking the fast, e.g., Gefilte Fish Mold, page 12.

Not what, but where, one eats is the concern of **Sukkot**, the harvest festival of thanksgiving. One dines in a sukkah, an outdoor, temporary structure decorated with colorful fall fruits and vegetables, with a roof of branches through which the sky can be seen. Traditionally, stuffed cabbage, e.g., Stuffed Cabbage Rolls, page 114, and meals featuring fruits and vegetables, e.g., Glazed Carrots and Apples, page 169, are served.

Oil is the operative word for **Chanukah**, the Festival of Lights. The well known potato latkes, or little cakes, go back to the biblical book of 2 Samuel, e.g., Potato Latkes, page 19. Chocolate coins are also a popular treat for Chanukah. The coin is significant because one of the first acts of the victors of the Chanukah story, the Maccabee family, was to coin their own money as a sign of their political independence.

Purim is the celebration of good over evil. Hamantashen, e.g., Raisin Hamantashen, page 217, are the most beloved Purim delicacies. The meaning of the word has long been debated. Some suggestions, beyond the "Haman's hat", are Haman's patches or Haman's pockets.

What one does not eat is usually the focus of **Passover**. All leavening is to be removed from one's dwelling place for this festival. The historical significance is the Exodus from Egypt. The "Seder" meal is served and eaten in a prescribed sequence as the story of the Exodus is told. Each family has its traditional favorite recipes that contain no flour or leavening agents, e.g., Passover Chiffon Cake, page 240.

Milchik! Why dairy foods are customary on **Shavuot**, the celebration of the spring harvest, is not truly known. The avoidance of meat probably goes back to a misunderstanding of a verse in the Bible where Mt. Sinai is referred to by a word that sounds like "cheese," therefore, dishes containing cheese are popular, e.g., Blintzes Supreme, page 93.

"L' Chaim," To Life.

T A B L E   O F   C O N T E N T S

D-Dairy
M-Meat
P-Parve

  Holiday

 Cornell Gourmet Club of Rochester

Beyond Chopped Liver

A P P E T I Z E R S

A P P E T I Z E R S

Chopped Liver

Meat • 2 cups

Meat grinder

. . . .

1 pound beef liver
3 tablespoons oil
3 medium-sized onions
  (divided)
2 hard-boiled eggs, sliced
2-3 slices of stale challah,
  soaked in water and
  squeezed almost dry
1 teaspoon mayonnaise
salt and pepper to taste
1 sprinkle paprika

1. Broil **liver** until juices run
   brown.
2. Heat **oil** in a skillet.
3. Sauté 2 sliced **onions** until
   lightly browned.
4. Alternately feed into grinder
   sautéed onions and liver.
5. Cut remaining onion into
   chunks.
6. Alternately, feed **eggs**, raw
   onion, and **challah** into grinder
7. Grind entire mixture again.
8. Add **mayonnaise**.
9. Add **salt** and **pepper**.
10. Place in a mold and refrigerate.
    Sprinkle with **paprika** for color.

Note:
A food processor can be used to
grind and blend ingredients.

I Can't Believe It's Not Chopped Liver

Meat • 2 cups

Cooking Time: 30 minutes
Chilling Time: 2 hours
3-quart covered saucepan

. . . .

2 cups water
1 cup lentils
2 bouillon cubes, chicken or
  vegetable
1 large onion, chopped
1 cup walnuts
salt and pepper to taste
parsley for garnish
cocktail rye bread
crisp raw vegetables

1. In **water**, cook **lentils** with
   bouillon cubes, covered, about
   30 minutes, or until tender. More
   water can be added if necessary.
   Drain.
2. Sauté **onion** until translucent.
3. In a food processor process
   lentils, onion, and **walnuts** until
   desired consistency. Season to
   taste with **salt** and **pepper**.
   Chill.
4. Serve mounded on a platter and
   garnish with chopped **parsley**.
   Surround with **bread** and/or
   vegetables.

Aunt Gussie's Famous Gefilte Fish

Parve • 24 to 36 small balls

Cooking Time: 2 hours
6 to 8-quart covered soup pot

BROTH

3 onions, sliced
2 carrots, sliced
1 teaspoon salt
2 teaspoons white pepper
bones of the fish
3 quarts water

1. Put **onions**, **carrots**, **salt**, **pepper**, and **fish bones** in pot. Add **water** to cover, plus at least one inch more.
2. Bring to a boil and simmer while preparing the fish.

FISH

1½ pounds pike, skinned and boned
1½ pounds fresh water whitefish, skinned and boned
1 large onion, grated
½ cup seltzer
1 teaspoon salt
1 teaspoon sugar
1 teaspoon white pepper
2 eggs
3 tablespoons matzoh meal (optional)

1. In a large wooden bowl, chop **fish** and **onion**.
2. Add **seltzer**, a little at a time. Add **salt**, **sugar**, and **pepper**.
3. Add **eggs**, one at a time. Keep chopping. This will take about one-half hour by hand.
4. Using a heaping tablespoon to measure, place fish on your wet hands, roll into a ball and drop into the boiling broth. Simmer, covered, for two hours.

Note:
1. If fish batter seems too loose, add **matzoh meal**. 2. Chopping may be done in a food processor, in several batches, then blended all together by hand.

Gefilte Fish Mold

Parve • Serves 4 to 6

Chilling Time: 4 hours
4-cup mold, greased

3 ounces lemon gelatin
½ cup boiling water
½ cup jelled broth from gefilte fish
¾ cup red horseradish
24 ounces gefilte fish balls

1. Dissolve **gelatin** in **boiling water**.
2. Add **fish broth** and **horseradish**. Mix well.
3. Place **fish** in prepared mold and pour gelatin mixture over fish.
4. Chill until firm.

Pacific Gefilte Fish

Parve • 18 gefilte fish ovals

Cooking Time: 3 hours
8-quart covered pot

FISH STOCK

. . . .

1 large onion, sliced
2 carrots, thickly sliced
3 stalks celery, thickly sliced
salt and pepper, to taste
3 quarts water
heads, skins, and bones of fish

1. Place **vegetables** for fish stock, **seasonings**, **water**, **heads**, **skins** and **bones** of **fish** into pot.
2. Cover and simmer 40 minutes. Strain stock and return it to pot.

FISH

. . . .

1 pound salmon, heads, skin and bones removed
1 pound pike, heads, skin and bones removed
1 pound filet of sole, or other mild white fish, heads, skin and bones removed
2 eggs (or 4 egg whites)
1 medium onion
1 stalk celery
1 medium parsnip, peeled
1 small carrot, peeled
½ cup matzoh meal
1½ teaspoons salt
½ teaspoon white pepper
1 tablespoon sugar
⅓ cup cold water, if needed

1. Using a food processor with metal blade attached, chop **fish** one pound at a time. Combine in a large bowl.
2. Beat **eggs** in food processor. Add **onion, celery, parsnip**, and **carrot** to eggs. Pulse until finely chopped.
3. Add **matzoh meal, spices,** and **sugar**. Pulse once or twice.
4. Add egg mixture to chopped fish. Mix. If mixture seems too stiff, gradually add about ⅓ cup of **water**. Refrigerate ½ hour.
5. Form fish mixture into ovals. Gently put fish ovals into simmering stock. Cover and simmer 1½ hours.

Note:
Wet hands to form ovals.

Making gefilte fish with my grandmother was not an exact science. She measured with a handful and a teacup. When it did not look like enough, she threw in more! One day about 10 years ago I took her handfuls and tea cups and measured them. So here is the recipe for my grandma's gefilte fish. I wish she was still able to make it with my mother and me today. Our holidays are not the same without her.

Tortilla Rolls

Dairy • 100 pieces

. . . .

10 soft 9-inch flour tortillas
24 ounces cream cheese,
    softened
Combination of the following
    finely chopped fillings to
    total 7 cups
chives
green olives
black olives
pimentos
mushrooms
water chestnuts
whole olives for garnish
scallions for garnish

Variation:
Fruited cream cheese is a
refreshing summertime filling.

1. Spread each **tortilla** with a thin
   layer of **cream cheese**.
2. Top with approximately ⅔ cup
   filling, leaving a 1 inch border.
   Roll into a tight roll. Place seam
   side down on cutting board.
3. Cut into ¾ inch slices. Turn
   slices onto side so spirals are
   visible.
4. Garnish with whole **olives** and
   scallions.

Note:
Can be prepared a day in advance,
covered with plastic wrap and
refrigerated.

Balsamic Marinated Mushrooms

Parve • 6 to 8 servings

Chilling Time: 3 hours
Large covered skillet

. . . .

1 pound small mushrooms
¼ cup balsamic vinegar
2 tablespoons olive oil
½ teaspoon crushed dried
    oregano
1 tablespoon chopped dried
    parsley
½ teaspoon minced garlic
½ teaspoon salt (optional)
½ teaspoon freshly ground
    pepper
parsley for garnish

1. Wash and trim **mushrooms**.
   Leave stems intact.
2. Place mushrooms in skillet.
   Cover with salted **water** and boil
   for 5 minutes. Drain.
3. Combine **vinegar, olive oil,
   oregano, parsley, garlic, salt**,
   and **pepper**. Add to mushrooms.
4. Place in a large jar, cover and
   refrigerate at least 3 hours, or
   overnight.
5. Drain. Garnish with **parsley**.

Company Caponata

Parve • 1½ quarts

Chilling Time: Overnight
Covered roasting pan

. . . .

1¾ pounds eggplant, cubed
  (peeling optional)
salt
⅔ cup olive oil (divided)
1 medium onion, chopped
2 cloves garlic, minced
1 cup thinly sliced celery
16 ounces tomato purée
½ cup water
½ teaspoon dried oregano
1 tablespoon fresh chopped
  basil
¼ teaspoon pepper
1¼ cups pitted black olives,
  halved
1¼ cups pimento stuffed olives,
  halved
2 tablespoons capers
1 tablespoon sugar
2 teaspoons red wine vinegar
2 tablespoons fresh parsley,
  chopped

1. Wash and dry **eggplant**.
2. Sprinkle with **salt**. Let stand 15
   minutes. Dry.
3. In a skillet, using half the **olive
   oil**, sauté half the eggplant,
   stirring often, until brown and
   tender.
4. Spoon into roasting pan.
5. Sauté remaining eggplant in
   remaining olive oil. Spoon into
   pan.
6. Sauté **onion, garlic**, and **celery**
   until onion is golden.
7. Transfer to pan. Add **tomato
   purée, water, oregano, basil,
   pepper**, and **olives**. Cover and
   simmer 30 minutes.
8. Add **capers, sugar, vinegar,
   and parsley**. Cover and simmer
   30 minutes more, or until
   eggplant is tender.
9. Cool, cover tightly and refrigerate overnight.

Note:
Can be frozen for up to six months.

Spinach Brownie

Dairy • 16 to 20 pieces.

Preheat oven to 350°
Cooking Time 30 to 35 minutes
13 x 9 x 2-inch pan, greased

. . . .

1 cup flour
1 teaspoon salt
1 teaspoon baking powder
2 eggs, beaten
1 cup milk
¼ cup butter, melted
½ medium onion, chopped
10 ounces frozen, chopped
  spinach thawed and drained
1 pound cheddar cheese,
  grated

1. Mix **flour, salt, baking powder,
   eggs, milk**, and **butter**.
2. Add **onion, spinach**, and
   cheese. Pour into prepared pan.
3. Bake.

Note:
Can be frozen. Defrost and bake for
10 minutes.

Yalangis (Grape Leaves Stuffed with Rice and Onion)

Parve • 50 yalangis

Cooking Time: 30 minutes
10-inch covered skillet

. . . .

4 large onions, chopped
4 tablespoons oil (divided)
1 cup rice, uncooked
1 teaspoon salt
¼ teaspoon pepper
2-3 tablespoons lemon juice
    (divided)
3 cups water (divided)
16 ounces grape leaves

1. Sauté **onions** in 2 tablespoons **oil** until lightly golden. Add **rice, salt, pepper**, one half of **lemon juice** and 2 cups of **water**. Cover and simmer for 10 minutes, or until liquid is absorbed.
2. Rinse **grape leaves**, remove stems, and spread each leaf flat, bottom side up. Place 1 tablespoon filling in center of each leaf and roll up. Tuck in sides.
3. Arrange seam side down in pan.
4. Combine remaining juice, oil, and water and pour over yalangis.
5. Simmer, partially covered, until grape leaves are soft.

Note:
Grape leaves can be purchased in jars or cans in specialty food shops, or tender, young, fresh grape leaves can be used. Fresh leaves should be precooked 2 minutes in boiling, salt water (1 teaspoon salt to 4 cups water).

Spicy Vegetable Dip

Parve • 1 cup

Chilling Time: Overnight

. . . .

1 cup mayonnaise
2 tablespoons grated onion
2 teaspoons tarragon vinegar
2 teaspoons chili sauce
2 teaspoons green onion or
    chives
⅛ teaspoon dried thyme
½ teaspoon curry powder
salt and pepper to taste
sliced raw vegetables

1. Mix **mayonnaise** thoroughly with **onion, vinegar, chili sauce, green onions**, or **chives, herbs**, and **spices**.
2. Serve with **vegetables**.

Note:
Refrigerating overnight allows flavors to blend.

Herbed Cheese Ball

Dairy • 3 cups   Chilling Time: 4 hours

. . . .

2 sticks unsalted butter
16 ounces cream cheese
2 large cloves garlic, minced
½ teaspoon dried basil
½ teaspoon dried marjoram
½ teaspoon dried chives
¼ teaspoon dried thyme
¼ teaspoon pepper
½ teaspoon salt
1 teaspoon dill weed
crackers
carrot and celery sticks

1. Whip **butter** and **cream cheese** together.
2. Add **herbs** and **spices**. Mix thoroughly.
3. Form into a ball. Refrigerate.
4. Serve with **crackers, carrot**, and **celery sticks**.

Note:
Preparing several hours in advance allows flavors to blend.

Chutney Cheese Spread

Dairy • 2 cups

. . . .

6 ounces cream cheese, softened
1 cup sharp cheddar cheese, grated
1 tablespoon dry vermouth or sherry
1½ teaspoons curry powder
8 ounces mango chutney
crackers or fresh vegetables
minced scallions for garnish (optional)

Variation:
Your favorite flavor of chutney can be used.

1. Mix **cheeses** together with a fork.
2. Add **vermouth** and **curry**. Mix until well blended.
3. Place on a piece of waxed paper and shape into a pie-shaped wedge or half-circle. Invert cheese onto a serving platter.
4. Spread with **chutney**.
5. Serve with **crackers** and/or **fresh vegetables**.
6. Garnish with **scallions**.

Curried Chicken Spread

Meat • 1½ cups

. . . .

1 cup cooked chicken, diced
1 thin slice of onion
1 teaspoon curry powder
salt to taste
½ cup mayonnaise
½ cup almonds, toasted
⅓ cup minced parsley

1. Put **chicken, onion, curry powder, salt,** and **mayonnaise** into a food processor. Process until almost smooth.
2. Add **toasted almonds**. Process until smooth.
3. Form into a ball and roll in **parsley**.

Note:
Preparing several hours in advance allows flavors to blend.

Roasted Red Pepper Hummus

Parve • 2 cups   2-cup bowl

. . . .

2 large garlic cloves
15 ounces chick peas, drained
⅓ cup sesame seed paste
⅓ cup fresh lemon juice
½ cup chopped sweet roasted
    red pepper from jar, drained
1 tablespoon olive oil
    (optional)
salt and pepper to taste
pita bread
crisp raw vegetables

1. With metal blade attached and food processor running, drop **garlic cloves** down the feed tube and mince. Scrape down sides of bowl.
2. Add **chick peas, sesame seed paste**, and **lemon juice**. Process until mixture is smooth.
3. Add **roasted red pepper**. Process until peppers are finely chopped. Season with **salt** and **pepper**.
4. Add **oil** drop by drop until mixture is spreadable.
5. Transfer hummus to a small bowl. Cover and chill. Bring to room temperature and serve with **pita bread** and **vegetables**.

Note:
Preparing several hours in advance allows flavors to blend.

❖ *Pesto and Sun Dried Tomato Torte*

Dairy • 10 servings

Chilling Time: 1 day
3-cup bowl

. . . .

1 cup coarsely chopped, fresh
   spinach leaves
1 cup loosely packed, fresh
   basil leaves
1 teaspoon minced garlic
⅛ cup olive oil
1 tablespoon fresh lemon juice
1 cup Parmesan cheese
salt and pepper to taste
4 ounces goat cheese
8 ounces cream cheese
¼ cup finely chopped almonds
   or pecans
¼ cup thinly sliced, well-
   drained, oil-packed sun-
   dried tomatoes
assorted crackers

1. Line bowl with plastic wrap, leaving a 4-inch overhang.
2. In a food processor, using metal blade, combine **spinach**, **basil**, and **garlic**. Finely chop.
3. Gradually add **oil** and **lemon juice**. Add **Parmesan cheese** and process until smooth. Season with **salt** and **pepper**.
4. In a separate bowl, combine **goat cheese** and **cream cheese** and blend until smooth.
5. Spread ⅓ of the cheese mixture in bottom of prepared bowl.
6. Spread half the spinach mixture on top.
7. Sprinkle with half the **nuts**. Add half of the **tomatoes**.
8. Add ⅓ more cheese mixture on top. Cover evenly.
9. Add remaining layers of spinach, nuts, and tomato mixture. Top with remaining cheese mixture.
10. Fold the plastic wrap over the top. Press down gently to compact the mixture. Refrigerate at least 1 day or up to 3 days. Serve with crackers.
11. Unfold plastic. Invert mixture onto a plate. Let stand 30 minutes at room temperature.

Sweet and Sour Herring

Dairy • 2 cups

Chilling Time: 1 hour

. . . .

16 ounces party snack herring
6 ounces whole cranberry
   sauce
½ cup sour cream
dark party rye bread

1. Drain **herring** and chop coarsely.
2. Combine with **cranberry sauce** and **sour cream**.
3. Chill and serve with **rye bread**.

APPETIZERS   1 9

Smoked Salmon Spread

Dairy • 1¼ cups   Chilling Time: Overnight

. . . .

½ pound lox (divided)
1½ cups cottage cheese
2 tablespoons vodka
2 tablespoons lemon juice
2 teaspoons Dijon mustard
fresh ground pepper
fresh dill for garnish
cocktail rye bread

1. Finely dice ⅓ of the **lox**. Cut remaining lox into chunks.
2. Line a sieve with cheese cloth. Put **cheese** in lined sieve. Drain overnight in refrigerator.
3. Transfer cheese to a food processor, add **lox chunks, vodka, lemon juice, mustard**, and **pepper**. Process until smooth.
4. Transfer to a bowl. Fold in the diced lox. Refrigerate overnight.
5. Garnish with **dill**. Serve with **cocktail rye bread**.

❖ Artichoke Appetizers

Dairy • 32 to 40 pieces   Preheat oven to 350°
                                 Cooking Time: 12 minutes
                                 Jelly roll pan

. . . .

15 ounces artichoke hearts, drained
32-40 sesame crackers
1 stick butter or margarine, melted
½ teaspoon garlic powder
salt and pepper to taste
2 tablespoons sesame seeds

1. Cut **artichokes** into quarters. Place each quarter, cut side up, on a **cracker**. Arrange on jelly roll pan.
2. Melt **butter** and add **herb** and **spices**. Spoon generously on top of artichokes.
3. Sprinkle with **sesame seeds**. Can be prepared to this point and baked later.
4. Bake for 10 minutes. Broil about 2 minutes, or until browned.

Baked Spinach Artichoke Dip

Dairy • 3 cups

Preheat oven to 350°
Cooking Time: 30 minutes
1-quart casserole, lightly greased

. . . .

10 ounces frozen, chopped
spinach, defrosted, and
drained
24 ounces marinated artichoke
hearts, drained.
2 cloves garlic
½ medium onion
1½ cups mayonnaise
1½ cups grated Parmesan
cheese
cocktail rye bread
fresh crisp vegetables

1. In a food processor, combine
   spinach, artichokes, garlic,
   and **onion**. Blend well.
2. In a large bowl, combine **vegetable** mixture with **mayonnaise** and **Parmesan cheese**.
3. Place in prepared casserole and
   bake until bubbly.
4. Serve with **bread** and **vegetables**.

Note:
Can be prepared ahead, refrigerated,
and then baked.

Chicken Fingers Kahlúa

Meat • 40 to 60 pieces

Large skillet

. . . .

4 chicken breasts, skinned and
boned
1 cup flour
½ stick margarine (divided)
3 ounces coffee-flavored
liqueur
1¼ cups non-dairy creamer
¼ teaspoon salt
¼ teaspoon garlic powder to
taste
¼ cup brown sugar

1. Cut **chicken** into ½ inch strips.
   Toss strips in **flour**.
2. Sauté half of the chicken in half
   of the **margarine** until golden
   brown. Set aside. Repeat with
   the remaining chicken. Return
   chicken to pan.
3. Add **liqueur** and ignite. As flame
   subsides, add **creamer, salt,
   garlic**, and **brown sugar**.
4. Heat to boiling and then reduce
   temperature to low. Let simmer
   until very little liquid remains.
5. Serve immediately with toothpicks and lots of napkins.

Sweet Ginger Wings

Meat • 6 to 8 servings

Preheat oven to 400°
Cooking Time: 40 minutes
Large roasting pan

. . . .

5 tablespoons brown sugar
2 teaspoons ginger
2 teaspoons paprika
2 teaspoons garlic powder
2 teaspoons coarse ground
   black pepper
4 pounds split chicken wings,
   tips removed

1. Combine **brown sugar** with
   spices.
2. Sprinkle half the spices on
   chicken wings.
3. Bake in oven 20 minutes.
4. Broil for a few minutes to make
   them crispy, monitoring them
   closely.
5. Turn over and repeat process,
   until desired crispness.

Note:
*These can be made ahead, frozen,
and re-heated.*

Montreal Garlic Wings

Meat • 3 to 4 servings

Preheat oven to 350°
Cooking Time: 2 hours
13 x 9 x 2-inch pan, greased

. . . .

3-4 pounds chicken wings
1 cup brown sugar
1 cup light soy sauce
1 cup water
4-6 cloves garlic, minced, to
   taste

1. Remove tips from **chicken
   wings**. Cut wings at joint, if
   desired.
2. Place in prepared pan.
3. In a separate bowl, combine
   **brown sugar, soy sauce,
   water**, and **garlic**. Stir and pour
   over wings.
4. Bake uncovered, basting every
   half hour or until wings are
   brown and syrup has caramelized.

Note:
*This dish can be frozen and
reheated.*

Middle Eastern Turkey in Phyllo

Meat • 30 to 36 pieces

Preheat oven to 325°
Cooking Time: 20 minutes
Baking sheet, greased

. . . .

½ cup golden raisins
¾ cup hot water
3 tablespoons oil
2 cups finely chopped onion
1 tablespoon minced garlic
1 pound ground turkey
2 teaspoons salt
2 teaspoons black pepper
1 teaspoon ground cinnamon
8 ounces stewed tomatoes,
    chopped and drained
⅓ cup honey
pinch cayenne pepper, or few
    drops Tabasco sauce
    (optional)
1 pound phyllo dough
1 stick margarine, melted

Variation:
For entrée, cut phyllo sheets into
3 strips and allow ⅓ cup of filling
for each portion. Proceed as for
appetizer. Yields 8 to 12 portions.

1. Plump up the **raisins** by covering them with **hot water** while preparing other ingredients.
2. Heat **oil** in a skillet. Add **onion** and **garlic** and sauté until transparent. Remove from skillet.
3. Add **turkey** to skillet and cook until no longer pink. Return onion and garlic to skillet.
4. Drain raisins. Add raisins, **spices, tomato**, and **honey** to skillet. Sauté all an additional 5 minutes. Cool.
5. Layer 3 **phyllo sheets**, brushing each with **margarine**. Cut layered phyllo sheets into 3-inch strips, cutting parallel to short side.
6. Allow 2 teaspoons filling for each portion. Follow directions on phyllo package for folding into triangular pockets. May be refrigerated, covered with barely damp cloth until ready to bake. Bake until golden.

Note:
To freeze, bake first. Defrost, and
bake for an additional 4 to 5
minutes, or until heated through.

Scallion Pancakes

Meat • 25 pancakes

Large skillet

. . . .

½ cup chicken stock
½ teaspoon salt
1 egg
⅔ cup sifted flour
⅔ cup minced scallions
3 tablespoons oil (divided)

1. Combine **stock, salt, egg, flour**, and **scallions**.
2. Heat skillet and coat with 1 tablespoon of **oil**.
3. Drop 1 tablespoon of batter onto hot skillet and fry pancakes until brown on both sides. Add oil as necessary.

Goat Cheese with Roasted Garlic and Sun-Dried Tomatoes

Dairy • 4 to 6 servings

Preheat oven to 350°
Cooking Time: 30 minutes
Oven-proof skillet

. . . .

6 cloves garlic
2 tablespoons olive oil
4-6 ounces goat cheese
1 teaspoon dried oregano
5 sun-dried tomatoes
fresh ground black pepper
  (optional)
1 loaf French bread

1. Cut **garlic** into small pieces.
2. In skillet, combine garlic and **olive oil**. Make sure cloves are well coated.
3. Place skillet under preheated broiler until garlic turns light brown or dark spots appear. You need to watch this carefully to make sure garlic does not burn.
4. Remove skillet and set aside to cool.
5. Cut **goat cheese** log into thin slices, approximately ¼-inch thick. Arrange slices carefully on serving dish.
6. Sprinkle cheese with **oregano**.
7. Reconstitute **sun-dried tomatoes** according to package directions.
8. Using kitchen scissors or sharp knife, slice sun-dried tomatoes into thin strips. Place strips over cheese. Sprinkle with **black pepper**, if desired.
9. When garlic and oil reach room temperature, scatter garlic cloves around cheese and drizzle garlic flavored oil over cheese. You may want to add additional fresh olive oil to be sure all cheese has been drizzled with oil.
10. Slice **bread** into ⅓-inch thick slices. Toast in oven until golden. Serve with cheese.

Stuffed Mushroom Caps with Béchamel Sauce

Dairy • 6 servings

Preheat oven to 350°
Cooking Time: 10 minutes
13 x 9 x 2-inch baking pan, lightly
greased

FILLING

5 tablespoons butter (divided)
½ cup chopped shallots
30 ounces frozen chopped
   spinach, defrosted and
   drained
1 cup béchamel sauce
18-24 (2-inch) mushroom caps

1. In a large skillet, melt 3 tablespoons **butter**. Add **shallots** and
   cook over moderate heat for 2
   minutes, or until soft, stirring
   frequently.
2. Add **spinach** and continue
   stirring for 3 to 4 minutes.
   Transfer mixture to a large bowl.
3. Prepare **béchamel sauce** and
   add to shallot mixture.
4. Stuff **mushrooms** with filling.
   Place filled mushrooms in
   prepared pan.
5. Dot with remaining 2 tablespoons butter. Bake in upper
   third of oven until mushrooms
   are tender and filling is lightly
   browned.
6. Serve immediately.

BÉCHAMEL SAUCE

2 tablespoons butter
3 tablespoons flour
1 cup hot milk
salt and pepper to taste

1. In 3-quart saucepan, melt **butter**
   over moderate heat.
2. Stir in **flour**. Cook for 2 minutes.
   Do not allow to brown.
3. Remove pan from heat. Add hot
   milk.
4. Return to high heat and cook
   until sauce comes to a boil,
   stirring constantly.
5. Reduce heat and simmer for 2 to
   3 minutes or until sauce is thick
   enough to coat a spoon.
6. Remove from heat, season with
   salt and **pepper**.

❖ *Madeira Mushroom Strudel*

Dairy • 30 to 36 slices

Preheat oven to 375°
Cooking Time: 15 to 20 minutes
Baking sheet, buttered

. . . .

2 tablespoons shallots, minced
1 pound fresh mushrooms,
   minced
3 tablespoons butter
1 teaspoon tarragon
1 teaspoon black pepper
2 tablespoons Madeira wine
½ cup sour cream
9 sheets phyllo
1 stick butter, melted (divided)
¾ cup bread crumbs

1. Sauté **shallots** and **mushrooms** in **butter**. Add **tarragon**, **pepper**, and **wine**.
2. Cook until vegetables are soft and liquid has evaporated. Cool. Add **sour cream**.
3. Slightly dampen a clean lint-free dish towel. Spread towel on working surface.
4. Place 1 sheet **phyllo** on towel. Brush lightly with melted **butter**. Sprinkle with 1 tablespoon **bread crumbs**. Top with another sheet of phyllo, brush with butter and sprinkle with bread crumbs again. Place third sheet on top and repeat.
5. Spoon ⅓ of filling along short end of pastry leaving a margin on both sides so filling won't ooze out when rolling strudel.
6. Starting with the filling end of phyllo, gently roll up dough.
7. Use towel to lift strudel and place strudel on prepared baking sheet. Brush top of strudel lightly with melted butter.
8. Repeat process with remaining sheets. Bake until strudel is golden brown.
9. Cool before slicing.

Hint:
To cut flaky pastry, use an electric knife.

Beyond
Chicken
Soup

S O U P S

SOUPS

Traditional Chicken Soup

Meat • 8 to 10 servings

Cooking Time: 3 hours
8-quart covered pot

. . . .

4 to 5 pound stewing chicken,
   quartered
4 quarts water
3 carrots, sliced
3 stalks celery with leaves, sliced
1-2 parsnips, sliced
1 medium onion
1 large sprig parsley
1 large sprig dill weed
salt and pepper to taste

1. Remove giblets from chicken cavities.
2. Place cleaned **chicken** in pot of **water**. Bring to a boil. Skim foam.
3. Add **vegetables, herbs**, and **spices**. Bring to a boil again. Simmer until chicken is tender.

Hint:
Most soups improve in **flavor,** if allowed to cool overnight. It also makes it easier to skim off excess fat.

✡ Scallion Matzoh Balls

Meat • 24 balls

Cooking Time: 25 minutes
Skillet

. . . .

7 green onions, finely chopped
8 tablespoons margarine, melted
6 large eggs
3 tablespoons chicken broth
2 teaspoons salt
½ teaspoon ground pepper
1½ cups matzoh meal

1. In a skillet, sauté **onions** in **margarine** until tender. Cool.
2. Beat **eggs, broth, salt**, and **pepper**.
3. Add to **matzoh meal** and onions.
4. Cover and refrigerate 2½ hours.
5. Roll rounded teaspoons of matzoh mixture into balls. Place on a baking sheet lined with plastic wrap. Refrigerate 30 minutes.
6. Bring large pot of salted water to boil. Drop matzoh balls into water.
7. Cover and cook 25 minutes. Remove with slotted spoon.

Note:
Can be made 2 days in advance and refrigerated.

Chicken Soup and Beyond

Meat • 16 servings

Cooking Time: 3 hours
12-quart stock pot

. . . .

6 carrots, peeled and sliced
3 stalks celery, sliced
3 parsnips, peeled and sliced
3 small boiling onions
1 yam, peeled
½ cabbage, tied together with a
  string
1 pound lean top rib or chuck
2 pounds short ribs or shank
½ cup lima beans
3 marrow bones
¼ teaspoon salt
½ teaspoon sugar
5 to 6 pound capon or pullet,
  cut in pieces

1. Place prepared **vegetables** in
   ice water.
2. Place **beef, lima beans, bones,
   salt**, and **sugar** in pot with
   enough water to cover all. Bring
   to a boil.
3. Reduce heat. Skim fat off the
   surface.
4. Cover and let simmer one hour.
5. Remove fat from **chicken** and
   discard. Add chicken pieces to
   soup. Simmer until just tender,
   about 1½ hours. Skim foam as
   needed.
6. Add prepared vegetables. Cook
   ½ hour more.
7. Remove chicken and beef from
   soup. Cut into chunks.
8 Remove vegetables from soup.
   Purée in a food processor.
9. Return puréed vegetables to
   soup. Add cut up chicken and
   beef.
10. Serve hot.

Note:
1. Omit lima beans at Passover.
Noodles or matzoh balls make this
extra special.
2. To easily remove excess fat from
soup, chill soup overnight.

When my mother was 10 years old, she was invited to a Seder with her family. She
wore her brand new Passover dress to dinner. The first course was matzoh ball soup.
The matzoh ball was too big to put into her mouth whole, so she tried to cut it with
her spoon. It was so hard, that it bounced out of her soup bowl and landed on her
lap, right on her new Passover dress. She was very embarrassed and did not know
what to do with the matzoh ball, so she put it in her pocket. She spent the rest of
the dinner with a wet matzoh ball in her pocket, afraid that her mother would be
angry at her for ruining her new dress.

Curried Chicken Soup with Sprouts

Meat • 6 servings

3-quart pot

. . . .

4 tablespoons margarine
1 onion, chopped
1 cup celery with leaves, thinly
   sliced
1 apple, peeled, cored, and
   chopped
¼ cup flour
4 cups chicken broth
½ teaspoon curry powder
2 cups cooked chicken, diced
1 cup bean sprouts
salt and pepper, to taste

1. Melt **margarine**.
2. Sauté **onion, celery**, and **apple** for 5 minutes, or until tender.
3. Stir in **flour**.
4. Gradually stir in **broth** and **curry powder**. Bring to a boil.
5. Add **chicken** and **sprouts**. Reduce heat, simmer for 5 minutes.
6. Season to taste with **salt** and **pepper**.

Hot and Sour Soup with Snow Peas

Meat • 4 servings

Cooking Time: 8 minutes
Wok or skillet

. . . .

¼ cup oil
1 small red bell pepper, diced
2 cups snow peas
1 cup sliced mushrooms
2 teaspoons chopped fresh
   ginger root
½ cup sliced water chestnuts
1 tablespoon reduced salt soy
   sauce
14 ounces chicken or vegetable
   broth
2 tablespoons white vinegar
2 teaspoons honey
⅛ teaspoon crushed hot red
   pepper flakes
¼ cup chopped green onions

1. Heat **oil** in pan. Stir fry **pepper** and **peas** for 2 minutes. Remove from wok.
2. Stir fry **mushrooms, ginger**, and **water chestnuts** for 2 minutes.
3. Add **soy sauce, broth, vinegar, honey**, and **pepper flakes**. Bring to a boil and simmer for 2 minutes.
4. Return pepper and peas to pan.
5. Reheat briefly and sprinkle with **green onions**.

Kreplach

Meat • 30 to 36 kreplach

Preheat oven to 325°
Cooking Time: 2 hours,
   20 minutes
Covered roasting pan

DOUGH

1 egg
½ teaspoon salt
1 teaspoon oil
¼ cup mashed potatoes
2 cups flour (divided)

1. Mix **egg, salt, oil**, and **potato** together.
2. Place 1½ cups **flour** on a pastry board. Make a well in the center and add potato mixture.
3. Mix flour into the center, a little at a time, using your hands.
4. Add remaining flour and enough **water**, a little at a time, until the dough sticks together and begins to form a ball.
5. Knead the dough for about 8 minutes, or until smooth and soft.
6. Roll the dough into a rectangle, 14 x 10-inches and about ⅛-inch thick.
7. Cut into 2-inch squares.

FILLING

2 onions, sliced
½ cup water
1 pound top rib or brisket
1 bay leaf
salt and pepper, to taste

1. Place **onion** in the bottom of pan. Add **water.**
2. Add **meat, bay leaf, salt**, and **pepper**.
3. Cover pan and roast for 2 hours, or until fork tender.
4. Grind meat and onion in a food processor.

ASSEMBLY AND COOKING

1. Place a generous teaspoon of filling in the center of each square of dough.
2. Place a little water around edges of dough.
3. Fold dough to make a triangle, and pinch edges together tightly.
4. Bring enough salted water to cover kreplach to a boil. Gently drop kreplach into pot.

Kreplach *(continued)*

Variation:
Seasoned mashed potatoes can be used for the filling.

5. Cover pot and boil 20 minutes. This may need to be done in 2 or 3 batches.
6. Remove with slotted spoon. Serve with your favorite chicken soup.

Hint:
To **freeze individual portions**, like kreplach, chicken breasts, or meatballs, place them on a baking sheet in the freezer and when frozen, transfer them to plastic freezer bags.

Black Bean Soup

Meat • 6 to 8 servings

Cooking Time: 30 minutes
6 quart pot

. . . .

¼ cup olive oil
1 large onion, chopped
1 red bell pepper, chopped
3 garlic cloves, minced
14½ ounces canned peeled tomatoes, chopped, with juice
4 ounces green chilies, diced
1 teaspoon dried thyme, crumbled
64 ounces canned black beans, drained and rinsed
2 cups low salt chicken broth
salt and pepper to taste
green onions for garnish
tortilla chips for garnish

1. Heat **oil** in pot over medium heat.
2. Add **onion, pepper**, and **garlic**. Sauté until onion is tender, about 10 minutes.
3. Mix in **tomato, chilies**, and **thyme**.
4. Reduce heat to low and simmer until vegetables are soft, about 10 minutes.
5. Add **beans** and **chicken broth**.
6. Purée in several batches in a food processor or blender.
7. Return soup to pot. Simmer to heat.
8. Season with **salt** and **pepper** to taste.
9. Garnish with **green onions** or **tortilla chips**.

Vegetable Bisque

Meat • 6 servings

Cooking Time: 30 minutes
2-quart covered saucepan

. . . .

¼ cup oil
1 medium onion, diced
1 large potato, diced
⅔ cup diced celery
1 clove garlic, minced
½ teaspoon pepper
3 cups chopped broccoli
5 cups chicken broth
1 tablespoon dried basil
salt to taste

1. Heat **oil** in saucepan. Sauté **onion** until tender.
2. Add **potato, celery, garlic**, and **pepper**. Cook 10 minutes, stirring occasionally.
3. Stir in **broccoli, broth**, and **basil**. Cover and simmer 20 minutes.
4. Pour small amounts into a blender or food processor and purée until smooth.
5. Taste and adjust seasonings. Serve hot or cold.

Broccoli Bisque

Meat • 4 to 6 servings

Chilling Time: 4 hours
2-quart saucepan

. . . .

26 ounces chicken broth
20 ounces frozen chopped broccoli
1 medium red onion, quartered
2 teaspoons margarine
1 teaspoon salt (optional)
1-2 teaspoons curry powder
dash of ground pepper
2 tablespoons lime juice
chopped chives for garnish

1. Combine **broth, broccoli, onion, margarine,** and **spices** and bring to a boil.
2. Reduce heat and simmer 8 to 10 minutes.
3. Pour small amounts into a blender and purée until smooth. Stir in **lime juice**.
4. Cover and refrigerate 4 hours.
5. Serve hot or cold in small bowls. Sprinkle with **chives**.

Cream of Broccoli Soup

Dairy • 4 to 5 servings

Cooking Time: 30 minutes
6-cup covered pot

SOUP

1 bunch broccoli
1 cup water
1 clove chopped garlic,
   (optional)
1 teaspoon chopped dill
1 envelope instant vegetable
   soup seasoning
salt and pepper to taste

1. Wash **broccoli**. Peel stems and slice into ½-inch thick slices. Separate flowerets.
2. Steam, covered, over **water** until tender, about 10 minutes.
3. Purée in blender, with cooking water, until smooth.
4. Stir in **herbs** and **vegetable soup seasoning, salt**, and **pepper**.
5. Blend in white sauce.
6. Heat, adding additional milk until desired consistency.

WHITE SAUCE

4 tablespoons flour
3 tablespoons margarine, melted
¼-½ cup milk

1. Add **flour** to **margarine**, stir until smooth.
2. Gradually add **milk**, stirring constantly until mixture thickens.

Traditional Cabbage Soup

Meat • 8 large servings

Cooking Time: 2½ to 3 hours
Large covered pot

. . . .

1 medium head cabbage
2 pounds beef chuck
beef bones (optional)
2 tablespoons oil
1 large onion, coarsely chopped
3 tablespoons flour
28 ounces canned crushed
   tomatoes, undrained
1 cup brown sugar
1 cup golden raisins
1 tablespoon black peppercorns
   (in cheese cloth bag) or 1
   tablespoon fresh ground
   pepper
1 teaspoon celery salt
1-1½ quarts water
1 cup white vinegar

1. Shred **cabbage** medium fine.
2. Cut **beef** into 1 inch cubes.
3. Brown meat and **bones** in **oil**
   over medium heat.
4. Add **onion** and continue to
   brown for 2 minutes.
5. Stir in **flour** and brown 1
   minute longer.
6. Add cabbage, **tomatoes, sugar,
   raisins,** and **spices**.
7. Add **water** and **vinegar**. Bring
   to a boil.
8. Reduce heat to low. Cover
   tightly and simmer. Add more
   vinegar or sugar to taste.
9. Simmer a total of 2½ to 3 hours,
   or until meat is tender.
10. After cooking, remove beef
    bones, and peppercorns. Cool
    and refrigerate.

Note:
Taste improves if made a day before
serving. It freezes well.

Cheddar Cheese Chowder with Cumin

Dairy • 6 to 8 servings

Cooking Time: 30 minutes
6-quart pot

. . . .

1 large potato, peeled and diced
2½ cups water, salted to taste
1 bay leaf
¼ teaspoon dried sage
½ teaspoon cumin seeds
3 tablespoons butter
1 medium onion, finely chopped
3 tablespoons flour
1¼ cups heavy cream
8 ounces corn kernels, drained
2 tablespoons chopped parsley
    and/or chives
¼ teaspoon nutmeg
salt and pepper to taste
4 ounces cheddar cheese, grated
4-5 tablespoons dry white wine

1. Boil **potato** in salted **water** with **bay leaf, sage**, and **cumin seeds** about 15 minutes, or until potato is tender. Remove bay leaf. Do not drain.
2. Melt **butter** in a saucepan. Add chopped **onion** and sauté until tender.
3. Blend in **flour**.
4. Over low heat, slowly blend in **cream**, stirring constantly. Mixture will thicken.
5. Pour this sauce into potato stock.
6. Add **corn, herbs**, and **spices**.
7. Simmer soup gently for 10 minutes. Stir in **cheese** and **wine**. Mix well. Heat until cheese is completely melted.

Healthy Corn Chowder

Dairy • 4 to 6 servings

Large covered pot

. . . .

1½ tablespoons oil
2 onions, chopped
1 stalk celery, chopped
1 red bell pepper, seeded and
    diced
3 cloves garlic, minced
½ teaspoon cumin
3½ cups vegetable stock
1 teaspoon thyme
1 bay leaf
2 cups frozen corn kernels
1 potato, peeled and diced
2 tablespoons corn starch
12 ounces evaporated skimmed
    milk
salt and pepper to taste

1. Heat **oil** over low heat.
2. Add **onions** and cook 5 minutes, or until translucent.
3. Add **celery, red pepper, garlic**, and **cumin**. Stir 2 to 3 minutes.
4. Add **stock, thyme**, and **bay leaf**. Bring to a boil. Reduce to a simmer and cook 10 minutes.
5. Add **corn** and **potato**. Continue to simmer 5 to 10 minutes, or until vegetables are tender.
6. Combine **cornstarch** and **milk**. Blend into soup.
7. Season with **salt** and **pepper**.

Hearty Fish Chowder

Meat • 3 to 4 quarts

CookingTime: 30 minutes
4-quart covered pot

. . . .

2 tablespoons margarine
2 stalks celery, diced
1 large onion, chopped
6 cups chicken broth
5 large potatoes, cubed
salt and freshly ground pepper
   to taste
10 ounces peas and carrots
10 ounces green beans
16 ounces stewed tomatoes,
   crushed, undrained
1¼ pounds cod fish, cut in
   2-inch cubes

1. Melt **margarine** in pot. Add **celery** and **onion**. Cook until onion is transparent.
2. Add **broth, potatoes, salt**, and **pepper**. Bring to a boil. Reduce heat, cover and cook over low heat for 20 minutes.
3. Add remaining **vegetables, tomatoes**, and **fish**. Cover and cook about 8 minutes, or until vegetables are tender and fish flakes easily.

Note:
You can use any combination of vegetables, fresh or frozen. White fish can be used.

Garden Vegetable Soup

Parve • 4 to 5 quarts

Cooking Time: 1 hour
6-quart covered pot

. . . .

½ head broccoli, chopped
½ head cauliflower, chopped
4 carrots, thinly sliced
4 stalks celery, thinly sliced
4 green onions, chopped
4 cloves garlic, minced
16 ounces canned whole
   tomatoes, with juice
16 ounces tomato purée
⅛ cup lemon juice, or more to
   taste
1 teaspoon dried basil, or more
   to taste
½ teaspoon dried oregano
salt and pepper to taste

1. Combine **broccoli, cauliflower, carrots, celery, green onions**, and **garlic** in pot.
2. Add **tomatoes, tomato purée, lemon juice, herbs**, and **spices**.
3. Bring to a boil, reduce heat and gently simmer, covered until vegetables are tender. Add water, as soup thickens, to get desired consistency.

Hint:
Soups freeze well, with the exception of those containing cubed potatoes.

Cozy Comfort Soup

Dairy • 10 to 12 servings

Cooking Time: 1 hour
5 to 6 quart covered pot

SOUP

3 quarts water
2 cups carrots, peeled, and sliced
2 cups white potatoes, peeled,
   and cubed
1 cup sweet potatoes, peeled,
   and cubed
1 cup turnip, peeled, and sliced
2 cups chopped onion
1 tablespoon salt
2 cups frozen green beans
1 cup kidney beans, drained
⅓ cup broken spaghetti
1 slice stale challah, crushed
⅛ teaspoon pepper
1 pinch saffron

1. Combine **water** with **carrots, white potatoes, sweet potatoes, turnip, onions**, and **salt**. Cook partially covered 45 minutes.
2. Add **greens bean, kidney beans, spaghetti, challah, pepper**, and **saffron**. Bring to a boil and simmer uncovered 15 minutes, or until vegetables are tender.
3. Stir **pistou** mixture into 1 cup of soup. Mix thoroughly. Add to pot of soup.

PISTOU

4 cloves garlic
4 tablespoons tomato paste
¼ cup chopped fresh basil
   (or 1½ tablespoons dried)
½ cup grated Parmesan cheese
¼ cup olive oil

1. Use food processor with metal blade attached to blend **garlic, tomato paste, basil**, and **Parmesan cheese**.
2. Slowly add **olive oil**.
3. Add 1 to 2 cups of soup to pistou.

Vegetable Stock

Parve

Cooking Time: 2 to 3 hours
8-quart covered pot

. . . .

1 stick margarine
6 carrots, sliced
4 leeks, sliced
3 cups chopped onions
6 stalks celery with leaves, sliced
2 large green bell peppers, diced
6 large potatoes, diced
4 small turnips, diced
1 small bunch parsley
1 tablespoon fresh thyme
1 tablespoon salt
9 peppercorns
4 quarts of water

1. Melt **margarine**. Add **carrots** and remaining six **vegetables**. Cook 20 minutes, stirring often.
2. Add **parsley, thyme, salt, peppercorns**, and **water**. Water should cover vegetables.
3. Bring to a boil. Cover and simmer until vegetables are soft. Strain.

Note:
Can freeze for up to 3 months.

Greens 'n' Beans

Parve • 4 servings

Cooking Time: 25 minutes
3-quart pot

. . . .

3 cloves garlic, minced
1 tablespoon olive oil
1 bunch escarole, coarsely chopped
1 quart vegetable broth
15 ounces canned white beans (cannelloni), drained
1 teaspoon oregano
1 teaspoon basil
½ cup couscous
salt and pepper to taste

1. Sauté **garlic** in **oil**.
2. Wash **escarole** to remove any sand. Add escarole to pot. Simmer until wilted.
3. Add **vegetable broth, beans, oregano**, and **basil**. Simmer 5 minutes.
4. Add **couscous** and simmer 10 minutes.
5. Add **salt** and **pepper** to taste.

Spicy Italian Soup

Meat • 5 quarts

Cooking Time: 2 hours
6-quart soup pot

. . . .

1½ pounds spiced sausage
2 cloves garlic, minced
½ teaspoon dried basil
3 tablespoons chopped dried
　parsley
1 teaspoon dried oregano
2 large onions, chopped
28 ounces canned Italian
　tomatoes, undrained
2 quarts beef broth
1½ cups burgundy wine
2 medium zucchini, chopped
1 cup bowtie noodles, uncooked

1. Remove **sausage** from casing.
2. Sauté sausage until brown.
　Drain.
3. Add **herbs, onions, tomatoes,
　broth**, and **wine**.
4. Simmer 1½ hours.
5. Add **zucchini** and **noodles**,
　simmer 30 minutes more.

Note:
Can be frozen.

Leek and Spinach Soup

Meat • 5 to 6 servings

Cooking Time: 30 minutes
4-quart pot

. . . .

¼ cup olive oil
2 leeks, white portion and 1 inch
　of green, thinly sliced
2 stalks celery, chopped
2 carrots, peeled and thinly
　sliced
2 medium baking potatoes,
　peeled and thinly sliced
2 quarts chicken broth
10 ounces frozen chopped
　spinach, defrosted and
　drained
Salt and pepper to taste

Variation:
For a heartier, main dish soup, after
soup is puréed, stir in ½ cup of long
grain white rice. Bring to a boil, and
simmer 20 minutes or until rice is
tender.

1. Heat **olive oil** over medium
　heat. Add **leeks, celery,
　carrots**, and **potatoes**. Sauté for
　10 minutes, or until vegetables
　are tender.
2. Add **broth** and bring to a boil.
　Lower heat and simmer for 10
　minutes.
3. Stir in **spinach** and simmer for
　10 minutes.
4. Pour small amounts into a
　blender or food processor and
　purée until smooth. Add **salt** and
　pepper to taste. Serve warm.

Note:
Vegetable broth can be used to make
this a parve soup.

Lentil Barley Soup

Parve • Serves 8 to 10

Cooking Time: 1 hour
6-quart covered soup pot

. . . .

3 tablespoons oil
1 large onion, diced
10 cups water
1 cup lentils
1 cup barley
2 large stalks celery, chopped
1 large carrot, chopped
1 large potato, diced
3 tablespoons minced fresh
   parsley
16 ounces canned tomatoes,
   chopped
2 bay leaves
1 teaspoon dried basil
1 teaspoon dried oregano
2 teaspoons salt
¼ teaspoon pepper

1. Heat the **oil** and sauté **onion** until translucent, about 5 minutes.
2. Add the **water, lentils, barley, vegetables**, and **spices**.
3. Bring to a boil.
4. Cover, reduce heat, and simmer for 1 hour, or until vegetables are tender and lentils are cooked. Stir occasionally. Add more water to get desired consistency.

Hints:

If a soup is **too salty**, add a raw potato and simmer for 15 minutes. Remove potato before serving. This also works for gravy.

When **sautéing**, heat pan before adding oil or butter to prevent sticking.

Red Lentil Soup

Meat • 8 servings

Cooking Time: 60 minutes
3-quart covered pot

. . . .

1 tablespoon oil
1 large onion, chopped
1 clove garlic, minced
1 tablespoon peeled ginger root, minced
1 jalapeño pepper, seeded, and minced
1½ tablespoons curry powder
1½ teaspoons cinnamon
1 teaspoon ground cumin
2 bay leaves
1½ cups lentils, rinsed and picked over
8 cups chicken stock
1 tablespoon fresh chopped cilantro or parsley
2 tablespoons fresh lemon juice
2 tablespoons mango chutncy
salt and freshly ground pepper to taste

1. In heavy pot, heat **oil** over medium heat.
2. Add **onion** and sauté until softened, 3 to 5 minutes.
3. Add **garlic, ginger, jalapeño pepper, curry powder, cinnamon, cumin**, and **bay leaves**. Cook, stirring for about 5 minutes longer.
4. Add **lentils, chicken stock** and bring to a boil.
5. Reduce heat to low and simmer, partially covered, for about 45 minutes or until lentils are tender.
6. Discard bay leaves. Stir in **cilantro** or **parsley, lemon juice**, and **chutney**. Season with **salt** and **pepper**.

Note:
If preparing early in the day, decrease cooking time by 10 minutes. When reheating, the time will be made up and the lentils will not get too soft. Any lentils can be used.

Hint:
Wear rubber gloves when working with **jalapeño pepper**. Do not touch face or eyes.

Fresh Mushroom Soup

Parve • 6 servings

Cooking Time: 20 minutes
6-quart covered pot

. . . .

4 tablespoons margarine, melted
1 cup chopped onion
1 stalk celery with leaves,
    chopped
¼ cup shredded carrots
1 pound mushrooms, sliced
16 ounces canned tomatoes
1 quart vegetable stock
1 teaspoon fresh rosemary
½ teaspoon pepper
salt to taste
2 tablespoons fresh parsley,
    chopped, for garnish
1 teaspoon basil (optional)

1. Cook **onion** in **margarine** until tender but not browned.
2. Add **celery** and **carrot**. Cook for 3 minutes, stirring often.
3. Add **mushrooms** and cook 3 minutes.
4. Add **tomatoes, stock, herbs**, and **spices**. Bring to a boil.
5. Simmer, covered, for 10 minutes.
6. Sprinkle with **parsley** and **basil**.

Mushroom Barley Soup

Meat • 12 servings

Cooking Time: 2 hours
8 quart covered pot

. . . .

2 tablespoons dried mushrooms
6 tablespoons hot water
10 cups chicken broth
4 medium onions, sliced
2 stalks celery, sliced
6 carrots, sliced
2 parsnips, sliced
14 ounces fresh mushrooms,
    sliced
1 cup pearl barley
4-5 stems fresh dill or 2
    tablespoons dry dill
1-2 teaspoons cumin (optional)
salt and pepper to taste

1. Reconstitute **mushrooms** in **hot water**.
2. Place **broth, vegetables, barley, herbs**, and **spices** in pot and bring to a boil. Keep pot partially covered.
3. Simmer for 2 hours.
4. Adjust seasonings.

Note:
Dried porcini mushrooms are excellent. This can be a salt free soup with a spicier taste by using cumin. Freezes well.

Split Pea Soup

Parve • 4 to 6 servings

Cooking Time: 2½ to 3 hours
8-quart covered soup pot

. . . .

4½ cups boiling water
¼ cup green split peas
3 celery stalks, cut in 1-inch
   pieces
4 large carrots, cut in 1-inch
   pieces
3 bay leaves
¼ teaspoon dried thyme
1½ teaspoon salt
generous sprinkling of freshly
   ground pepper and powdered
   thyme
1 large carrot, grated

1. Combine **water** with **split peas,
   vegetables**, and **spices**.
2. Simmer gently until the peas are
   thoroughly dissolved and carrots
   are tender.
3. Season to taste.

Note:
Can be frozen. All herbs are
important to the flavor.

Fat Free Split Pea Soup

Parve • 4 quarts

Cooking Time: 4 hours
6-quart covered pot

. . . .

5 quarts water
1 pound green split peas
½ cup barley
1 large onion, chopped
3 stalks celery, chopped
¼ teaspoon dried oregano
¼ teaspoon dried marjoram
½ teaspoon dried sweet basil
¼ teaspoon dried rosemary
¼ teaspoon dried thyme
2-3 tablespoons parsley, fresh or
   dried
2 tablespoons salt
¼ teaspoon pepper
4-5 carrots, chopped

1. Simmer, covered, **water, split
   peas, barley, onion, celery,
   herbs**, and **spices** 3 hours.
2. Add **carrots** and cook one hour
   longer. Add more water to get
   desired consistency.

Note:
This can be frozen.

Reuben Soup

Meat • 4 servings

Cooking Time: 10 minutes
2-quart pot

. . . .

4 tablespoons margarine
½ cup chopped onion
1½ tablespoons Dijon mustard
⅓ pound cooked corned beef,
   shredded
¼ pound sauerkraut, rinsed,
   drained and chopped
½ teaspoon black pepper
½ teaspoon caraway seed
6 tablespoons flour
5 cups beef broth

1. Melt **margarine** and sauté
   onion until tender, but not
   brown.
2. Add **mustard, corned beef,
   sauerkraut, pepper, caraway
   seeds**, and **flour**. Stir to combine thoroughly.
3. Slowly stir in the **beef broth** to
   make a smooth mixture.
4. Simmer, stirring occasionally.

Note:
Purchase corned beef at deli
counter. This can be frozen.

Suggestion:
Serve hot, accompanied with
pumpernickel or rye bread.

Hint:
To avoid tears when **cutting onions**, place in freezer briefly before cutting. Do not
cut stem end of onion until the very end.

Butternut Squash Soup with Leeks

Meat • 12 cups

Cooking Time: 40 minutes
4-quart pot

. . . .

2 medium butternut squash
  (about 7 cups)
2 leeks
1 medium white onion, diced
1 clove garlic, minced
2 tablespoons olive oil
8 cups chicken stock
1 medium Idaho potato, peeled
  and thinly sliced
salt and black pepper to taste
pinch nutmeg
12 rusks
1 stick margarine, melted
½ teaspoon cayenne pepper
1 tablespoon minced chives

1. Peel and thinly slice **squash**.
   Thinly slice white part of **leeks**,
   rinsing thoroughly to remove
   any sand.
2. Over medium heat, cook squash,
   leeks, **onion**, and **garlic** in
   olive oil until tender, about 20
   minutes.
3. Add **chicken stock** and **potato**.
   Bring to a boil, simmer 20
   minutes or until vegetables are
   soft. Adjust seasoning with **salt**,
   black pepper, and **nutmeg**.
4. Purée, in small amounts, in a
   blender.
5. Brush **rusks** with **melted
   margarine**. Sprinkle each with a
   small amount of **cayenne
   pepper**.
6. To serve, heat soup and ladle
   into bowls. Place seasoned rusk
   on top of soup and garnish with
   chives.

Hearty Veggi Chili

Dairy • 8 servings

Cooking Time: 30 minutes
6-quart pot

. . . .

2 tablespoons oil
1-2 cloves garlic, minced
1 green bell pepper, chopped
1 stalk celery, chopped
1 small onion, chopped
1 carrot, chopped
1 medium zucchini, sliced
15 ounces canned tomatoes with
  juice
8 ounces tomato sauce
¼ cup water
15 ounces canned kidney beans,
  rinsed
15 ounces canned garbanzo
  beans, rinsed
15 ounces canned black beans,
  rinsed
8 ounces frozen corn kernels
½-1 teaspoon chili powder
½ teaspoon black pepper
¼-½ teaspoon Tabasco sauce
1 teaspoon dried basil
1 teaspoon dried oregano
cheddar cheese, shredded, for
  garnish

1. In **oil**, sauté **garlic, green
   pepper, celery, onion, carrot**,
   and **zucchini** about 5 minutes.
   Vegetables should not be limp.
2. Stir in **tomatoes, tomato sauce,
   water, beans, corn, spices**, and
   herbs.
3. Bring to a boil, uncovered, then
   reduce heat to medium. Cook 5
   minutes, lower heat to simmer.
   Cook 15 to 20 minutes.
4. Garnish with **cheddar cheese**.

Note:
Serve over couscous or rice.
Can easily be doubled or tripled.
Reheats well.

New Wave Chili

Parve • 6 to 8 servings

Cooking Time: 1 hour
Large heavy covered skillet

. . . .

12 ounces canned whole tomatoes

14 ounces canned red kidney beans

15 ounces canned garbanzo beans

¾ cup bulgur

2 tablespoons oil

1 medium onion, coarsely chopped

3 stalks celery, coarsely chopped

3 carrots, peeled and coarsely chopped

5 tablespoons chili powder

4 medium garlic cloves, minced

1 teaspoon ground cumin

1 teaspoon dried basil, crumbled

1½ teaspoons salt

1 teaspoon ground pepper

1 tablespoon fresh lemon juice

1 tablespoon fresh lime juice

½ cup coarsely chopped green bell peppers

2 cups cocktail vegetable juice or tomato juice

¾ cup raw cashews (optional)

½ cup raisins (optional)

1. Drain **tomatoes** and **beans**, reserving liquid.
2. Chop tomatoes coarsely and set aside.
3. Bring 1 cup of the reserved liquid to a boil in microwave oven or saucepan. Remove pan from heat and stir in the **bulgur**. Cover and let stand while cooking the vegetables.
4. Heat **oil** in skillet over medium-low heat.
5. Add **onion** and cook until translucent, stirring frequently, about 10 minutes.
6. Add tomatoes, **celery, carrot, herbs, spices, lemon**, and **lime juices**. Cook until vegetables are almost tender, stirring frequently, about 15 minutes.
7. Add **green pepper** and cook until tender, stirring frequently, 10 minutes.
8. Mix in bulgur, kidney beans, garbanzo beans and **tomato** or **vegetable juice**. Reduce heat to low and simmer 25 minutes, stirring occasionally.
9. Add **cashews** and **raisins** and simmer an additional 5 minutes. Add remaining liquid from tomatoes and beans, if necessary, to thin.

Cranberry Borscht

Meat • 7 servings

Chilling Time: 4 hours
2-quart saucepan

. . . .

1 medium onion, coarsely
  chopped
1 tablespoon margarine
16 ounces beets with juice
28 ounces chicken broth
12 ounces cranberries, washed
½ cup sugar
1 tablespoon grated orange zest
orange slices, peeled, for garnish

1. In a pan, over low heat, sauté **onion** in **margarine** for 3 to 4 minutes.
2. Purée **beets** and **liquid** in a blender. Place in a 3 quart container. Add cooked onion.
3. In saucepan, over medium heat, combine **broth, cranberries**, and **sugar**. Simmer, uncovered, until berries begin to pop, 5 to 7 minutes.
4. Purée berries and broth mixture in blender, about 2 cups at a time. Strain each batch and discard skins. Add berries to beets.
5. Stir in **orange zest**.
6. Cover and chill 4 to 6 hours or overnight.
7. Serve garnished with an **orange slice**.

Hint:
Before **peeling oranges,** cover with boiling water and let stand for 5 minutes. The silver-white membrane can then be easily removed.

Gazpacho

Parve • 10 to 12 servings

Chilling Time: 4 hours
3-quart covered container

· ·

2 cups finely chopped peeled
  ripe tomatoes
1 cup finely chopped celery
1 cup finely chopped cucumber-
  peeling optional
1 cup finely chopped green bell
  pepper
½ cup finely chopped onion
4 teaspoons snipped parsley or
  chives
½ teaspoon minced garlic
2 teaspoons salt
½ teaspoon pepper
1 teaspoon Worcestershire sauce
6 tablespoons wine vinegar
46 ounces tomato juice

1. Place **vegetables, herbs, spices,
   Worcestershire sauce, vinegar**,
   and **tomato juice** in container.
   Mix well.
2. Chill at least 4 hours or overnight in refrigerator. Serve cold.

Chilled Strawberry Soup

Dairy • 6 servings

Chilling Time: 1 hour

· ·

3 pints fresh strawberries
2½ cups orange juice
¼ cup orange flavor liqueur
3 tablespoons sugar
1 cup sour cream

1. Purée **strawberries** in a food
   processor or blender until
   smooth. Pour into a bowl.
2. Stir in **orange juice, liqueur**,
   and **sugar**. Add **sour cream** and
   whisk until well blended.
3. Cover and chill for at least one
   hour.

Strawberry Rhubarb Soup

Dairy • 6 to 8 servings

Chilling Time: 2 hours
2-quart saucepan

. . . .

1 pound rhubarb, cut into 3-inch
    pieces
3 cups water
½ cup sugar
1 teaspoon grated orange zest
2 cups strawberries
sour cream (optional)

Substitution:
Frozen rhubarb can be used.

1. Cook **rhubarb**, uncovered, in **water** with **sugar** and **orange zest** until it comes to a boil.
2. Simmer 20 minutes. Cool.
3. Combine with **strawberries**.
4. In blender or food processor, blend small amounts of fruit mixture.
5. Chill. Serve in bowls with a tablespoon of **sour cream**.

Note:
For casual entertaining, serve in mugs. For elegant entertaining, serve in large wine glasses with hors d' oeuvres. Tie a ribbon around stem of glasses.

Hint:
Rhubarb is most tender when young. If you find it tough, peel it back like celery and remove the coarsest strings before cooking. In either case, use as little water as possible. Never cook the leaves, as they are heavy in toxic oxalic acid.

Beyond Lettuce

SALADS & DRESSINGS

Wheat Garden Salad

Parve • Ten ½ cup servings   Chilling Time: 3 hours

. . . .

¼ cup olive oil
⅓ cup lemon juice
1 clove garlic, minced
½ teaspoon dried oregano
1 teaspoon salt
dash cayenne pepper
1 cup boiling water
1 cup bulgur
¼ cup chopped scallions
1 bunch fresh parsley, chopped
2 tomatoes, chopped
½ tablespoon fresh dill, chopped
½ tablespoon fresh mint,
    chopped
2-¼ cups sliced black olives
lettuce or flowering kale
    (optional)

1. In a small jar, with a tight fitting lid, combine **olive oil, lemon juice, herbs**, and **spices**. Shake well.
2. Pour boiling **water** over **bulgur** and let stand ½ hour.
3. Add **scallions, parsley, tomatoes, dill, mint**, and **olives** to bulgur.
4. Add dressing to bulgur-vegetable mixture. Chill.
5. Serve on a bed of **lettuce** or **flowering kale** for an attractive presentation.

Crunchy Munchy Salad

Parve • 6 to 8 servings

. . . .

6 cups torn greens
½ cup zesty sprouts
½ cup raw sunflower seeds
1 cup drained mandarin oranges

DRESSING

¼ cup oil
2 tablespoons sugar
½ teaspoon salt
2 tablespoons balsamic vinegar
Dash Tabasco sauce
Pepper to taste

1. Mix **greens** with **sprouts, sunflower seeds**, and **mandarin oranges** in a large salad bowl.
2. Combine **oil, sugar, salt, vinegar, Tabasco,** and **pepper** in a separate container.
3. Toss salad with just enough dressing to coat greens.

Note:
1. Romaine, red lettuce, or a combination of your favorite lettuces can be used. 2. Zesty sprouts are a combination of radish and alfalfa sprouts. Plain alfalfa sprouts can be used.

Salad Niçoise

Parve • 6 servings

Chilling Time: 1 hour

. . . .

1 head romaine lettuce, washed and torn
1 head leaf lettuce, washed and torn
12 ounces tuna, drained and broken into pieces
2¾ ounce can flat anchovies, drained
1 cup green and/or black olives
1 medium sweet onion, sliced
10 ounces frozen green beans, steamed crisp
2 small potatoes, boiled, cooled, and thinly sliced
½ red bell pepper, sliced
½ green bell pepper, sliced

DRESSING

½ cup olive oil
¼ cup wine vinegar
2 tablespoons mayonnaise
salt and pepper to taste
garlic powder to taste

1. Toss **lettuce** with **tuna, anchovies, olives**, and **vegetables** in a large serving bowl. Chill.
2. Combine **oil, vinegar, mayonnaise**, and **spices**. Chill.
3. At serving time, toss salad with dressing.

Note:
Vidalia or red onions may be used.

___

Hint:
Wilted **salad greens** and spinach can be restored to crispiness by soaking in cold water to which a slice of lemon has been added.

Springtime Salad

Parve • 6 servings

. . . .

3 cups cut up broccoli
6 cups assorted lettuce, washed
   and torn
1 cup fresh strawberries, sliced
2 oranges, peeled and sectioned

DRESSING

2 tablespoons honey
⅓ cup oil
2 tablespoons wine vinegar
2 tablespoons Dijon mustard
1 tablespoon fresh lemon juice
2 teaspoons grated onion
salt and pepper to taste
1 tablespoon poppy seeds

1. Toss **broccoli, lettuce, straw-berries**, and **oranges** together.
2. Combine **honey** with **oil** and **seasonings**, in blender or food processor. Add **poppy seeds**.
3. Gently mix dressing with salad.

Note:
Mandarin oranges, drained, may be used.

Red, White and Green Salad

Parve • 4 to 6 servings

. . . .

2½ pounds red potatoes,
   unpeeled
1 pound fresh green beans
1 small red onion, chopped
¼ cup fresh parsley, chopped
2 tablespoons fresh basil,
   chopped
2 tablespoons fresh mint,
   chopped
¼ -½ pound feta cheese,
   crumbled (optional)

DRESSING

¼ cup balsamic vinegar
2 tablespoons Dijon or coarse
   grained mustard
1 tablespoon lemon juice
⅛ teaspoon Worcestershire sauce
1 clove garlic, minced
¼ cup olive oil
¼ cup oil
salt and pepper to taste

1. Cut **potatoes** into 1-inch cubes. Cook in salted water until tender. Do not overcook. Drain and cool.
2. Cut **green beans** into 2-inch pieces. Steam until crisp and tender. Cool.
3. Combine **onion** with **herbs** and **feta cheese**.
4. Whisk **vinegar** with **mustard, lemon juice, Worcestershire sauce**, and **garlic**. Gradually whisk in **oils**, **salt**, and **pepper**.
5. Add dressing to vegetables. Toss lightly to coat. Refrigerate.

Note:
Salad is best at room temperature.

❖ California Salad

Parve • 6 to 8 servings

. . . .

1 avocado, peeled and sliced
1 teaspoon fresh lemon juice
2 navel oranges, peeled and
   thinly sliced
1 red onion thinly sliced
1 head of romaine washed and
   torn

D R E S S I N G

½ cup oil
2 tablespoons walnut oil
3 tablespoons cider vinegar
1 tablespoon soy sauce
1 teaspoon honey
½ teaspoon grated fresh ginger
½ cup walnuts, coarsely
   chopped

1. Sprinkle **avocado** with **lemon juice**.
2. Arrange avocado, **oranges** and **onion slices** on a bed of **romaine**.
3. In a blender combine both **oils, cider vinegar, soy sauce, honey**, and **ginger** in blender until smooth.
4. Pour dressing on salad, and sprinkle with **nuts**.

Note:
Lemon juice prevents avocado discoloration.

Apple Salad with Honey Lime Dressing

Parve • 4 to 6 servings   Chilling Time: 2 hours

. . . .

4 tart apples (divided)
¼ cup chopped crystallized
   ginger
½ cup raisins
½ cup chopped walnuts
3 tablespoons honey
⅓ cup fresh lime juice
1 cup chopped celery
lettuce leaves

1. Peel 3 **apples**. Core and slice all 4 apples into julienne strips.
2. Add **ginger, raisins**, and **nuts**.
3. Combine **honey** and **lime juice**. Mix well. Add to apple mixture.
4. Add **celery** and toss.
5. Serve on lettuce leaves.

Hint:
To get the most juice from **citrus fruits**, bring them to room temperature and roll them on the counter while pressing down with the flat of your hand.

Mandarin Spinach Salad with Almonds

Parve • 6 to 8 servings

. . . .

1 pound fresh spinach
11 ounces mandarin orange
   segments, drained
¼ cup slivered almonds

D R E S S I N G

¼ cup oil
¼ cup wine vinegar
2 tablespoons sugar
¼ teaspoon salt
¼ teaspoon almond extract

1. Rinse and tear **spinach** leaves.
2. Add **oranges** and **almonds**.
3. Blend together **oil, vinegar, sugar, salt**, and **almond extract**.
4. Add dressing to salad and toss.

Hint:

To make **wine vinegar**, add one part wine to three parts vinegar. Use white wine with white vinegar, and red wine with cider vinegar.

Spinach and Cashew Salad

Parve • 4 to 6 servings

. . . .

⅓ cup sugar
¼ cup vinegar
1 teaspoon salt
1 teaspoon grated onion
1 teaspoon dry mustard
1 cup oil
1 teaspoon celery seeds
   (optional)
1 package fresh spinach, rinsed
   and torn into bite size pieces
6 ounces cashews

1. Blend **sugar, vinegar, salt, onion**, and **mustard**.
2. Whisk in **oil** and **celery seeds**.
3. Pour over **spinach** and toss.
4. Add **cashews**. Serve.

Spinach Salad with Cucumber and Orange

Parve • 10 to 12 servings

. . . .

1 large cucumber, peeled and
  seeded
20 ounces fresh spinach
22 ounces mandarin oranges,
  drained
10 medium mushrooms, sliced

DRESSING

1 cup low fat mayonnaise
2 tablespoons oil
1 scallion, sliced
2 tablespoons wine vinegar
2 tablespoons fresh lemon juice
3 teaspoons fresh, minced
  parsley
Worcestershire sauce,
salt and pepper, to taste
⅓ cup toasted almonds

1. Cut **cucumber** into julienne strips.
2. Mix **spinach, oranges, cucumber**, and **mushrooms** in salad bowl. Cover and chill.
3. Combine **mayonnaise, oil**, and **scallion** with **vinegar, lemon juice**, and **seasonings**. Cover and chill.
4. Toss salad with dressing immediately before serving.
5. Sprinkle **almonds** on top.

Hints:

To clean **mushrooms**, wipe with a clean cloth which has been moistened with lemon juice. This will also prevent discoloration.

Domestic mushrooms are **freshest** when the cap is closed and the gills do not show.

Store mushrooms in a brown paper bag in the refrigerator.

Spinach Salad with Dates and Citrus

Parve • 4 servings

. . . .

1 pound spinach, rinsed, stems
    removed
2 large oranges, peeled and cut
    into thin slices
12 dates, pitted and halved
1 tablespoon slivered almonds

HONEY DRESSING

¼ cup honey
¼ cup balsamic vinegar
2 tablespoons vegetable oil
1 teaspoon Dijon mustard
¼ teaspoon salt
¼ teaspoon freshly ground
    pepper

Variation:
Canned mandarin oranges can be
substituted for oranges.

1. Dry **spinach**. Arrange on 4 salad plates.
2. Equally distribute **oranges, dates**, and **almonds** on top of spinach.
3. Combine **honey, vinegar, oil**, and **spices**.
4. Drizzle over salad before serving.

Picnic Potato Salad

Parve • 8 servings   Chilling Time: 1 hour

. . . .

3 pounds potatoes
½ cup minced scallions
½ cup sweet onion, thinly sliced
1 red bell pepper, diced
½ cup diced celery

DRESSING

½ cup low-fat mayonnaise
3 tablespoons Dijon mustard
salt and pepper to taste
1 teaspoon Worcestershire sauce
4 teaspoons white wine vinegar

1. Scrub **potatoes** and cover with water. Simmer, covered, gently for 18 to 22 minutes, or until tender.
2. Drain and dry potatoes.
3. Peel and cut into cubes.
4. Add remaining **vegetables**.
5. Mix **mayonnaise** with **mustard** and **seasonings** and toss with potato vegetable mixture.
6. Chill 1 hour or longer.

German Potato Salad

Parve • 4 to 6 servings   Chilling Time: 1 hour

. . . .

1 medium head Romaine lettuce, washed, coarsely chopped
4 whole green onions, finely chopped
½ cup fresh dill, finely chopped
2 medium potatoes, boiled, peeled, and diced
½ cup olive oil
5 tablespoons red wine or balsamic vinegar
2 tablespoons mayonnaise
salt and pepper (fresh ground) to taste

GARNISH

2 hard-boiled eggs, finely chopped
2 dill pickles, sliced
2 tablespoons capers

1. In a large bowl, combine **lettuce, onions, dill**, and **potatoes**.
2. In a small bowl, combine **oil, vinegar, mayonnaise, salt**, and **pepper**. Mix until smooth.
3. Garnish with **eggs, pickles**, and **capers**. Serve chilled.

Hints:

To determine if an **egg** is raw or hard-boiled, spin it on its side. A hard-boiled egg spins; a raw egg does not.

Shells are easier to remove from hard-boiled eggs if eggs are immediately placed in cold water until cool.

I still remember a phone call from my son at college. "Mom, I boiled my egg for 30 minutes and it's getting harder. My potatoes would get soft after boiling them for only 20-30 minutes. How long does it take for eggs to get soft?"

❖ *Mandarin Beef Salad*

Meat • 12 servings

Marinating Time: Overnight
Broiler

BEEF

3 pounds flank steak
⅓ cup soy sauce
⅓ cup honey
1 clove garlic, minced
⅓ cup pineapple juice
1 teaspoon minced ginger root

1. Marinate **flank steak**, overnight, in a mixture of **soy sauce, honey, garlic, pineapple juice**, and **ginger**.
2. The next day, broil the steak until medium. Some center pinkness should remain. Chill and slice the steak into thin slices.

POPPY SEED DRESSING

¾ cup sugar
1 teaspoon dry mustard
1 teaspoon salt
⅓ cup cider vinegar
2 tablespoons minced onion
1 cup salad oil
1½ tablespoons poppy seeds
lettuce leaves
12 oranges sectioned, with the membranes removed
1 small red onion, thinly sliced into rings
½ cup slivered almonds, toasted

1. In a food processor, combine **sugar, mustard, salt, vinegar**, and **onion**. Process until well combined.
2. Gradually drizzle in **oil** while the machine is running. The mixture should be thick and smooth.
3. Stir in **poppy seeds**.
4. Line a large platter or individual serving plates with **lettuce**.
5. Arrange beef slices and **orange sections** on it.
6. Top with **red onion** and **almonds**.
7. Drizzle dressing over the salad and serve.

Note:
This dressing keeps well, covered, in the refrigerator.

❖ Curried Chicken Salad

Meat • 6 servings

Chilling Time: 3 hours

. . . .

22 ounces mandarin orange
  segments, with juice
½-¾ cup mayonnaise
2 teaspoons curry powder
2 teaspoons soy sauce
4 cups cooked, cubed, chicken
  breasts
8 ounces water chestnuts,
  drained and sliced
1 cup chopped celery
½ cup chopped pecans
lettuce leaves

1. Drain juice from **oranges**,
   reserving 2 tablespoons of juice.
2. Beat **mayonnaise** with mandarin orange juice, **curry powder**,
   and **soy sauce**.
3. Combine with oranges, **chicken,
   water chestnuts, celery**, and
   pecans. Chill.
4. Serve on **lettuce leaves**.

Note:
Prepare several hours in advance to
allow flavors to blend.

Tropical Chicken Salad

Meat • 6 to 8 servings

Chilling Time: 30 minutes

. . . .

⅓ cup mayonnaise
1 tablespoon cider vinegar
¼ teaspoon salt
⅛ teaspoon pepper
⅓ cup golden raisins
4 scallions, thinly sliced
⅓ cup celery
¼ cup chopped chutney
4 cups cubed cooked chicken or
  turkey
½ cup red seedless grapes, cut in
  half
curly leaf lettuce
strawberries and/or kiwi for
  garnish

1. Combine **mayonnaise, vinegar,
   salt, pepper, raisins, scallions**,
   and **celery**.
2. Add **chutney** and mix.
3. Add **chicken** and **grapes**. Mix
   well.
4. Chill to allow flavors to blend.
   Serve on a bed of leaf **lettuce**.
   Garnish with **strawberries**
   and/or **kiwi**.

Variation:
Cantaloupe and apples can be
substituted for the raisins and
grapes.

Chinese Chicken Salad

Meat • 4 servings   Marinating Time: 3 hours

. . . .

2 boneless, skinless, chicken
  breasts
1 cup cut-up broccoli
¾ cup pea pods, trimmed
½ cup fresh mushrooms,
  quartered
½ medium, red bell pepper, cut
  into 1-inch strips
½ cup bean sprouts

DRESSING

3 tablespoons soy sauce
2 teaspoons rice vinegar
1 tablespoon oil (optional)
2 teaspoons sugar
2 tablespoons cooking sherry
1 clove garlic, minced
1 tablespoon sesame seeds

1. Poach **chicken breasts** and cut
   into cubes.
2. Steam **broccoli, pea pods,
   mushrooms**, and **pepper**,
   separately. Vegetables should be
   steamed crisp. Rinse under cold
   water and set aside.
3. Place chicken in a medium sized
   bowl. Add vegetables and **bean
   sprouts**.
4. In a small bowl, whisk together
   **soy sauce, vinegar, oil, sugar,
   sherry, garlic**, and s**esame
   seeds** with a wire whisk. Pour
   over chicken and vegetables.
5. Marinate in refrigerator for 3
   hours minimum, mixing
   frequently.

Variations:
You can substitute water
chestnuts, or canned baby corn for
pea pods or bean sprouts. Left over
chicken, turkey, or beef can be used.

Note:
May be prepared 24 hours ahead.

Hint:
To **poach chicken**, simmer chicken in enough broth or water to cover, approximately
fifteen minutes, or until juices run clear. Remove from liquid and cool.

Great Wall Chicken Salad

Meat • 4 to 6 servings

Preheat oven to 350*
Chilling Time: 8 hours
Baking sheet, greased

. . . .

1 garlic clove, minced
¼ teaspoon salt
2 tablespoons hoisin sauce
2 tablespoons soy sauce
1 tablespoon sesame oil
4 scallions, chopped fine
   (divided)
pepper to taste
1½ pounds skinless, boneless
   chicken breasts, cut into 1"
   strips
8 cups mixed torn lettuce leaves
¼ cup finely chopped fresh
   coriander
7 ounces canned baby corn
1 cup snow peas, lightly steamed

DRESSING

¼ cup hoisin sauce
¼ cup lemon juice
3 tablespoons olive oil
3 tablespoons vegetable oil
3 tablespoons sesame oil
¼ cup sugar
2 tablespoons soy sauce
1 clove garlic, minced
½ teaspoon hot red pepper
   flakes
salt and pepper to taste
cashews and sliced fresh fruit for
   garnish

1. Mash **garlic** to a paste with **salt**.
2. In a shallow dish, stir together **hoisin sauce, soy sauce**, garlic paste, **oil**, half the **scallions** and **pepper**.
3. Add the **chicken** and toss until chicken is well coated.
4. Chill mixture, covered, for at least 8 hours or overnight.
5. Arrange chicken on baking sheet and bake 30 minutes in middle of the oven until cooked through.
6. Let chicken cool on baking sheet for 10 minutes.
7. Mound the **lettuce** in the middle of a large serving dish, sprinkle with **coriander** and remaining scallions. Arrange the chicken decoratively over the lettuce mixture.
8. Blanch **corn** in boiling water for 30 seconds. Drain.
9. Arrange corn and **snow peas** decoratively around the chicken.
10. To make the dressing, combine **hoisin sauce** with **lemon juice, oils, sugar, soy sauce, herbs** and **spices**. Whisk until the dressing ingredients are well combined.
11. Pour half of the dressing over salad. Sprinkle salad with **cashews** and garnish with **fruit**.
12. Serve the remaining dressing separately.

❖ *Turkey Salad with Strawberries*

Meat • 6 to 8 servings

. . . .

1 pound asparagus
2 cups fresh strawberries, sliced
6 cups assorted salad greens
3 cups cooked turkey, cut into
　½-inch cubes
¼ cup pecans halves for garnish

D R E S S I N G

¾ cup sugar
1 teaspoon dry mustard
1 teaspoon salt
⅓ cup cider vinegar
2 tablespoons minced onion
1 cup oil
1 tablespoon orange juice
1 teaspoon grated orange zest
1½ tablespoons poppy seeds

1. Cut **asparagus** into 1-inch pieces. Discard woody ends. Cover with water and cook until crisp tender, about 5 minutes. Drain and rinse with cold water.
2. Combine asparagus, **berries, greens**, and **turkey**.
3. In a food processor, combine **sugar, mustard, salt, vinegar**, and **onion**.
4. Gradually add the **oil, orange juice, orange zest**, and **poppy seeds**.
5. Toss the dressing with salad ingredients. Top with **pecans**.

Variation:
Fresh blueberries can be used.

Hints:
Berries do not ripen after being picked. Do not wash or hull them until ready to use.

Nuts keep best in their shells. Once shelled, store in a sealed container at 40° F, or in the freezer. This keeps the oils in the nuts from spoiling.

Chilled Asparagus Salad

Parve • 4 to 6 servings   Chilling Time: 1 hour

1-2 pounds asparagus
1 red bell pepper, thinly sliced
1 avocado, peeled and sliced

1. Steam **asparagus** until crisp tender. Quickly "blanch" in ice water to prevent further cooking.
2. Arrange asparagus, **red pepper slices**, and **avocado slices** on a platter.

DRESSING

½ cup soy sauce
¼ cup sesame oil
1-2 tablespoon fresh lemon juice
2 cloves garlic, minced
1 teaspoon rice vinegar
1 dash ginger
1 dash dry mustard
1 dash red pepper flakes
sesame seeds for garnish

1. Blend **soy sauce, sesame oil, lemon juice, garlic, vinegar, ginger, mustard**, and **pepper flakes**. Pour dressing over asparagus.
2. Sprinkle with **sesame seeds**. Chill until ready to serve.

Salmon Pasta Salad with Lemon

Parve • 10 servings

1½ pounds fresh salmon
2 cups vegetable broth
1½ pounds angel hair pasta
8 ounces small frozen peas
1 medium to large red bell pepper, diced
2½ tablespoons fresh chopped parsley
3 tablespoons fresh chopped dill
¼-⅓ cup lemon vinaigrette
lemon and lime slices for garnish
dill sprigs for garnish

VINAIGRETTE

2 teaspoons Dijon mustard
⅔ cup fresh lemon juice
2 teaspoons fresh chopped chives
1 teaspoon salt
½ teaspoon ground pepper

1. Poach **salmon** in **broth** 5 minutes. Cool, skin, and bone. Rinse with cold water in colander. Dice and set aside.
2. Cook and drain **pasta** according to package directions. Rinse and cool.
3. Combine pasta with **peas, red pepper, parsley**, and **dill**.
4. For vinaigrette, mix together **mustard, lemon juice**, and **chives**. Add **salt** and **pepper** to taste.
5. Add vinaigrette to salmon. Toss with pasta mixture. Garnish with **dill sprig, lemon**, and **lime slices**.

Note:
Extra vinaigrette can be served on the side. It can be kept refrigerated for up to 2 weeks. Also good on greens.

Broccoli Surprise Salad

Parve • 6 to 8 servings

. . . .

4 cups fresh broccoli, coarsely
  chopped
½ cup raisins
½ cup chopped onion
½ cup peanuts

DRESSING

¾ cup mayonnaise
3 tablespoons vinegar
¼ cup sugar

1. Combine **broccoli, raisins, onion**, and **peanuts**. Chill.
2. Combine **mayonnaise, vinegar**, and **sugar**. Blend well.
3. Add dressing to salad no more than 1 to 2 hours before serving. Keep refrigerated.

Colorful Carrots

Parve • 8 to 10 servings   Chilling Time: Overnight

. . . .

2 pounds carrots
1 medium red onion, sliced
10 ounces frozen peas
1 green bell pepper, sliced
12-14 broccoli flowerets
   (optional)
10 ounces condensed tomato
   soup
½ cup oil
¾ cup sugar
¾ cup cider vinegar
1 teaspoon prepared mustard
salt and pepper to taste

1. Peel and slice **carrots** diagonally.
2. Place in a saucepan or microwave dish with a small amount of water.
3. Cook 5 minutes or until crisp and tender.
4. Immerse in cold water to stop cooking. Drain and cool.
5. Separate **onion slices** into rings.
6. In a bowl alternate layers of cooked carrots, **peas, onion rings, green pepper**, and **broccoli**.
7. In another bowl, mix **tomato soup** with **oil, sugar, vinegar**, and **seasonings**, until smooth.
8. Pour over vegetables. Cover and refrigerate overnight.

Note:
Can be refrigerated for up to a week.

❖ Marinated Tomato Salad

Parve • 6 servings   Chilling time: 3 hours

½ cup oil
⅓ cup red wine vinegar
½ teaspoon dried oregano
½ teaspoon dried basil
1 clove garlic, minced
1 teaspoon salt
½ teaspoon pepper
4 large tomatoes, thinly sliced
½ cup red onion, finely chopped
½ cup chopped fresh parsley

1. Combine **oil, vinegar, herbs**, and **spices** in a covered jar. Chill for at least 1 hour.
2. Layer **tomatoes** in a large shallow dish. Top with **onion** and **parsley**.
3. Shake the marinade well and pour over tomatoes.
4. Refrigerate, covered, at least 2 hours.

Herbed Tomatoes with Goat Cheese

Dairy • 4 servings

2 large tomatoes
salt and pepper to taste
1 tablespoon red wine vinegar
3 tablespoons olive oil
1 tablespoon finely chopped
  fresh parsley
1 tablespoon finely chopped
  fresh basil
¼ cup goat cheese

1. Core and slice **tomatoes**.
2. Arrange tomatoes on serving platter.
3. Season with **salt** and **pepper**.
4. Blend **vinegar** and **oil** with **parsley** and **basil**.
5. Pour mixture over tomatoes.
6. Sprinkle with **cheese** and serve.

Vegetables in Balsamic Vinegar

Parve • 10 to 12 servings   Chilling Time: 2 hours

. . . .

½ pound fresh green beans
½ pound fresh waxed beans
½ pound fresh sugar snap peas
½ pound summer squash
½ bunch broccoli, cut into
  flowerets

DRESSING

¾ teaspoon salt
2 tablespoons minced shallots
1 clove garlic, minced
½ cup olive oil
½ cup oil
¼ cup cider vinegar
2 tablespoons balsamic vinegar
½ cup sliced radishes
1 pint cherry tomatoes, cut in
  half
¼ cup chopped chives for
  garnish

1. Steam **beans**, just to crisp
   tender. Immerse in cold water.
2. Repeat process with the remaining **vegetables**.
3. In a large bowl combine **salt,
   shallots, garlic, oils**, and
   vinegars.
4. Whisk until dressing is blended
   and thickened. Add **radishes**
   and **tomatoes** to dressing and
   pour over steamed vegetables.
5. Toss to coat, refrigerate. Toss
   occasionally before serving.
6. Just before serving arrange on
   plates and sprinkle with **chives**.

Variation:
Additional vegetables that could be
added: sliced mushrooms, sliced
zucchini, and cauliflower flowerets.

Maple Raspberry Dressing

Parve • 1 cup

. . . .

4 tablespoons raspberry vinegar
4 tablespoons olive oil
4 tablespoons oil
4 tablespoons maple syrup
2 teaspoons Dijon mustard
2 teaspoons crumbled fresh
  tarragon leaves
½ teaspoon salt

1. Combine **raspberry vinegar**
   with **oils, maple syrup, mustard**, and **spices**.
2. Shake well. Serve over salad.

Note:
Excellent with curly leaf lettuce and
radicchio.

Papaya Dressing

Parve • 1½ cups   Chilling Time: 4 hours

. . . .

1 ripe papaya
½ cup oil
¼ cup sugar
salt to taste
½ teaspoon dry mustard
½ cup minced onion

1. Peel **papaya**, reserving 2 table-spoons seeds.
2. Put seeds in a food processor.
3. Add **oil, sugar, salt, mustard**, and **onion**.
4. Purée until smooth and seeds are pulverized.
5. Cut papaya into small chunks.
6. Toss dressing and fresh papaya with your favorite combination of lettuce.

Note:
Dressing keeps up to 5 days in refrigerator.

Cranberry Gel

Dairy • 6 to 8 servings   Chilling Time: 4 hours
                                   6-cup mold

. . . .

6 ounces cherry gelatin
16 ounces cranberry sauce
2 cups hot water
8 ounces sour cream
½ cup chopped walnuts
    (optional)

1. Mix **gelatin** with **hot water**.
2. Blend in **cranberry sauce**.
3. Chill until semi-set, about 1 hour.
4. Blend in **sour cream**.
5. Add **walnuts**.
6. Pour into mold and refrigerate until set.

As we were leaving a holiday dinner at grandmas, she would always say "I forgot to serve the jello", and made us all take some home. After this happened many times, we finally convinced her to stop making jello, since it always ungelled in our car on the way home.

❖ Cranberry Raspberry Ring

Parve • 6 to 8 servings

Chilling Time: 5 hours
5-cup mold

. . . .

1½ cups boiling water
3 ounces raspberry gelatin
3 ounces lemon gelatin
10 ounces frozen raspberries
1 cup cranberry-orange relish
1 cup lemon-lime carbonated
    soft drink
orange slices for garnish

1. Dissolve **gelatins** in **water**.
2. Stir in the frozen **raspberries**
   and **relish**.
3. Chill until cold but not set.
4. Add the **carbonated drink**. Stir
   gently.
5. Chill slightly. Pour into a 5 cup
   mold and chill until firm, about 5
   hours.
6. Unmold. Garnish with **orange
   slices**.

Lemon Jello Mold

Dairy • 20 servings

Chilling Time: 3 hours
12-cup mold

. . . .

12 ounces lemon flavored gelatin
5 cups boiling water
12 ounces frozen lemonade,
    defrosted
16 ounces whipped topping
6 tablespoons orange
    marmalade

1. Dissolve **gelatin** in water. Chill
   until thickened about 1 hour.
2. Add **lemonade, whipped
   topping**, and **marmalade**. Beat
   with beater until blended.
3. Pour into mold and chill.

Note:
Can easily be cut in half and used
with a 6-cup mold.

Hint:
Moisten top of **gelatin mold** and serving plate. The moist surfaces make it
easier to slide the gelatin to the center of the plate after it has been unmolded.

❖ Lemon-Blueberry Gelatin

Dairy • Serves 8

Chilling Time: 4 hours
9 x 9 x 2-inch pan

. . . .

3 ounces lemon gelatin
3 ounces black raspberry gelatin
1 cup boiling water
½ cup cold water
1 tablespoon lemon juice
21 ounces blueberry pie filling
¼ cup powdered sugar
1 cup sour cream

1. Dissolve **gelatins** in boiling **water**.
2. Add cold **water** and **lemon juice**.
3. Gradually stir mixture into **pie filling**.
4. Pour into pan.
5. Chill until firm.
6. Fold **powdered sugar** into **sour cream**. Spread on top of gelatin.

Quick and Easy Fruit Ring

Dairy • 16 to 20 servings

Chilling Time: 5 hours
12-cup mold, lightly greased

. . . .

9 ounces raspberry gelatin
2 cups boiling water
20 ounces crushed pineapple, drained, reserve juice
15 ounces blueberries, drained, reserve juice
16 ounces frozen, whipped topping
1 cup chopped nuts

1. Dissolve **gelatin** in **boiling water**.
2. Combine **fruit juices** to make 2 cups. Add to gelatin.
3. Set aside 2 cups of gelatin mixture at room temperature.
4. Add **fruit** to remaining gelatin. Pour into mold and chill until firm, about 3 hours.
5. Whip reserved gelatin until egg white consistency. Fold in **whipped topping** and **nuts**.
6. Pour over firm layer in mold and chill until firm, about 2 hours.

Hint:
Use warm water to **unmold gelatin**. Hot water will melt the gelatin. Dip the mold just to the rim in the warm water, about 10 seconds. Lift from water, shake slightly to loosen the gelatin from the mold. Invert onto moistened plate.

Beyond Challah

B R E A D S

B R E A D S

Challah

Parve • 4 breads

Preheat oven to 325°
Cooking Time: 25 minutes
2 baking sheets, greased

. . . .

B R E A D

2½ cups warm water (90°-115°)
  (divided)
3 scant tablespoons, or 3
  packages active dry yeast
5 tablespoons honey (divided)
5 egg yolks
¾ cup oil
1 tablespoon salt
pinch of saffron
8 cups unbleached white bread
  flour

W A S H

2 egg whites
2 teaspoons water
poppy seeds (optional)

Note:
This recipe requires about 2 hours of
rising time.

Suggestion:
Bread may be baked in four
9 x 5 x 3-inch loaf pans.

1. Combine ½ cup **water, yeast**
   and 1 tablespoon **honey** in a
   small bowl. Allow yeast to
   proof 5-10 minutes. Mixture will
   start to bubble.
2. Beat **egg yolks** in a large bowl.
3. Stir **oil, salt**, remaining honey,
   saffron, and yeast mixture, in
   this order, into the beaten eggs.
4. Let this sponge rest for five
   minutes.
5. Add 4 cups of **flour**, one cup at
   a time, beating well after each
   addition.
6. Add additional 3 to 4 cups of
   flour, enough to make a firm
   dough, alternately with remaining 2 cups of warm water. Mix
   until smooth. Cover with a
   towel and let rest ten minutes.
7. Knead 8 to 10 minutes, or until
   smooth and elastic.
8. Place dough in an oiled bowl,
   turning to bring oiled side up.
9. Cover with waxed paper. Allow
   to rise until double in size,
   approximately 1 to 1½ hours.
10. Divide dough into 4 parts.
    Divide each of these parts into
    3 parts. Roll each part into a
    rope 12 inches long. Braid three
    ropes together, pinching ends
    to seal.
11. Place two loaves on each
    prepared baking sheet. Cover
    with waxed paper and allow to
    rise until doubled, about 45
    minutes.
12. Combine **egg whites** with 2
    teaspoons **water**. Brush mixture
    on braids. Sprinkle with **seeds**.
13. Bake 10 minutes at 325°. Raise
    temperature to 350° and bake
    an additional 15 minutes, or
    until golden brown.

No Knead Wheat Germ Bread

Dairy • 1 loaf

Preheat oven to 375°
Cooking Time: 40 minutes
1½- quart casserole, greased

. . . .

2½-3 cups unsifted flour
  (divided)
½ cup wheat germ
2 packages active dry yeast
2 teaspoons salt
1½ cups very warm water
2 tablespoons butter or
  margarine, softened
2 tablespoons molasses

Variation:
At the start, adding ¼ to ½ cup
chopped onion or instant onion
flakes makes this an onion bread.
Method can be adjusted for use in a
bread machine.

1. Combine 1 cup of the **flour, wheat germ, yeast**, and **salt** in a large bowl. Add **water, butter**, and **molasses**. Beat 2 minutes at medium speed with an electric mixer.
2. Add ½ cup additional flour. Beat at high speed 2 minutes, scraping down sides of bowl.
3. With a wooden spoon, beat in enough flour to make a stiff batter. Cover bowl with a clean towel. Let rise in a warm place, away from drafts, 45 minutes or until doubled in bulk.
4. Punch dough down. Beat vigorously for 30 seconds with wooden spoon. Place in prepared casserole.
5. Bake until bread sounds hollow when tapped. Remove from casserole. Serve warm or cool completely.

Since I was three years old I remember baking challah with my grandmother every Friday. She always made the best challah. One day my grandmother burned the challah, so my mother thought something must be wrong. My grandmother never complained so my mother called the doctor to examine her. She knew her mother never burnt the challah. My grandmother died three days later.

Rise and Shine Cinnamon Rolls

Parve • 24 rolls

Preheat oven to 375°
Cooking Time: 20 to 25 minutes
13 x 9 x 2-inch pan, greased

. . . .

2 packages rapid rise yeast
1 cup warm water (110°-115°)
½ cup sugar
1 teaspoon salt
2 eggs
½ cup soft shortening or
  margarine (divided)
4½-4¾ cups flour (divided)

T O P P I N G

2 tablespoons cinnamon
½ cup sugar

Variation:
½ cup raisins and ½ cup chopped
nuts may be sprinkled on top of
dough before rolling.

1. Dissolve **yeast** in **water**.
2. Add **sugar, salt, eggs, shortening**, and 2½ cups of **flour**. Mix until smooth.
3. Add remaining 2 cups of flour. If dough is sticky, add remaining flour.
4. Knead until smooth on a lightly floured board, about 5 minutes.
5. Place in a greased bowl, turn dough to bring greased side up. Cover. Let rise in a warm place until doubled, about 45 minutes.
6. Punch down. Let rise again until almost doubled, about 15 minutes.
7. Combine **cinnamon** with **sugar**.
8. Roll half of the dough into an 8 x 20-inch oblong. Spread lightly with ¼ cup margarine. Sprinkle with ⅓ of cinnamon-sugar mixture.
9. Beginning at the wide side, tightly roll up dough. Pinch the edge well to seal the roll.
10. Cut roll into 1½ inch slices. Place in prepared pan so you can see swirls.
11. Repeat with second half of dough, having 6 rows, 4 rolls each.
12. Cover. Let rise for 20 minutes. Sprinkle with remaining cinnamon-sugar.
13. Bake until lightly golden brown.

Note:
These freeze well. A glass pan allows
you to check the underside for
doneness.

Hint:
When cooking in **glass pans** reduce temperature by 25 degrees.

❖Pull-Apart Herb Rolls

Dairy • 12 rolls

Preheat oven to 400°
Cooking Time: 15 to 20 minutes
12 cup muffin pan, greased

. . . .

1 package active dry yeast
1 cup warm water
1 stick melted butter or
  margarine (divided)
3-3½ cups flour (divided)
2 tablespoons sugar
1½ teaspoons salt
¼ teaspoon dried thyme
¼ teaspoon dried oregano
¼ teaspoon dried dill

1. Dissolve **yeast** in **warm water**.
   Add ¼ cup **butter**, 2 cups **flour**,
   sugar, salt, thyme, oregano,
   and **dill**.
2. Mix in an electric mixer, with
   dough hook attached, for 2
   minutes, or until well blended.
   Add remaining flour, ½ cup at a
   time, until dough clings to dough
   hook, and cleans side of the
   bowl.
3. Knead dough for about 7
   minutes. Dough should be
   smooth and elastic.
4. Place dough in a greased bowl,
   turning to bring greased side to
   the top. Cover with a clean towel
   and let rise in a warm place 1
   hour, or until doubled in bulk.
5. On a lightly floured surface
   punch down the dough. Roll
   dough into a 12 x 9-inch rectangle. Brush with remaining
   butter.
6. Slice dough into 6 strips, each
   1½ x 12-inches. Stack the strips
   and cut the stack into 12 1-inch
   pieces.
7. Place the pieces, cut side up, in
   the prepared muffin cups. Cover
   and let rise in a warm place 45
   minutes, or until doubled in
   bulk.
8. Bake until light brown. Remove
   from cups immediately and cool
   on wire racks.

Note:
If dough hook is not available, mix
ingredients in a large bowl with a
wooden spoon until ingredients are
well blended. Knead by hand until
dough is smooth and elastic.

Bread Machine Onion Focaccia

Dairy • 10 to 12 servings

Preheat oven to 400°
Cooking Time: 15 minutes
Baking sheet, lightly greased

. . . .

¾ cup water
2 tablespoons olive oil
2 cups bread flour
1 tablespoon sugar
1 teaspoon salt
1½ teaspoons active dry yeast

ONION TOPPING

2 medium onions, sliced
2 cloves garlic, minced
3 tablespoons olive oil
2 tablespoons grated Parmesan
   cheese

1. Place **water, olive oil, flour, sugar, salt** and **yeast** in bread machine. Proceed as directed by manufacturer on dough/manual cycle to knead. Remove dough.
2. Pat dough onto baking sheet. Cover and let rise in a warm place about 30 minutes.
3. Meanwhile, in a sauce pan over moderate heat, cook **onions** and **garlic** in 3 tablespoons **olive oil** for 15 to 20 minutes, stirring occasionally until onion is brown and caramelized. Remove from heat.
4. Make a depression in dough. Spread onion mixture over dough. Sprinkle with **Parmesan cheese**.
5. Bake until edges are brown. Remove and cool on a wire rack.

Note:
This wonderful flat onion bread can be used for open face sandwiches.

❖ *Harvest Bread*

Parve • 2 loaves

Preheat oven to 325°
Cooking Time: 45 to 60 minutes
Two 9 x 5 x 3-inch loaf pans,
  greased

. . . .

2 eggs
2 cups sugar
½ cup oil
½ cup applesauce
¼ cup white wine
2 teaspoons vanilla
1 teaspoon cinnamon
1 teaspoon nutmeg
1 teaspoon salt
3 teaspoons baking soda
1 teaspoon baking powder
3 cups flour
3 cups grated zucchini
1½ cups walnuts or pecans,
  chopped
1½ cups raisins

1. Beat **eggs** in large bowl until foamy.
2. Gradually add **sugar**. Mix thoroughly.
3. Add **oil, applesauce, wine**, and **vanilla**. Add **cinnamon, nutmeg, salt, baking soda**, and **baking powder**. Mix until blended.
4. Add **flour** alternately with **zucchini**.
5. Fold in **nuts** and **raisins**.
6. Bake until toothpick inserted in center of loaf comes out clean.

Note:
This bread can be frozen.

Hint:
Pans should be **greased** with shortening, butter, or margarine. Do not use oil, as dough seems to absorb oil and will invariably stick.

Chocolate Zucchini Bread To Go

Dairy • 3 loaves

Preheat oven to 350°
Cooking Time: 1 hour
3 loaf pans, 8 x 4 x 2½ inch,
   lightly greased

. . . .

3 eggs
2 cups sugar
1 cup oil
1 teaspoon vanilla
3 cups flour
1 teaspoon baking soda
¼ teaspoon baking powder
1 teaspoon cinnamon
¼ teaspoon salt
½ cup sour cream
2 cups grated unpeeled zucchini
½ cup raisins
1 cup chopped nuts
¼ cup chocolate chips

1. Beat **eggs, sugar, oil** and **vanilla** together.
2. Mix **flour** with next four **dry ingredients**. Blend into egg mixture.
3. Beat in **sour cream**.
4. Mix in **zucchini, raisins, nuts**, and **chips**, making sure all are well blended.
5. Pour into prepared pans and bake until tester comes out dry or the top is golden and springs back to the touch.

Poppy Seed Bread

Dairy • 2 loaves

Preheat oven to 350°
Cooking Time: 1 hour
Two loaf pans, 8½ x 4½ x 2½-
   inch, greased and floured

. . . .

3 eggs, slightly beaten
2¼ cups sugar
1½ cups oil
1½ cups milk
3 cups flour
1½ teaspoons baking powder
1½ teaspoons salt
1½ tablespoons poppy seeds
2 teaspoons almond extract

1. Beat together **eggs, sugar, oil**, and **milk**.
2. Combine **flour, baking powder**, and **salt**. Beat into egg mixture.
3. Stir in **poppy seeds** and **almond extract**. Divide batter into prepared pans.
4. Bake for 1 hour or until top is golden brown, springs back to the touch and toothpick inserted into centers comes out clean.
5. Cool breads in pans for 10 minutes, then run thin knife around edges of pans. Remove breads. Cool on wire racks.

Wilma's Corn Bread

Dairy • 12 to 16 servings

Preheat oven to 350°
Cooking Time: 30 to 40 minutes
9-inch square pan, greased

. . . .

½ cup sugar
½ cup shortening
1 egg
1 teaspoon baking soda
1 cup buttermilk or sour milk
¾ cup cornmeal
1 cup flour
1 teaspoon salt

1. Beat **sugar, shortening, egg,**
   and **baking soda** at low speed.
2. Gradually beat in **buttermilk** or
   sour milk.
3. Add **cornmeal, flour**, and **salt**.
   Stir until no lumps remain.
4. Pour batter into prepared pan.
5. Bake until toothpick comes out
   clean.

Note:
*Double recipe for a 13 x 9 x 2-inch
pan.*

Hint:
To make **sour milk,** put 1 tablespoon lemon juice or vinegar in a 1 cup measure. Add
milk to make 1 cup. Skim or low fat milk can be used.

Autumn Pumpkin Loaves

Parve • 2 loaves

Preheat oven to 350°
Cooking Time: 1 hour
Two 9 x 5 x 3-inch loaf pans,
  greased

. . . .

3 cups flour
2 cups sugar
2 teaspoons baking soda
½ teaspoon baking powder
1 teaspoon ground cloves
1 teaspoon cinnamon
1 teaspoon nutmeg
1 teaspoon salt
16 ounces canned pumpkin
⅔ cup oil
3 eggs slightly beaten

1. In a large bowl mix **flour,
   sugar, baking soda, baking
   powder**, and **spices**.
2. Add **pumpkin, oil,** and **eggs**.
   Blend.
3. Pour batter into prepared pans.
   Bake until a toothpick inserted in
   the center comes out clean.
4. Cool pans on wire rack 10
   minutes. Remove loaves and
   cool on rack.

Note:
Do not use pie filling.

❖ Zesty Lemon Bread

Dairy • 3 loaves

Preheat oven to 350°
Cooking Time: 55 to 60 minutes
Three loaf pans, 9 x 5 x 3-inch,
   greased and floured

BREAD

2 sticks butter or margarine
4 eggs, separated
2 cups sugar
3¼ cups flour
2 teaspoons baking powder
1 teaspoon salt
1¼ cups milk
1 cup finely chopped nuts
grated zest from 2 lemons

1. Cream **butter**. Blend in **egg yolks** and **sugar**. Beat well.
2. Mix together **flour, baking powder**, and **salt**. Add to egg yolk mixture, alternating with milk. Blend until just mixed.
3. Beat **egg whites** until stiff.
4. Add egg whites, **nuts**, and **lemon zest**.
5. Pour into prepared pans and bake until toothpick inserted in the center comes out clean.
6. Glaze when hot. Cool 1 hour before removing from pans.

GLAZE

½ cup sugar
2-3 tablespoons lemon juice

1. Combine **sugar** and **lemon juice**.
2. Pierce top surface of bread with toothpick.
3. Spoon lemon-sugar mixture over hot loaves.

Hint:
Remove only the thinnest layer of rind, or **zest**, with a parer or sharp knife. Be careful not to cut into the pith, the bitter white layer beneath the color.

Basic Banana Cake

Parve • 18 servings

Preheat oven to 375°
Cooking Time: 25 minutes
Two 8 x 8-inch pans, greased

· ·

1⅓ cups sugar
2 eggs
1 stick margarine
2 cups flour
1 teaspoon baking powder
1 teaspoon baking soda
¼ teaspoon salt
½ cup plus 2 tablespoons
   pineapple, orange or lemon
   juice
1 cup mashed bananas
½ cup chopped nuts

1. Cream **sugar, eggs**, and **margarine**.
2. Combine **dry ingredients** and add alternately with **fruit juice**. Add **banana** and **nuts**.
3. Beat until just blended.
4. Pour batter into prepared pans.
5. Bake until tester comes out clean and top is browned.

Variation:
Nuts can be ground and sprinkled on the top before baking.

Hint:
Peeled **bananas** can be frozen. Cover tightly with plastic wrap and place in a plastic bag. Defrost and use in any recipe calling for mashed bananas. Or, mash bananas first, and then place in freezer containers.

Banana Oatmeal Muffins

Dairy • 12 muffins

Preheat oven to: 375°
Cooking Time: 20 minutes
12 cup muffin pan, greased

. . . .

½ cup sugar
1 stick butter or margarine
2 eggs
3 medium bananas, mashed
¾ cup honey
1½ cups flour
1 teaspoon baking soda
1 teaspoon baking powder
1 cup quick cooking rolled oats

1. In a large mixing bowl, cream **sugar** and **butter**. Beat in **eggs, bananas**, and **honey**.
2. Stir in **flour, baking soda**, and **baking powder**. Beat until well blended.
3. Stir in **oats**.
4. Fill prepared muffin cups ¾ full.
5. Bake until golden and a tooth-pick inserted in center comes out clean. Remove from pan and cool on rack.

Hints:

If the **batter** does not fill all the cups, put a few tablespoons of water in the empty forms, to protect the pans and to keep the muffins moist.

3 to 4 medium-sized **bananas** equal 2 cups mashed bananas. If you do not have enough fresh bananas you can make up the difference with jars of baby fruit.

Apple Streusel Muffins

Dairy • 12 muffins

Preheat oven to 425°
Cooking Time: 20 minutes
12 cup muffin pan, greased or
paper lined.

BATTER

2 cups flour
½ cup sugar
1 teaspoon salt
3 teaspoons baking powder
1 stick margarine
1 egg
⅔ cup milk
1 cup pared, diced apple
1 teaspoon grated lemon zest

1. Sift together **flour, sugar, salt**, and **baking powder**.
2. Cut in **margarine** until crumbly.
3. Set aside ½ cup of this crumb mixture for streusel topping.
4. Beat **egg** well. Stir in **milk, apple**, and **lemon zest**.
5. Combine dry and wet mixtures. Spoon into prepared muffin pans, filling ⅔'s full.

STREUSEL TOPPING

½ cup reserved crumb mixture
1 teaspoon grated lemon zest
2 tablespoons sugar
¼ cup chopped nuts

1. Blend reserved crumb mixture, **lemon zest, sugar**, and **nuts** to make topping. Sprinkle on each muffin.
2. Bake until muffins are rounded on top, and slightly brown.

Note:
Stir, do not beat muffin batter. The ingredients should be moist and lumpy.

Old Fashioned Blueberry Muffins

Dairy • 12 muffins

Preheat oven to 300°
Cooking Time: 30 minutes
12 cup muffin pan, greased and
  floured

. . . .

1 stick margarine
1 cup sugar, plus 2 teaspoons
  (divided)
2 eggs
2 cups flour
2 teaspoons baking powder
½ cup milk
1 teaspoon vanilla
2 cups blueberries

1. With electric mixer on low
   speed, cream **margarine** and
   1 cup **sugar** until fluffy.
2. Add **eggs**, one at a time, and
   mix until well blended.
3. Sift **flour** and **baking powder**
   together. Add alternately with
   milk and **vanilla**.
4. Gently stir in **blueberries** by
   hand with a wooden spoon.
5. Spoon mixture into prepared
   pan, piling high. Sprinkle tops
   liberally with remaining 2
   teaspoons sugar.
6. Bake at 300° for 7 to 10 minutes.
   Increase heat to 375° and bake
   for 30 minutes more. This is very
   important to insure that muffins
   puff up.

Note:
Muffins can be frozen.

✡ *Passover Vegetable Muffins*

Meat • 10 to 12 muffins

Preheat oven to 350°
Cooking Time: 45 minutes
12 cup muffin pan, greased

. . . .

3 tablespoons oil
2 small onions, finely chopped
1 clove garlic, minced
2 stalks celery, finely chopped
1 cup mushrooms, finely
  chopped
½ green bell pepper, finely
  chopped
¼ teaspoon dried thyme
3 cups matzoh farfel
2 cups chicken broth, heated
3 eggs, beaten
salt and pepper to taste

Variation:
Use vegetable broth and this is
parve.

1. Heat **oil** in a large, heavy skillet. Sauté **onions** and **garlic** until the onion is translucent.
2. Add **celery, mushrooms, green pepper**, and **thyme**. Sauté 2 minutes.
3. Soak the **farfel** in the warm **broth** until soft. Add the vegetables and **eggs**.
4. Season with **salt** and **pepper**. Mix thoroughly.
5. Mound moist mixture in prepared muffin pan. Bake until top is browned.
6. Let cool 5 minutes before removing from pan. Serve warm as a bread or a vegetable.

Hints:
Avoid soaking **vegetables** after slicing; you will lose much of the nutritional value.

Save **vegetable juices** from cooking; they can be used for vegetable soup or sauces. Freeze in ice cube containers and use as many as needed.

Beyond Pancakes and Punch

BRUNCH & BEVERAGES

Brunch & Beverages

Blintzes Supreme

Dairy • 10 servings

Preheat oven to 350°
Cooking Time: 1 hour 30 minutes
13 x 9 x 2-inch baking pan,
   greased

BLINTZES

3 eggs
1½ cups flour
1½ cups milk
oil for cooking

1. Beat **eggs** and add **flour** alternately with **milk**.
2. Place skillet over medium heat and brush with **oil**.
3. Pour approximately 2 tablespoons of batter into pan to make a very thin pancake, rotate to cover entire pan.
4. Cook until browned on one side only.
5. Turn pancake out onto waxed paper, browned side down.
6. Repeat with remaining batter.

FILLING

1½ pounds pot cheese or farmer cheese
2 egg yolks
sugar and cinnamon to taste

1. Combine **cheese** with **egg yolks, sugar**, and **cinnamon**.
2. Place 1 tablespoon of filling on non-browned side of pancake.
3. Fold sides of pancake over filling to form a square.
4. Place in prepared pan.

TOPPING

1½ pints sour cream
4 eggs
4½ sticks margarine, melted
1 cup sugar
1 teaspoon vanilla

1. Blend **sour cream** with **eggs, margarine, sugar**, and **vanilla**.
2. Pour over blintzes.
3. Bake until puffed and golden brown. Check after one hour.

Breakfast Apple Soufflé

Dairy • 4 to 6 servings

Preheat oven to 425°
Cooking Time: 20 minutes
12-inch quiche pan

. . . .

6 eggs
1½ cups milk
1 cup flour
3 tablespoons sugar
1 teaspoon vanilla
½ teaspoon salt
¼ teaspoon cinnamon
4 tablespoons margarine
2 tart apples, peeled and sliced
2 tablespoons brown sugar

1. In a large bowl, mix **eggs, milk, flour, sugar, vanilla, salt**, and **cinnamon** until blended.
2. Melt **margarine** in quiche pan. Add **apple slices** and bake in pan in the oven for 3 to 5 minutes. Do not allow apples to brown.
3. Remove pan from the oven and pour batter over the apples. Sprinkle with **brown sugar**.
4. Bake until puffed and brown. Serve immediately.

Note:
Equivalent egg substitute can be used.

Cheesy Egg Soufflé

Dairy • 8 to 12 servings

Preheat oven to 325°
Cooking time: 40 minutes
13 x 9 x 2-inch pan, greased

. . . .

6 eggs, beaten
1 cup milk
2 teaspoons sugar
1 teaspoon salt
½ pound Monterey Jack cheese, cubed
3 ounces cream cheese
8 ounces cottage cheese
2 tablespoons butter, cubed
1 teaspoon baking powder
½ cup flour
chives or parsley for garnish

1. In a large bowl, beat **eggs, milk, sugar**, and **salt** together.
2. Add **Monterey Jack cheese, cream cheese, cottage cheese**, and **butter**. Blend.
3. At this point, dish may be refrigerated up to one day.
4. Just before baking, blend in **baking powder** and **flour**. Pour into prepared pan.
5. Bake until set.
6. Garnish with **chives** or **parsley** before serving.

Note:
Will hold shape 10 to 15 minutes with oven turned off.

French Toast with Orange Zest

Dairy • 3 servings

Cooking Time: 3 to 5 minutes
Large skillet

. . . .

3 eggs
¾ cup milk
grated zest of 2 oranges
6 (½-inch) slices challah or
    brioche bread
oil
powdered sugar
maple syrup

Variation:
Add ¼ teaspoon vanilla to batter.

1. Mix **eggs, milk**, and **orange zest** in a deep-sided dish. Add 3 slices **bread**. Soak and turn over.
2. Heat small amount of **oil** in skillet. Brown bread on both sides.
3. Serve with **powdered sugar** and **syrup**.
4. Repeat with remaining bread.

Overnight French Toast

Dairy • 6 to 8 servings

Preheat oven to 450°
Chilling Time: Overnight
13 x 9 x 2-inch baking pan,
    greased

. . . .

1 loaf French bread
1¼ cups egg substitute
¾ cup skim milk
¼ teaspoon baking powder
1 tablespoon vanilla
20 ounces frozen whole
    strawberries
4 bananas, sliced
½ cup sugar
3 packets granulated sugar
    substitute
1 teaspoon nutmeg
1 teaspoon cinnamon

1. Cut **French bread** into 8 thick slices. Place in an ungreased baking dish.
2. Combine **egg substitute, milk, baking powder**, and **vanilla**.
3. Pour mixture over bread. Cover and refrigerate overnight.
4. Next day, combine **strawberries, banana, sugar, sugar substitute, nutmeg**, and **cinnamon**.
5. Place fruit in greased baking pan and top with prepared bread.
6. Bake 20-25 minutes, or until bread is puffed and golden brown.

TOPPING

¼ cup sugar
1 tablespoon cinnamon

. . . .

1. Combine **sugar** with **cinnamon**.
2. Sprinkle on top of bread.

Note:
This is a low fat recipe.

Veggie Cheddar Strata

Dairy • 8 servings

Preheat oven to 350°
Chilling Time: Overnight
13 x 9 x 2-inch pan, greased

. . . .

1½ cups finely chopped onion
1 cup finely chopped scallions
¾ pound mushrooms, thinly
 sliced
3 tablespoons olive oil
2 medium red bell peppers cut
 into thin strips
2 medium green bell peppers,
 cut into thin strips
salt and pepper to taste
9 cups Italian bread cut into 1-
 inch cubes (1½ loaves)
2½ cups grated cheddar cheese
1 cup grated Parmesan cheese
12 eggs
3½ cups milk
3 tablespoons Dijon mustard
Tabasco sauce to taste

Variations:
Substitute leftover cooked
vegetables for mushrooms and
peppers. Egg substitute, skim milk,
and low fat cheese can be used.

1. Sauté **onions, scallions**, and
 mushrooms in **olive oil** over
 low heat, stirring until onions
 soften.
2. Add **red** and **green peppers,
 salt**, and **pepper** and cook over
 medium heat, stirring until all
 liquid is evaporated and peppers
 are tender.
3. Arrange ½ the **bread** in prepared
 baking pan. Spread ½ the
 vegetable mixture over bread
 and sprinkle with ½ of each
 cheese.
4. Cover with rest of bread,
 remaining vegetables and
 remaining cheese.
5. In a large bowl, whisk together
 eggs, milk, mustard, and
 Tabasco sauce. Pour evenly
 over casserole. Cover and chill
 overnight.
6. Bring to room temperature. Bake
 50-60 minutes, or until puffed,
 golden and cooked through.

Mini Puffs

Dairy • 12 muffins

Preheat oven to 350°
Cooking Time: 20 minutes
12 cup muffin pan, greased

. . . .

1½ cups flour
½ cup sugar
1½ teaspoons baking powder
¼ teaspoon ground nutmeg
⅛ teaspoon salt
1 egg
½ cup milk
⅓ cup melted margarine

1. In a mixing bowl, combine **flour, sugar, baking powder, nutmeg,** and **salt**. Make a well in the center.
2. In another bowl, beat **egg** slightly. Stir in **milk** and **margarine**. Add egg mixture to flour mixture. Stir just until moistened. Batter may be slightly lumpy.
3. Fill prepared cups ½ full with batter. Bake until golden.

TOPPING

¼ cup sugar
½ teaspoon ground cinnamon
⅓ cup melted margarine

1. In a shallow bowl, combine **sugar** and **cinnamon**.
2. When muffins are baked, immediately brush them with melted **margarine** and sprinkle sugar-cinnamon mixture over tops.

Classic Coffee Cake

Dairy • 10 servings

Preheat oven to 350°
Cooking Time: 60-70 minutes
9-inch Bundt pan, greased

. . . .

3 cups sifted flour
1½ teaspoons baking powder
1½ teaspoons baking soda
1½ cups sour cream
1½ sticks butter or margarine
2 cups sugar (divided)
2 teaspoons vanilla
3 eggs
½ cup chopped walnuts
2 teaspoons cinnamon
½ cup chocolate chips

Variation:
Add ½ cup golden raisins to the nut mixture.

1. Combine **flour** with baking powder and set aside.
2. Mix **baking soda** with **sour cream** and set aside.
3. Cream **butter** until fluffy. Add 1½ cups **sugar**, beating again. Mix in **vanilla**.
4. Add **eggs**, one at a time, and beat until mixture is light and fluffy.
5. Add dry ingredients, a little at a time, alternating with sour cream mixture. End with sour cream.
6. Spoon half the batter into prepared pan.
7. Mix together **nuts**, remaining ½ cup sugar, **cinnamon**, and **chocolate chips**. Sprinkle half of this mixture on top of batter.
8. Spoon in remaining batter and sprinkle remaining nut mixture on top.
9. Twirl knife in batter to create a marbled effect.
10. Bake until cake tester inserted in center of cake comes out clean.

Putter Kuchen

Dairy • 6 to 8 servings

Chilling Time: overnight
Preheat oven to 350°
9-inch square dish, greased

DOUGH

2½ cups flour (divided)
1 (0.6 ounce) yeast cake
¼ cup warm water
4 tablespoons sugar
½ teaspoon salt
4 tablespoons butter, melted
½ cup sour cream
2 eggs, well beaten

1. Put 2 cups of **flour** in a large bowl and make a well in the center.
2. Dissolve **yeast** in **warm water** and let stand until yeast starts to bubble.
3. Pour yeast mixture into well in flour. Add **sugar, salt, butter, sour cream**, and **eggs**.
4. Knead with hands until dough leaves sides of bowl.
5. As you knead, add approximately ½ cup flour so dough isn't sticky and the butter gets absorbed.
6. Cover with waxed paper and refrigerate overnight.

FILLING

2 tablespoons butter, melted
2 teaspoons cinnamon, divided
2 tablespoons sugar, divided
½ cup raisins

1. The next day, remove dough from refrigerator and cover it with several heavy cloth towels.
2. Place dough in a warm place to rise for about 2 hours or until doubled in bulk.
3. Put dough on a floured board and knead.
4. Roll into a large rectangle ⅛ to ¼-inch thick. Brush top with 1 tablespoon melted **butter**.
5. Combine **cinnamon** and **sugar** and sprinkle half of mixture, along with **raisins**, over the brushed butter.
6. Roll dough up and cut into 1 to 1½-inch slices.
7. Place slices flat in prepared pan about 1-inch apart.
8. Cover with a towel and let rise in a warm place until doubled.
9. Brush top with remaining melted butter and sprinkle with remaining cinnamon and sugar mixture.
10. Bake 15 to 20 minutes, or until the top is golden.

Schnecken

Dairy • 36 to 40 muffins

Chilling Time: overnight
Preheat oven to 350°
36 muffin cups

DOUGH

. . . .

1½ packages active dry yeast
¼ cup warm water
1 teaspoon sugar
1 cup milk less 2 tablespoons
1 stick butter, softened
⅓ cup sugar
1 teaspoon salt
4 cups sifted flour (divided)
2 eggs
1 stick butter, melted

1. Dissolve **yeast** in **warm water**. Add 1 teaspoon **sugar**. Let stand until yeast bubbles.
2. Scald **milk**. Add **softened butter, sugar**, and **salt**. Cool to lukewarm.
3. Add 2 cups **flour** and dissolved yeast. Beat well.
4. Add **eggs** and remaining flour. Beat until mixture is smooth.
5. Pour into greased bowl. Cover with towel and refrigerate overnight.
6. Next day, remove dough from refrigerator. Let rest about 2 hours. Meanwhile, prepare topping and filling.
7. Divide dough into thirds.
8. On a floured board, roll one-third of dough into a rectangle ¼-inch thick and 12 inches long.
9. Sprinkle rectangle with one third of **cinnamon** and **sugar** mixture and one third of the **raisins**.
10. Starting from the long side of the rectangle, roll the dough tightly and pinch to seal.
11. Slice roll into 1-inch pieces or to fill half of each muffin cup. Place on topping.
12. Press down and brush tops with **melted butter**.
13. Cover with towel or plastic wrap. Let rise until puffy. Repeat process with remaining two parts of dough and remaining cinnamon mixture, raisins, and melted butter.
14. Bake 15 minutes, on middle shelf of oven, or until golden brown. When muffins are done, turn pan upside down immediately onto waxed paper to cool.

Schnecken *(continued)*

TOPPING

2 sticks butter
1 cup brown sugar
2 tablespoons light corn syrup
1½ teaspoons water
1¼ cups coarsely chopped
    pecans

1. Cream **butter**. Add **brown sugar** gradually. Add **syrup** and **water**. Mix well.
2. Spread 2 level teaspoons of this mixture in bottom of each muffin cup.
3. Sprinkle with **chopped pecans**.

FILLING

1 tablespoon cinnamon
¼ cup sugar
1 cup raisins (divided)

1. Mix **cinnamon** and **sugar** together.
2. Reserve **raisins**.

Note:
Place waxed paper onto a cookie sheet. Place this on top of muffin pan, then invert.

Microwave Marmalade

Parve • 1 to 1½ cups   Cooking Time: 6 minutes

1 seedless navel orange
sugar

Variation:
Grapefruit, lemon or lime marmalade can be made the same way.

1. Slice **orange** into several pieces. Using a food processor fitted with a steel blade, finely chop the entire orange. Measure the amount. Place in a microwave bowl.
2. Measure an equal amount of **sugar**. Add to bowl with orange. Mix well.
3. Cook at high power in microwave oven for 6 minutes, stirring every 2 minutes.
4. Pour into a clean jar. Refrigerate.

Pear Chutney

Parve • 4 cups

Cooking Time: 50 to 60 minutes
Chilling Time: Overnight
Large covered saucepan

. . . .

4 pounds Anjou pears
1 scant cup honey
¾ cup fresh lemon juice
½ teaspoon ground cloves
2 teaspoons cinnamon
½ cup golden raisins

1. Peel and cut **pears** into 1-inch pieces. Cook pears, **honey, lemon juice, clove**, and **cinnamon** over moderate heat. Stir, until mixture begins to simmer.
2. Simmer 35 to 45 minutes or until thickened.
3. Add **raisins** and simmer, partially covered, for 15 minutes. Stir occasionally.
4. Transfer to bowl. Cover, cool, and chill overnight or up to a week.

Note:
Preparing a day in advance allows the flavors to blend. Conserve will continue to thicken as it ages in refrigerator.

Hints:
When planning to **cook pears**, make sure to use them while they are still firm.

To **ripen pears** for eating, store in a paper bag.

Refrigerate **ripe fruit**.

Cranberry Chutney

Parve • 1½ quarts

Cooking Time: 40 to 45 minutes
4-quart pot

. . . .

4 small oranges, peeled
4 cups fresh cranberries
1 cup diced unpeeled apple
½ cup seedless raisins
2 cups sugar
½ cup orange juice
¼ cup chopped walnuts
1 tablespoon vinegar
½ teaspoon powdered ginger
½ teaspoon cinnamon

1. Separate **oranges** into segments.
2. In pot, combine **fruits** with **sugar, juice, walnuts, vinegar**, and **spices**. Cook over medium heat, shaking pot occasionally, until all cranberries pop.
3. Refrigerate. Chutney will thicken.

Note:
Flavor improves if made a few days ahead. It will keep 2 to 3 weeks.

Hints:
Fresh **cranberries** can be frozen in the original package, unrinsed, for 5 to 6 months. Rinse in a colander and use still frozen.

When **freezing foods**, label each container with the contents and the date it was put into the freezer.

Tropical Tea Punch

Parve • 12 (6-ounce) servings   Chilling Time: 2 hours

. . . .

8 tea bags
4 cups water
6 ounces frozen orange juice
    concentrate
6 ounces frozen pineapple juice
    concentrate
½ pint fresh strawberries
32 ounces club soda
ice

1. Brew **tea** in boiling **water** for
   five minutes.
2. Remove tea bags. Chill.
3. At serving time, combine tea
   with **juice concentrates** and
   strawberries in a punch bowl.
4. Add **soda** and **ice**.

Tea Punch

Parve • 16 cups   Chilling Time: 3 hours

. . . .

4 tea bags
2 cups hot water
5 cups orange juice
1 cup lemon juice
2 quarts ginger ale
sugar to taste
1 quart lemon sherbet

Variation:
8 teaspoons loose tea may be used.
Be sure to strain leaves before
adding sherbet.

1. Brew **tea** leaving tea bags in
   water.
2. Add **juices, ginger ale**, and
   sugar. Chill.
3. Remove tea bags.
4. Add **sherbet** just before serving.

Note:
Loose tea can be placed in a tea ball
or cheesecloth.

Fire Island Margaritas

Parve • 4 to 6 servings

. . . .

4-6 tablespoons fresh lime juice
6 ounces frozen limeade
    concentrate
6 ounces tequila
2 ounces triple sec
10 ice cubes
lime slices for garnish

1. Place **lime juice, limeade,**
   tequila and **triple sec** in a
   blender.
2. Fill blender to top with **ice**
   cubes.
3. Blend until smooth.
4. Garnish with **lime slices**.

Beyond Brisket

ENTRÉES

ENTRÉES

Traditional Brisket of Beef

Meat • 10 to 12 servings

Preheat oven to 400°
Cooking Time: 3 hours
Large covered roasting pan

. . . .

5 pounds potatoes, peeled and
　quartered
2 pounds carrots, cut in chunks
3-4 stalks celery, cut in chunks
2 large onions, sliced
1 cup water
pepper to taste
garlic powder to taste
14 ounces ketchup
5-7 pound beef brisket

1. Place **potatoes, carrots, celery**,
   and **onions** in pan.
2. Add enough **water** to cover
   vegetables.
3. Add **pepper** and **garlic
   powder**.
4. Mix **ketchup** with water.
5. Place **brisket** on top of vegetables and pour ketchup mixture
   over meat.
6. Bake, covered. Turn brisket over
   and baste after 1½ hours. Baste
   as needed. Continue baking until
   meat is easily pierced with a
   fork.
7. Slice brisket across the grain.
   Serve with warmed pan juices.

Hint:
Brisket is best when prepared ahead of time, as it is easier to slice the meat
when cold, and to remove the fat from the gravy.

✡ *Brisket with Shiitake Mushrooms*

Meat • 8 to 10 servings

Preheat oven to 300°
Cooking Time: 4½ hours
Large covered roaster

. . . .

5-8 pound beef brisket
salt and pepper to taste
24 pearl onions
6 parsley sprigs
1 rosemary sprig
1 thyme sprig
2 bay leaves
2 tomatoes, peeled and chopped
2 large carrots, coarsely chopped
3 cloves garlic, minced
4 cups boiling chicken broth
¼ cup matzoh cake meal
4 tablespoons margarine
   (divided)
½ pound shiitake mushrooms
2 tablespoons fresh parsley,
   minced

Note:
To braise is to cook slowly in very
little liquid.

1. Season **brisket** with **salt** and
   pepper. Line broiler pan with
   foil. Broil brisket 4 inches from
   heat for 4 to 6 minutes on each
   side.
2. Blanch **onions** in boiling water
   one minute. Peel. Set aside.
3. Combine fresh **herb sprigs** and
   bay leaves in a cheesecloth
   bag.
4. Transfer brisket to roasting pan.
   Add **tomatoes, carrots**,
   onions, cheesecloth bag, **garlic**,
   and **broth**. Braise, 3 to 3½
   hours, covered, in a 300° oven.
5. Raise temperature to 375°. Baste
   and cook uncovered for an
   additional 45 minutes, or until
   easily pierced with a fork. Let
   stand 20 minutes and slice.
6. Reserve 3 cups of braising
   liquid along with vegetables.
   Skim fat.
7. In a small saucepan, brown the
   cake meal over moderately
   high heat, stirring constantly for
   6 minutes. Add 2 tablespoons of
   margarine. Add 2 cups of
   reserved braising liquid in a
   stream and whisk until mixture
   is smooth.
8. Cook **mushrooms** in the
   remaining 2 tablespoons
   margarine over moderate heat,
   stirring until the liquid has
   evaporated. Stir in **parsley**, salt,
   and pepper to taste.
9. Add cake meal mixture to
   mushrooms. Add enough left
   over braising liquid mixture
   until gravy is desired consistency. Warm gravy.
10. Serve gravy with brisket.

Chili Spiced Brisket

Meat • 8 to 10 servings

Preheat oven 350°
Cooking Time: 3 hours
Covered roasting pan

. . . .

4-5 pounds brisket of beef
salt and pepper to taste
3-4 peppercorns
1 bay leaf
8 ounces chili sauce
1½ cups diced onions
1 tablespoon Worcestershire
   sauce
1½ cups beef bouillon
1½ tablespoons brown sugar
dash garlic salt

1. Sear **beef** on all sides in a hot skillet. Place in roaster.
2. Top beef with **peppercorns, bay leaf, chili sauce**, and **onions**. Combine **Worcestershire sauce, bouillon, brown sugar**, and **garlic salt** and pour over and around beef.
3. Cover and bake. After 2½ hours, test for tenderness with a fork.
4. For gravy, strain liquid and onions through a fine strainer. Discard pulp.
5. Let meat rest 10 to 15 minutes before slicing. Cover with gravy and serve.

Note:
If preparing in advance, refrigerate gravy and unsliced meat separately. When ready to serve, skim fat from top of gravy and slice meat. Cover with gravy and heat.

Cranberry Brisket

Meat • 8 servings

Preheat oven to 350°
Cooking Time: 3 hours
Covered roasting pan

. . . .

4 pounds brisket
1 (1 ounce) envelope dry onion
   soup mix
16 ounces whole cranberry sauce
1 cup red wine, Burgundy
   preferred

1. Rinse **brisket**. Place in pan.
2. Combine **soup mix, sauce**, and **wine**. Pour over beef.
3. Cover pan and bake until easily pierced with a fork.
4. Slice across the grain. Serve with gravy.

Hint:
When slicing or **cutting meat**, cut across grain for most tender results.

Southwestern Brisket

Meat • 4 to 6 servings

Preheat oven to 325°
Cooking Time: 2 to 2½ hours
3-quart covered roasting pan

. . . .

3-4 pound beef brisket
5-6 onions, sliced
½ cup cold water
½ cup chili sauce
2 tablespoons brown sugar
1½ tablespoons vinegar
dash Worcestershire sauce

1. Sear **beef** browning on both sides.
2. Place in baking dish and cover with sliced **onions**.
3. Mix **water** with **chili sauce, brown sugar, vinegar**, and **Worcestershire sauce**. Pour over onions and beef.
4. Bake, covered, until meat is easily pierced with a fork.
5. Cool and slice against the grain. Serve with gravy.

Note:
This can be prepared on top of the stove at a gentle simmer.

My grandfather used to tell us that Nana was the prettiest girl at the party. But that's not why he married her. He'd pause, waiting for our full attention. "It was her pot roast," he'd whisper, "now come eat." And we would. Who could resist a meal that could steal a young man's heart?

Tzimmes

Meat • 8 servings

Cooking Time: 3 hours
Large covered roasting pan

1 tablespoon oil
1½ pounds boneless chuck or
   brisket
3-4 pounds carrots, thickly sliced
½ cup orange juice
salt to taste
3 tablespoons brown sugar

1. Heat pan. Add **oil** and quickly
   brown **meat** on all sides.
2. Add enough cold water to just
   cover the meat. Bring water to a
   boil and reduce heat to simmer.
3. Cover and cook meat until
   tender, about 1½ hours.
4. Skim off the foam that rises to
   the top.
5. Remove the meat from pan and
   slice. Keep covered in the
   refrigerator. The water should
   be reduced to about half.
6. Add **carrots** to pan. Stir well.
7. Bring to a boil. Reduce heat to
   simmer.
8. Cook 45 minutes. Stir frequently
   to prevent sticking.
9. Add **orange juice, salt**, and
   brown sugar to carrots. If less
   than 1 cup liquid remains, add
   cold water to equal 1 cup. Bring
   to a boil and simmer for 15
   minutes.
10. Cool, drain and reserve carrot
    stock.

E I N B R E N   (T H I C K E N I N G)

3 tablespoons flour
3 tablespoons shortening
1 cup reserved carrot stock
4 ounces chopped candied
   ginger

1. Brown **flour** in a small, dry
   skillet over medium heat. Stir to
   prevent burning.
2. When flour is very light brown,
   remove from heat and slowly
   add **shortening**. Stir until
   smooth.
3. Slowly add **carrot stock** to
   mixture. It bubbles up.
4. Stir to make a smooth paste.
   Add to the carrots in pan.
5. Continue to simmer until the
   stock has thickened, about 10
   to 15 minutes.
6. Add **ginger** to the pan. Stir. If
   added too soon, the ginger
   tends to dissolve and taste
   diminishes.
7. Return the meat to tzimmes or
   reheat in a sauce of your
   choice.

Sauerbraten

Meat • 4-6 servings

Marinating Time: 4 days
Cooking Time: 2-3 hours
Covered roasting pan

. . . .

3 pounds beef, chuck or shoulder
1 tablespoon salt
½ teaspoon pepper
2 onions, sliced
1 carrot, sliced
1 stalk celery, chopped
4 whole cloves
4 peppercorns
2 bay leaves
2 cups red wine vinegar
5 cups water
2 tablespoons oil
6 tablespoons margarine

1. Wipe **beef** with damp cloth. Season with **salt** and **pepper**. Place in large bowl.
2. Combine **onions, carrot**, and **celery**, with **spices, vinegar, and water**. Heat and pour over meat. Refrigerate, covered, for 4 days.
3. On 5th day, drain meat and reserve marinade.
4. Sauté meat in **oil** and melted **margarine**.
5. Add marinade and simmer 2 to 3 hours, covered, until easily pierced with a fork.
6. Drain marinade and reserve 1½ cups.
7. Serve with Gingersnap Gravy.

GINGERSNAP GRAVY. . . . .

2 tablespoons sugar
5 tablespoons flour
1½ cups hot marinade
½ cup water
⅔ cups gingersnap crumbs

1. Melt **sugar** in skillet until golden brown. Carefully add **flour**.
2. Gradually stir in hot **marinade** and **water**.
3. Add **gingersnap crumbs**.
4. Cook, stirring, until mixture thickens.

Hint:
Most marinades contain acidic ingredients, therefore always marinate in a non-metallic container.

Traditional Stuffed Cabbage

Meat • 12 servings

Preheat oven to 350°
Cooking Time: 2½ hours
Covered roasting pan

. . . .

1 large head of cabbage
3 pounds ground beef
½ cup bread crumbs
2 eggs
¼ cup ketchup
¼ cup grated carrot
1 large onion, sliced
8 cups diced tomatoes or tomato
    purée
½ cup sugar
½ cup brown sugar
1 teaspoon sour salt
1 teaspoon salt
¼ teaspoon pepper
2 tablespoons lemon juice

1. Soften **cabbage** leaves. Separate leaves from softened cabbage. Chop any odd cabbage pieces and reserve.
2. Mix **beef, bread crumbs, eggs, ketchup**, and **carrot**.
3. Place ½ cup beef mixture in the center of each leaf and roll up, tucking in the ends securely as you roll.
4. Spread **onion** in bottom of pan and place cabbage rolls on top, seam side down.
5. Pour **tomatoes** and **sugars** over cabbage. Sprinkle with **sour salt, salt**, and **pepper** and reserved chopped cabbage.
6. Simmer, covered, on top of stove for 30 minutes. Spoon sauce from bottom of pan over the top of cabbage rolls and place pan in oven.
7. Bake, covered, for one hour. Add **lemon juice** and bake, uncovered for 1 hour.

Note:
Cabbage rolls freeze well.

Hint:
To soften **cabbage leaves**, freeze cabbage overnight, and defrost. Cabbage leaves will separate easily.

Stuffed Cabbage Rolls

Meat • 6 to 8 servings

Preheat oven to: 375°
Cooking Time: 3 hours
Covered roasting pan

CABBAGE ROLLS

1 large green cabbage, about
  3⅓ pounds
1 pound lean ground beef
½ cup raw white rice
¼ cup water
1 small onion, grated
2 eggs, beaten
½ teaspoon salt
¼ teaspoon pepper
⅛ teaspoon allspice
1 large onion, sliced

1. In a large kettle, bring 3 quarts of water to a boil. Add whole **cabbage** and simmer 3 to 5 minutes or until leaves are pliable. Drain cabbage, reserving water.
2. Carefully remove 12 large leaves from the cabbage. Trim thick rib from center of each leaf. If leaves are not soft enough to roll, return them to boiling water for another minute.
3. In a large bowl, combine **beef, rice, water, grated onion, eggs, salt, pepper,** and **allspice**. Mix until well blended.
4. Place ¼ cup of meat mixture in hollow of each leaf. Fold sides of leaf over stuffing. Roll up from thick end of leaf.
5. Place a few of the remaining cabbage leaves in the pan. Arrange rolls, seam side down, on leaves. Top with **onion slices**.
6. Prepare sauce and pour over cabbage rolls.
7. Bring to a boil over medium heat. Sprinkle with **brown sugar**.
8. Cover and bake 2½ hours. Uncover and bake ½ hour longer.

SAUCE

16 ounces tomato sauce
28 ounces canned stewed
  tomatoes, crushed
⅓ cup lemon juice
¼ cup water
½ teaspoon salt
⅛ teaspoon pepper
¼ cup light brown sugar

1. In a large bowl, combine **tomato sauce, tomatoes, lemon juice**, **water, salt,** and **pepper**.
2. Reserve for use later.

Note:
Cabbage rolls can be frozen.

Unstuffed Cabbage

Meat • 10 to 12 servings

Preheat oven to 350°
Cooking Time: 2 hours, 20 minutes
Large covered roasting pan

MEAT BALLS

3 pounds ground beef
1½ cups raw rice
1 onion, diced
2 whole eggs
3 egg whites
1 teaspoon salt
1 teaspoon pepper
1 teaspoon garlic powder
2 teaspoons dried parsley
1 large cabbage, shredded

1. Combine **meat** with **rice, onion, eggs, egg whites, salt, pepper**, and **herbs**. Shape into medium balls.
2. Place **cabbage** in bottom of pan.

SAUCE

48 ounces tomato juice
12 ounces chili sauce
1 cup ketchup
2½ cups water
¼ cup brown sugar
8-10 ginger snaps, crushed
1½ tablespoons lemon juice

1. Combine **juice, chili sauce, ketchup, water, sugar, ginger snaps**, and **lemon juice**. Pour sauce mixture over cabbage.
2. Bring to a boil.
3. Place meat balls into sauce. Simmer, covered, 20 minutes.
4. Transfer covered pan to oven and bake 2 hours or until cabbage is soft and sauce is thickened.

Note:
Can prepare in advance and freeze.

Sweet and Sour Stew

Meat • 6 servings

Cooking Time: 1½ hours
Covered roasting pan

. . . .

¼ cup flour
2 teaspoons salt (divided)
pepper to taste
2 pounds stew beef, cubed
3 tablespoons oil
1 cup water
½ cup ketchup
¼ cup brown sugar
¼ cup vinegar
1 tablespoon Worcestershire
    sauce
1 cup chopped onion
2 large carrots, sliced

1. Combine **flour**, 1 teaspoon **salt** and **pepper**. Coat **beef** with the flour mixture.
2. In roasting pan, brown meat in **oil**.
3. Combine **water, ketchup, brown sugar, vinegar, Worcestershire sauce**, and remaining salt. Pour over meat.
4. Add **onion** to pan and cover. Cook on low heat for 45 minutes.
5. Add **carrots**. Cook another 45 minutes, or until meat and vegetables can be pierced easily with a fork.

Sherried Beef

Meat • 6 to 8 servings

Cooking Time: 45 minutes
3-quart roasting pan

. . . .

2 tablespoons oil
2 pounds beef, cut in 1 inch
    cubes
2 tablespoons cream sherry,
    heated
24 small white onions, peeled
12 mushrooms, quartered
1-2 teaspoons tomato paste
3 beef bouillon cubes
3 tablespoons flour
½ cup water
1 cup red wine (divided)
salt and pepper to taste
1 teaspoon dried parsley
¼ teaspoon dried thyme
1 small bay leaf
chopped fresh parsley for
    garnish

Note:
This dish freezes well.

1. Heat **oil** in skillet. Brown **beef** quickly. Add **sherry**. Remove beef from pan.
2. Brown **onions** quickly in same pan. Add **mushrooms** and cook for 1 minute. A liquid will form.
3. Combine **tomato paste, bouillon cubes**, and **flour** with **water**, stirring until smooth. Add mixture to onions in pan and stir until mixture comes to a boil.
4. Add ¼ cup **wine**, browned beef, **salt** and **pepper**. Wrap **herbs** in small piece of cheesecloth. Add to pot.
5. Simmer uncovered, 30 minutes. Add remaining ¾ cup wine. Simmer additional 15 minutes, or until tender.
6. Sprinkle with **parsley**. Serve in casserole.

Five Star Meat Loaf

Meat • 6 to 8 servings

Preheat oven to 375°
Cooking Time: 1½ hours
9 x 5 x 3-inch loaf pan

· ·

2 pounds ground beef
1 cup regular oatmeal
6 ounces tomato juice
1 onion, chopped
2 eggs, beaten
2 teaspoons paprika
¼ cup horseradish
2 teaspoons salt
1 teaspoon dry mustard
½ cup ketchup

1. Mix **beef** with **oatmeal, juice, onion, eggs**, and **spices**.
2. Place in pan and spread **ketchup** over the top.
3. Bake until top is browned and meat is firm.

Note:
Can be frozen.

Sweet and Sour Meatballs

Meat • 4 to 6 servings

Cooking Time: 1½ hours
4-quart covered saucepan

· ·

2 pounds ground beef
1 egg
2 tablespoons bread crumbs
1 (1 ounce) envelope dry onion
  soup mix
2 tablespoons ketchup
10 ounces condensed tomato
  soup
8-12 ounces tomato sauce
1 onion, diced
6 ounces water
8 ounces sauerkraut, drained,
  and rinsed
¾ cup brown sugar

1. Mix **beef, egg, bread crumbs, onion soup**, and **ketchup** until well blended. Form into small meatballs.
2. In saucepan, mix **tomato soup, tomato sauce, onion, water, sauerkraut**, and **brown sugar**.
3. Add meatballs to sauce and cook over low heat, covered, for 1½ hours. Sauce will be thick and dark.

Note:
This dish freezes well.

Armenian Meatballs in Egg Lemon Sauce

Meat • 4 servings

2-quart sauce pan

MEATBALLS

1 pound ground beef
1 egg
¼ cup finely chopped fresh
  parsley
½ cup onion, chopped
1 cup unseasoned bread crumbs
½ teaspoon cumin
1 teaspoon salt
1 teaspoon white pepper
¼ cup flour

1. Combine **beef, egg, parsley, onion, bread crumbs, cumin, salt**, and **pepper** in a medium mixing bowl and mix well.
2. Roll into small meatballs. Place **flour** in shallow dish. Roll meatballs in flour.

SAUCE

4-6 cups beef broth
2 eggs
juice of 1 lemon

1. Bring **beef broth** to a boil. Lower heat to simmer and add meatballs. Cook approximately 10 to 15 minutes. Remove meatballs and set aside. Continue to simmer broth.
2. In a large bowl whisk **eggs** together with **lemon juice** until frothy. Add broth to egg mixture, a small amount at a time, whisking well after each addition. If hot broth is added to egg mixture too rapidly, eggs will curdle. When all broth is incorporated, pour over meatballs and serve.

Note:
If you like food more heavily seasoned, double the parsley and cumin.

Beef Skillet Fiesta

Meat • 4 servings

Medium covered skillet

. . . .

1 pound ground beef
1 tablespoon oil
¼ cup diced onion
2 teaspoons salt
1 teaspoon chili powder
¼ teaspoon pepper
16 ounces canned tomatoes,
   drained
12 ounces whole kernel corn,
   drained
½ cup thin strips green pepper
¼ cup bouillon
1½ cups instant rice, uncooked

1. Brown **beef** in **oil** on high heat,
   separating beef into coarse
   chunks.
2. Add **onion**. Reduce heat to
   medium and cook until onion is
   tender but not brown.
3. Add **salt, chili powder, pepper, tomatoes, corn, green
   pepper**, and **bouillon**. Bring to
   a boil.
4. Stir in **rice**, turn off heat, cover
   and let stand 5 minutes. Fluff
   with a fork.

Sausage Ragout

Meat • 6 servings

Cooking Time: 40 minutes
3-quart covered pot

. . . .

4 tablespoons olive oil
2 large onions, sliced
2 large green bell peppers,
   seeded, and sliced
4 ounces sliced pimentos
¼ teaspoon crushed red pepper
1 teaspoon dried marjoram
½ teaspoon dried oregano
1 teaspoon caraway seeds
1 bay leaf
½ teaspoon paprika
1½ teaspoons salt
½ teaspoon black pepper
6-8 knockwurst, sliced
2 medium potatoes, peeled and
   cubed
3 ripe tomatoes, peeled, cut into
   chunks
3 medium zucchini, sliced
   diagonally
2 teaspoons minced fresh parsley

Variation:
1½ to 2 cups of canned tomatoes,
drained, may be used instead of
fresh tomatoes.

1. Heat **oil** in a skillet. Sauté
   onions and **green peppers** in
   oil for l0 minutes, or until very
   soft. Transfer to pot.
2. Add **pimentos, herbs**, and
   spices.
3. Bring to a boil. Add
   knockwurst and **potatoes**.
4. Cover and simmer mixture for 30
   minutes.
5. Add **tomatoes** and **zucchini**.
   Simmer another 10 minutes or
   until vegetables are tender.
6. Taste and adjust seasoning.
7. Garnish with minced **parsley**
   and serve.

Suggestion:
Serve with thick slices of black bread
and beer.

Note:
Can be frozen.

Tongue in Cranberry Sauce

Meat • 6 servings

Cooking Time: 2 hours
Covered roasting pan

. . . .

1-2 pounds tongue
14 ounces chili sauce
1½ cups water
6 ounces black currant jam
6-8 tablespoons orange juice
1 orange, peeled and sliced
⅓ cup craisins (dried
 cranberries)
salt and pepper to taste

Variation:
Sear a 3 pound chuck roast. Cook
covered for 2 hours. Drain stock and
reserve for use in a soup. Slice meat
and add to sauce, continuing as in
step 4.

1. Early in the day, boil **tongue**
 until tender, allowing about 20
 minutes per pound. Peel, cool
 thoroughly, and cut into thin
 slices.
2. Melt **chili sauce, water**, and
 jam in a sauce pan.
3. Add **orange juice, orange,
 craisins, salt**, and **pepper**.
 Simmer 10 minutes.
4. Combine tongue and sauce in
 roasting pan. Cover and simmer
 an additional 50 minutes. Add
 more water if necessary.

Veal Almondine

Meat • 4 servings

Cooking Time: 6 minutes
Large skillet

. . . .

3 egg whites
1 cup bread crumbs
½ cup finely chopped parsley
grated zest of 1 lemon
½ cup almonds, ground
salt and pepper to taste
14 ounces veal cutlets, pounded
 thin
8-12 tablespoons margarine

1. Pour **egg whites** into flat dish.
 Beat lightly.
2. Combine **crumbs, parsley,
 lemon zest, almonds, salt**, and
 pepper in a separate bowl.
3. Dip **veal** into egg whites and
 then crumbs.
4. Heat **margarine** in skillet over
 high heat. Cook veal 3 minutes
 per side until golden brown.

Veal Marengo

Meat • 8 to 10 servings

Preheat oven to 500°
Cooking Time: 60 minutes
4-quart covered casserole

. . . .

4 tablespoons olive oil
3 pounds veal, cubed
2 tablespoons flour
1 teaspoon salt (optional)
½ teaspoon pepper
1 teaspoon dried thyme
¾ cup finely chopped onion
¼ cup finely chopped shallots
½-1 teaspoon finely chopped
   garlic
½ cup dry white wine
1½ cups beef stock
1 cup diced canned tomatoes,
   drained
2 (2-inch) strips lemon peel
¾ pound mushrooms, quartered
1 tablespoon oil
2 tablespoons chopped parsley,
   for garnish

H E R B   B O U Q U E T

4 sprigs parsley
1 celery top
1 large bay leaf

Note:
Herb bouquet ingredients can be
placed in a large tea ball.

1. Heat **olive oil** in a large skillet.
   Brown **veal**, in batches, until
   dark brown. Toss veal with
   flour, salt, pepper, and **thyme**.
2. Transfer veal to casserole. Place,
   uncovered, in upper third of
   500° oven for 10 minutes. Turn
   veal pieces until slightly crusted
   and flour traces disappear.
   Remove casserole from oven.
   Reduce oven temperature to
   325°.
3. Add more oil to sauté pan, if
   necessary, and cook **onion,
   shallots**, and **garlic** about 10
   minutes or until soft.
4. Add **wine** and **stock** to onion in
   frying pan. Bring to a boil over
   high heat, scraping crust into
   liquid. Pour into casserole.
5. Make an **herb bouquet** by tying
   parsley, celery top, and **bay
   leaf** together, or placing in
   cheesecloth. Stir **tomatoes,
   lemon peel**, and herbs into
   casserole. With casserole on top
   of the stove, bring mixture to a
   boil.
6. Cover casserole and place on
   center oven shelf. Bake 50
   minutes.
7. Sauté **mushrooms** in **oil** and
   add mushrooms, and liquid that
   is produced, to casserole. Bake
   about 10 minutes more. Remove
   veal from casserole, discard
   bouquet and 1 lemon peel.
8. Skim fat from liquid in casserole.
   On top of stove, boil sauce and
   reduce to half. Return veal to
   sauce. There should be just
   enough to moisten veal. Sprinkle
   with **parsley**.

Veal and Mushrooms

Meat • 8 servings

Cooking Time: 30 minutes
Large skillet

. . . .

½ cup flour
salt and pepper to taste
3 pounds lean veal cut in 2-inch
  cubes
¼ cup olive oil
1 large onion, chopped
1 cup dry white wine
1 cup chicken stock
4 tomatoes, cut in ½-inch slices
1½ teaspoons minced garlic
1½ teaspoons dried tarragon
1 teaspoon dried thyme
2 tablespoons grated orange zest
12 ounces mushrooms, sliced
½ cup chopped fresh parsley

1. Season **flour** with **salt** and
   pepper and place in a plastic
   bag. Add **veal** and shake to coat
   pieces.
2. Heat **oil** in skillet. Add veal.
   Brown quickly on all sides, and
   remove from pan.
3. Add **onion** to pan and sauté 5
   minutes. Add **wine** and **chicken
   stock**.
4. Return veal to pan. Add
   **tomatoes, garlic, tarragon,
   thyme**, and **zest**. Simmer,
   uncovered, stirring for 15
   minutes.
5. Add **mushrooms** and cook for
   10 minutes.
6. Remove solids and reduce sauce
   until thick. Return solids.
   Sprinkle with **parsley**.

Layered Veal

Meat • 5 to 6 servings

Preheat oven to 325°
Cooking Time: 1 hour
2 quart baking pan, greased

. . . .

1 cup seasoned bread crumbs
½ teaspoon garlic powder
½ teaspoon dried oregano
2 tablespoons minced fresh
  parsley
1½ pounds veal, cubed
1 egg, beaten
½ cup olive oil
½ pound mushrooms, sliced
10 ounces frozen, chopped
  spinach, thawed and drained
½ teaspoon salt
½ cup chopped green onion
2 cups tomato sauce
1 cup water

Variation:
May substitute 1 cup of white wine
for 1 cup of tomato sauce.

1. Combine **crumbs, garlic powder, oregano**, and **parsley**. Set aside.
2. Dip each piece of **veal** into beaten **egg**, then into crumb mixture. Reserve extra crumb mixture.
3. Heat **oil** in a skillet over medium heat. Add veal and brown lightly. Drain on paper towel.
4. Add reserved crumb mixture to skillet drippings. Brown lightly. Set aside.
5. In same skillet, sauté **mushrooms**. Set aside.
6. Spread **spinach** in prepared pan. Sprinkle with **salt**.
7. Place **green onion** on top of spinach, layer mushrooms over green onion and end with a layer of veal.
8. Combine **tomato sauce** and **water**. Gently pour into the casserole. Top with reserved crumbs. May be refrigerated up to 24 hours at this point. Bring to room temperature before baking.
9. Bake, uncovered, until veal is tender.

Bubbe's Chicken Fricassee

Meat • 4 servings

Cooking Time: 1½ hours
Covered roasting pan

SAUCE

. . . .

1 pound chicken giblets
¼ pound chicken necks
4-6 chicken wings
1 onion, chopped
1 tablespoon chicken fat or oil
1 large carrot, chopped
1 stalk celery, chopped
2 cloves garlic, minced
1 tablespoon dried parsley
¼ teaspoon salt
¼ teaspoon pepper
1 teaspoon paprika
2 teaspoons powdered chicken
  soup mix
2 teaspoons ketchup
1 tablespoon flour
3 tablespoons water

1. Sauté **giblets, necks, wings**, and **onion** in hot **fat**.
2. Add **carrot, celery, garlic, parsley, spices, soup mix**, and **ketchup**. Mix together.
3. Add enough water to pan until ingredients are barely covered.
4. Simmer covered for 45 minutes.
5. Remove necks and giblets from mixture. Use or discard as desired.
6 Mix **flour** and **water** until smooth paste forms. Stir into pot and cook until thickened.

MEATBALLS

. . . .

¾ pound ground beef
2 tablespoons onion, minced
1 tablespoon matzoh meal
1 egg
1 garlic clove, minced
1 tablespoon dried parsley
¼ teaspoon salt
¼ teaspoon pepper

1. Mix **beef** with **onion, matzoh meal, egg, herbs**, and **spices**, and form into tiny balls.
2. Blanch meatballs by placing in a sieve and dipping into boiling water for 10 seconds. Drain.
3. Add meatballs to sauce and simmer 10 to 15 minutes before serving.

Lemon-Rosemary Roast Chicken

Meat • 4 to 6 servings

Preheat oven to 350°
Cooking Time: 2 hours
13 x 9 x 2-inch baking pan,
  ungreased

. . . .

4-5 pound chicken
3 sprigs fresh rosemary
1 lemon
6 small white potatoes, cut in
  quarters
8 baby pearl onions, peeled
giblets from chicken
⅓ cup water
lemon-pepper seasoning to taste
salt to taste

1. Rinse **chicken** in cold water.
   Place chicken, breast side up, in
   pan.
2. Place **rosemary sprigs** and
   whole unpeeled **lemon** deep
   into chicken cavity.
3. Place **potatoes, onions**, and
   giblets in pan around chicken.
   Pour **water** around chicken.
4. Sprinkle **lemon-pepper seasoning** over chicken and giblets.
   Salt as desired.
5. Bake, uncovered, until juices run
   clear. Remove rosemary and
   lemon from chicken before
   serving.

French Chicken

Meat • 4 to 6 servings

Preheat oven to 325°
Cooking Time: 1 hour
Covered roasting pan

. . . .

1 medium onion, chopped
1 carrot, cut in ½-inch slices
1 large garlic clove
3 tablespoons margarine
2 small chickens, quartered
2 tablespoons flour
2 tablespoons minced dried
  parsley
½ teaspoon dried thyme
1 teaspoon salt
⅛ teaspoon pepper
1½ cups sherry

1. Sauté **onion, carrot**, and **garlic**
   in **margarine**. Add **chicken**
   pieces and brown lightly.
2. Combine **flour, herbs, spices**,
   and **sherry**. Add to pan.
3. Cover and bake until vegetables
   are tender and chicken feels
   firm.

Glazed Chicken Rosemary

Meat • 6 to 8 servings

Preheat oven to 400°
Cooking Time: 2 hours
Roasting pan

. . . .

1 lemon
roasting chicken, about 7 pounds
1 large onion, quartered
salt and pepper to taste
2 teaspoons dried rosemary
½ cup water

1. Squeeze juice from **lemon** and sprinkle juice inside and outside **chicken**. Keep rind.
2. Place **onion** and lemon rind inside of chicken.
3. Season chicken with **salt, pepper**, and **rosemary**.
4. Add **water** to the pan.
5. Roast for 30 minutes, uncovered, at 400°. Reduce heat to 350°. Roast 1 more hour.
6. Brush glaze on chicken. Roast ½ hour more, or until glaze is shiny and drumstick moves easily.

G L A Z E

. . . .

2 tablespoons margarine
2 tablespoons Dijon mustard
2 tablespoons honey
1 tablespoon orange or apricot jam
2 tablespoons orange flavored liqueur

1. In a small saucepan simmer **margarine, mustard, honey**, and **jam** for 2 minutes. Remove from heat, and add **orange flavored liqueur**.
2. Set glaze aside.

Fast and Easy Company Chicken

Meat • 4 to 6 servings

Preheat oven to 350°
Cooking Time: 40 minutes
13 x 9 x 2-inch covered pan, greased

. . . .

1 cup orange marmalade
8 ounces Dijon mustard
¼ cup honey
1 tablespoon lemon juice
1 tablespoon curry powder
2 cut-up frying chickens

Variation:
6 chicken breasts can be used.

1. In a small saucepan, mix **marmalade** with **mustard, honey, lemon juice**, and **curry powder**. Simmer 5 minutes.
2. Place **chicken** in prepared pan. Pour sauce over chicken. Bake, covered, 30 minutes. Uncover and continue baking until chicken feels firm. Occasionally baste chicken with pan juices to glaze.

Chicken Hunter

Meat • 8 to 10 servings

Preheat oven to 350°
Cooking Time: 30 minutes
13 x 9 x 2-inch roasting pan

CHICKEN

6 chicken breasts, boned
flour to coat chicken
3 tablespoons margarine
½ pound mushrooms, sliced
2 shallots, chopped

1. Flatten **chicken breasts** by pounding lightly. Dust each breast with **flour**.
2. In a skillet, sauté coated chicken in **margarine** until tender. Place in roasting pan.
3. Sauté **mushrooms** and **shallots** in skillet in which chicken was prepared.
4. Place mushrooms and shallots on top of chicken.
5. Pour sauce over chicken. Bake until chicken feels firm and is cooked through.

SAUCE

2 tablespoons brandy
½ cup dry white wine
2 tablespoons tomato sauce
1 cup chicken broth
1 tablespoon minced fresh parsley

1. In a small saucepan, boil **brandy** and **wine** to reduce to half.
2. Add **tomato sauce, chicken broth**, and **parsley**.
3. Simmer until reduced to 1 cup.

After returning from our honeymoon, my husband and I invited our parents over for dinner. We decided to make a simple dinner of roasted chicken and potatoes. As we were carving the chicken, giblets started falling out of the cavity. My mother exclaimed, "Didn't you clean the chicken?" I said "Of course I did mom." She started laughing, realizing that I didn't know to clean out the inside of the chicken and remove all the parts before cooking. Oh well, live and learn.

Chicken Athena

Meat • 6 servings

Cooking Time: 40 minutes
Large covered skillet

· ·

1 small eggplant
1½ teaspoons salt (divided)
6 chicken breast halves, skinned
  and boned
3 tablespoons lemon juice
½ teaspoon pepper
3 tablespoons oil
3 tablespoons margarine
1 cup finely chopped onions
1 pound tomatoes, peeled and
  chopped
½ cup dry white wine
1 stick of cinnamon
2 cloves
2 tablespoons fresh parsley,
  finely chopped

1. Peel **eggplant**, cut into ½-inch
   slices. Sprinkle with ½ teaspoon
   salt. Set aside for 20 minutes.
2. Rub **chicken** with **lemon juice**.
   Sprinkle with remaining salt and
   pepper.
3. Heat **oil** and **margarine** in
   frying pan. Brown chicken on
   both sides. Remove from pan.
4. Brown eggplant on all sides.
   Remove from pan.
5. Sauté **onions** until tender but
   not brown. Add **tomatoes,
   wine, cinnamon**, and **cloves**.
   Bring to a boil. Add chicken and
   eggplant.
6. Cover and simmer until juice
   from chicken runs clear.
7. Sprinkle with **parsley**.

Chicken Versailles

Meat • 3 to 4 servings

Preheat oven to 350°
Cooking Time: 45 minutes
11 x 7 x 2-inch pan

· ·

2 pounds boneless chicken
  breasts
2 tablespoons margarine
¼ teaspoon pepper
½ teaspoon minced garlic
½ cup dry white wine (divided)
¼ teaspoon onion powder
2 teaspoons chicken stock
½ cup tomato sauce
½ pound sliced, fresh
  mushrooms
2 teaspoons fresh chervil
  (divided)

1. In a skillet, brown **chicken** in
   margarine.
2. Season with **pepper** and **garlic**.
3. Add 2 tablespoons **wine**. Place
   in pan.
4. Combine **onion powder,
   chicken stock**, remaining wine,
   tomato sauce, and **mushrooms**.
5. Pour over chicken.
6. Top with 1 teaspoon **chervil**.
7. Cover and bake 35 minutes.
8. Uncover and bake another 10
   minutes to brown.
9. Sprinkle with remaining chervil.

A B C Chicken
(Artichoke Baked Chicken)

Meat • 4 servings

Preheat oven to 350°
Cooking Time: 1½ hours
13 x 9 x 2-inch covered pan

. . . .

2 tablespoons oil
3 pounds chicken parts
1 cup flour seasoned with salt,
    pepper, and garlic powder
¾ pound fresh mushrooms
12 ounces marinated artichoke
    hearts, drained
2 cloves garlic, minced
1¼ teaspoons salt
½ teaspoon pepper
½ teaspoon dried oregano
42 ounces canned large tomatoes
½ cup sherry

1. Heat **oil** in a frying pan. Dredge **chicken parts** in seasoned **flour** and brown.
2. Place chicken in pan with **mushrooms** and **artichokes**.
3. Stir **garlic** and **spices** into **tomatoes**. Pour over chicken.
4. Cover pan and bake one hour. Add **sherry**.
5. Bake an additional ½ hour, or until chicken is tender. Baste several times while chicken is baking.

Note:
This recipe can be made one day in advance. Keep casserole refrigerated and covered. If you make ahead, bake ½ hour the day of preparation. Bake ½ hour the next day, add sherry. Bake another ½ hour. Sherry needs to be added when dish is warm.

Sesame Chicken with Peanut Apricot Sauce

Meat • 4 servings

Large skillet

CHICKEN

½ cup bread crumbs
½ cup flour
1 tablespoon paprika
½ teaspoon garlic powder
2 whole chicken breasts, skinned and boned
salt and pepper to taste
2 tablespoons oil

1. Mix together **bread crumbs, flour, paprika**, and **garlic powder**.
2. Cut **chicken** into 1-inch strips. Sprinkle with **salt** and **pepper**. Roll chicken in crumb mixture. Chicken can be refrigerated at this point.
3. Sauté chicken in **oil** until golden brown.
4. Place chicken in a heated chafing dish. Pour sauce over chicken just prior to serving. Serve with toothpicks.

SAUCE

1 cup apricot jam
¼ cup peanut butter
2 tablespoons lemon juice
2 tablespoons ketchup
2 tablespoons sesame seeds

1. In a small pan, mix **jam** with **peanut butter, lemon juice, ketchup**, and **sesame seeds**.
2. Slowly heat on top of stove until jam is melted and sauce is hot.

Grilled Maple Chicken Breasts

Meat • 4 servings

Marinating Time: 2 hours
Broiler

2 whole chicken breasts, skinned and boned
salt and pepper to taste
2 tablespoons low sodium soy sauce
2 tablespoons maple syrup
1 tablespoon olive oil
1½ teaspoons red wine vinegar
1 teaspoon minced garlic

1. Sprinkle **chicken** with **salt** and **pepper**.
2. Blend **soy sauce, maple syrup, oil, vinegar**, and **garlic**.
3. Marinate chicken at least 2 hours in refrigerator.
4. Broil 7 to 10 minutes per side.

Citrus Chicken Cutlets

Meat • 8 servings

Marinating Time: 45 minutes
Broiler

. . . .

1¼ cups orange juice
¾ cup dry white wine
1 cup olive oil
¼ cup minced shallots
1 tablespoon grated orange zest
4 cloves garlic, minced
1 teaspoon dried thyme
1 teaspoon dried oregano
1½ teaspoons dried basil
½ teaspoon salt
½ teaspoon pepper
8 chicken cutlets

1. Combine **juice, wine, oil, shallots**, and **orange zest** with **herbs** and **spices** to make marinade. Marinate **chicken** for 45 minutes.
2. Remove chicken and reserve marinade.
3. Place broiler pan, with chicken, 6-inches from broiler. Broil 10 minutes, or until juices run clear.
4. Remove chicken from pan, reserving juices. Keep chicken warm.
5. In a small pan over medium heat, boil marinade and cooking juices 5 minutes. Top breasts with sauce.

Ginger Chicken with Raspberries

Meat • 4 servings

Broiler or grill

. . . .

¾ cup raspberries
1½ teaspoons ginger, minced
1 tablespoon rice vinegar
pepper to taste
½ teaspoon fresh lime juice
1 teaspoon fresh lemon juice
4 chicken breast halves, skinned and boned

1. Place **raspberries, ginger, vinegar, pepper, lime juice**, and **lemon juice** in a sauce pan. Simmer on low heat for 10 minutes, stirring occasionally. Cool.
2. Pour cooled berry mixture into blender and blend well. Strain through a sieve to remove seeds.
3. Grill or broil **chicken breasts** 3 to 4 minutes per side.
4. Spoon sauce over chicken and serve.

Note:
Fresh raspberries enhance the flavor of the sauce.

Chicken Jubilee

Meat • 8 to 12 servings

Cooking Time: 55 minutes
13 x 9 x 2-inch pan, greased

. . . .

8 chicken breasts skinned and
boned
2 teaspoons salt
½ cup melted margarine
¼ teaspoon pepper
1 teaspoon garlic salt
½ cup water
½ cup raisins
½ cup brown sugar
2 medium onions, sliced
12 ounces chili sauce
1 tablespoon Worcestershire
sauce
16 ounces pitted bing cherries,
drained
1 cup sherry

1. Split **chicken breasts** in half.
   Arrange breasts in prepared pan.
   Season with **salt** and drizzle with
   margarine.
2. Checking frequently, broil until
   lightly browned, about 10
   minutes.
3. Set oven temperature to 325°
4. Combine **pepper, garlic salt,
   water, raisins, sugar, onions**,
   and **sauces**. Pour over chicken,
   cover with foil and bake 30
   minutes.
5. Add **cherries** and **sherry**. Cover
   and bake an additional 15
   minutes.

Note:
Can be prepared a day in advance.
Freezes well.

Pollo Kon Prunes
(Chicken with Prunes)

Meat • 8 servings

Cooking Time: 30 minutes
Covered roasting pan

. . . .

4 tablespoons olive oil
10 boneless chicken breast
   halves, cut in pieces
salt and pepper to taste
2 large onions, sliced
6 cloves garlic, minced
24 ounces tomato purée
1 teaspoon cinnamon
1 teaspoon coriander
1 teaspoon cayenne pepper
24 ounces pitted prunes
½-1 cup red wine (optional)
12 ounces chicken broth

1. Heat **olive oil** in skillet. Brown **chicken**. Season with **salt** and **pepper**.
2. Transfer chicken to roasting pan.
3. Add **onions** and **garlic** to oil remaining in skillet and sauté until onions are transparent. More oil may be needed.
4. Add **tomato purée, cinnamon, coriander, cayenne**, and **prunes**.
5. Simmer over low heat. If sauce seems too thick, add **red wine**.
6. When rich sauce has formed, pour it over chicken.
7. Add enough **broth** to cover the chicken.
8. Simmer tightly covered, until tender.

Note:
This tastes better if made in advance and reheated. It can be frozen.

Tagine of Chicken with Prunes and Almonds

Meat • 6 to 8 servings

Cooking Time: 35 to 40 minutes
Large covered skillet

. . . .

2 tablespoons oil
1 medium onion, finely chopped
3 pounds chicken cutlets
1 cup water
2 teaspoons cinnamon
½ teaspoon ginger
freshly ground pepper to taste
pinch of salt to taste
2 cups pitted prunes
1 tablespoon honey or sugar
½-1 cup slivered almonds - to
  taste

1. Heat **oil** in pan. Sauté **onion** until tender, but not brown.
2. Add **chicken** and lightly brown on both sides.
3. Mix **water** with **cinnamon, ginger, pepper**, and **salt**. Pour over chicken and bring to a boil. Cover tightly, lower heat and simmer 15 minutes, turning chicken occasionally.
4. Add **prunes** and **honey**, distributing evenly. Be sure prunes are covered with liquid. Cover and simmer about 20 minutes, or until chicken and prunes are tender. If sauce appears dry or sticky, add water.
5. Transfer the chicken to a large serving platter.
6. Stir **almonds** into the sauce. Spoon sauce over chicken. Garnish with additional almonds.

Lime Grilled Chicken with Black Bean Sauce

Meat • 4 to 6 servings

Marinating Time: 8 hours
Grill or broiler

. . . .

3 tablespoons fresh lime juice
2 tablespoons oil
¼ teaspoon cayenne pepper
4 cloves garlic, minced
4 chicken breasts, skinned and
    boned
½ cup diced red bell pepper
1 tablespoon chopped red onion
2 cups boiling water

S A U C E

1 cup canned black beans,
    drained
½ cup orange juice
2 tablespoons balsamic vinegar
¼ teaspoon salt
⅛ teaspoon black pepper
2 cloves garlic, minced

1. Combine **lime juice, oil, cayenne pepper**, and **garlic**. Place **chicken** in this marinade and refrigerate for 8 hours.
2. Blanch **red pepper** and **onion** for 30 seconds in the boiling **water**. Drain and cool immediately with ice water. Set aside.
3. In a food processor, process **beans, orange juice, vinegar, salt, pepper** and **garlic** until smooth. Set aside.
4. Drain marinade from chicken. Grill chicken about 5 minutes per side, turning once. Chicken should feel firm.
5. Spoon ¼ bean sauce onto each plate. Place chicken over it and top with pepper and onion mixture.

Pepper-Pepper-Pepper Chicken

Meat • 2 to 3 servings

Preheat oven to 350°
Cooking Time: 80 minutes
Covered shallow baking dish

. . . .

2 chicken breasts, skinned and boned
12 plum tomatoes, chopped
1 yellow bell pepper, thinly sliced
1 red bell pepper, thinly sliced
1 orange bell pepper, thinly sliced
2 tablespoons sundried tomatoes, marinated in olive oil
1 tablespoon capers, drained
2 cloves garlic, minced
¼ teaspoon red pepper flakes
¼ teaspoon Italian parsley
½ cup chopped fresh basil (divided)
¼ cup olive oil

1. Rinse **chicken** and pat dry. Arrange in baking dish and surround with **tomatoes, peppers, sun dried tomatoes**, and **capers**.
2. In a bowl, combine **garlic, red pepper flakes, parsley**, and ¼ cup **basil**. Add **olive oil**. Pour over chicken and cover.
3. Bake, covered, for 30 minutes. Uncover and bake another 40 minutes, basting every 10 to 15 minutes. Sprinkle with remaining basil and baste well. Remove remaining liquid and bake 10 minutes.

Arroz Con Pollo

Meat • 4 servings

Cooking Time: 30 minutes
Large covered skillet

· ·

4 chicken breast halves, skinned and boned
½ teaspoon salt (divided)
½ teaspoon ground pepper (divided)
½ teaspoon paprika (divided)
2 teaspoons olive oil
1 large green bell pepper, chopped
¾ cup chopped onions
1½ teaspoons minced garlic
1 cup raw rice
15 ounces chicken broth
½ cup dry white wine
⅛ teaspoon saffron powder (optional)
16 ounces stewed tomatoes, undrained
1 tablespoon chopped fresh parsley

1. Cut **breasts** into 3-4 pieces. Combine ¼ teaspoon each **salt, pepper**, and **paprika**. Rub over chicken.
2. Heat **oil** in nonstick skillet over high heat. Add chicken and cook until golden on all sides. Place chicken on a plate.
3. Add **green pepper, onions**, and **garlic** to skillet. Cook until vegetables are tender.
4. Add **rice** and cook, stirring, until rice is opaque, 1 to 2 minutes.
5. Stir in **broth, white wine, saffron**, remaining salt, pepper, paprika, and **tomatoes** with their liquid. Return to a boil. Cover and simmer 20 minutes more, stirring once, until chicken and rice are tender and liquid is absorbed. Stir in **parsley**.

Marinated Turkey

Meat • 10 to 15 servings

Marinating Time: Overnight
Preheat oven to 425°
Large roasting pan

. . . .

10-15 pound turkey
6-10 cloves unpeeled garlic
¾ cup water
½ cup oil
2 tablespoons salt
2 tablespoons paprika
½ teaspoon pepper
1 cup orange pineapple or
    apricot juice

1. Remove giblets. Rinse **turkey** inside and out. Dry thoroughly.
2. Cook **garlic** in boiling water for 2 minutes. Reserve water.
3. Peel garlic, combine with ½ cup garlic water, **oil, salt, paprika**, and **pepper**. Purée in an electric blender.
4. A day before roasting, season as follows: Loosen skin on entire bird. Using your hands, spread marinade under skin and inside cavity. Reserve any unused marinade for basting. Place turkey in plastic bag and refrigerate overnight.
5. If stuffing, prepare stuffing of your choice. Make ¾ cup of stuffing per pound up to 15 pounds. Stuff turkey only ¾ full, just before roasting.
6. Preheat oven to 425°. Remove turkey from plastic bag.
7. Place turkey in pan, breast side up. Add **fruit juice** and water. Form an aluminum foil tent over bird.
8. Bake 20 to 25 minutes per pound if turkey is stuffed, 15 minutes per pound unstuffed. After 30 minutes, lower the temperature to 350°. Continue roasting, turning occasionally and basting to brown evenly. Add water to pan as liquid evaporates.
9. To test for doneness, prick skin of thigh to see if the juice runs clear or the drumstic moves easily.

G L A Z E

1 cup water
½ cup red currant jelly
juice of one lemon

. . . .

1. In a small saucepan, combine **water, jelly**, and **lemon juice**. Heat until the jelly has melted.
2. Remove turkey from oven and brush on glaze.
3. Let the glazed turkey rest at least 20 minutes before carving.

Piquant Turkey Loaf

Meat • 4 servings

Preheat oven to 350°
Cooking Time: 50 minutes
9 x 5 x 3-inch loaf pan, lightly
    greased

. . . .

1 pound ground turkey
1 small onion, finely chopped
½ green bell pepper, finely
    chopped
¾ cup whole wheat bread
    crumbs
½ cup plus 2 tablespoons tomato
    sauce
2 egg whites
1 teaspoon salt
⅛ teaspoon ground pepper
1 tablespoon Worcestershire
    sauce

1. Mix **turkey** with **vegetables,
   bread crumbs, tomato sauce,
   egg whites, spices**, and
   Worcestershire sauce.
2. Place in prepared pan.
3. After baking 30 minutes, pour off
   any fat and return to oven for 20
   minutes, or until firm.

Hints:

Turkey or chicken should be stuffed just before placing in the oven. After serving,
extra **stuffing** should be removed from the bird and refrigerated separately.

Allow a roast of beef or a roasted turkey to rest at least 20 minutes before
carving.

Asian Turkey Patties

Meat • 5 servings   10-inch skillet

PATTIES   . . . .

1¼ pounds fresh, lean, ground
  turkey
¼ cup dry bread crumbs
½ teaspoon salt
¼ teaspoon garlic powder
1 egg
1 tablespoon oil

1. In a medium bowl, combine
   **turkey, bread crumbs, salt,
   garlic powder**, and **egg**. Blend
   until well mixed.
2. Form into five (½-inch) thick
   patties.
3. Heat **oil** in skillet over medium-
   high heat, or until oil sizzles.
4. Add turkey patties. Cook 3 to 5
   minutes on each side, or until
   browned and no longer pink in
   the center. Remove patties from
   skillet.

SAUCE   . . . .

1 cup sliced celery
1 medium green bell pepper, cut
  into ¾ inch strips
1 tablespoon sugar
2 teaspoons cornstarch
⅛ teaspoon ground ginger
1 cup chicken broth
3 tablespoons soy sauce
2 teaspoons vinegar
2 medium tomatoes, cut into
  wedges

1. Add **celery** and **green pepper**
   to skillet in which patties were
   browned.
2. Combine **sugar, cornstarch,
   ginger, broth, soy sauce**, and
   vinegar in a small bowl. Blend
   well.
3. Add cornstarch mixture to celery
   and green peppers.
4. Bring mixture to a boil, reduce
   heat to low. Simmer, stirring
   occasionally, until vegetables are
   tender.
5. Stir in **tomatoes**, simmer until
   thoroughly heated.
6. Serve patties with heated sauce.

❖ *Fast-n-Fancy Fish*

Dairy • 6 servings

Preheat oven to 500°
Cooking Time: 30 minutes
Baking sheet, ungreased

. . . .

2-3 pounds halibut fillets
4-6 tablespoons lime juice
salt and pepper to taste
½ cup low-fat mayonnaise
¼ cup grated Parmesan cheese
¼ cup dried dill or tarragon

Variation:
Salmon or haddock can be used.

1. Marinate the **fish** in **lime juice** for at least 30 minutes, turning once.
2. Line baking sheet with foil. Place fish on baking sheet and season with **salt** and **pepper**.
3. Spread the **mayonnaise** ⅛ inch thick over fish.
4. Top with **cheese** and **tarragon**.
5. Immediately place fish in oven.
6. Turn off oven.
7. Leave fish in oven for 30 minutes without opening door.

Pesce Marinara

Parve • 3 servings

Cooking Time: 15 minutes
Large covered skillet

. . . .

1 teaspoon olive oil
2 cloves garlic, minced
2 tablespoons minced fresh
   parsley
28 ounces canned crushed
   tomatoes
2-3 anchovy fillets, minced
1 teaspoon capers
1 green bell pepper, cut in
   ½-inch strips
½ onion thinly sliced
½ cup chopped celery
1 pound flounder fillets
½ pound linguine

Variation:
Try snapper or perch fillets.

1. Heat **oil** in skillet.
2. Sauté **garlic** and **parsley** for 30 seconds.
3. Stir in **tomatoes, anchovies**, and **capers**. Simmer 5 minutes.
4. Add **pepper, onion**, and **celery**.
5. Add **fish**, spooning sauce over fish. Simmer, covered, for 10 minutes.
6. Meanwhile, cook and drain **linguine** per package directions. Serve fish and sauce over pasta.

❖ *Heart-n-Sole*

Dairy • 4 servings

Preheat oven to 375°
Cooking Time: 15 minutes
9 x 9-inch buttered baking dish

. . . .

5 tablespoons butter or
 margarine (divided)
1 teaspoon minced garlic
1 medium tomato, peeled,
 seeded, and chopped
2 tablespoons grated Parmesan
 cheese
1 tablespoon chopped fresh
 parsley
2 pounds fillet of sole

1. Heat 4 tablespoons **butter** in a
 small saucepan and cook until
 bubbly. Add **garlic** and **tomato**.
 Cook 30 seconds, stirring constantly.
2. Turn off heat and add **cheese**
 and **parsley**.
3. Spread ½ of each **fillet** with
 some of the mixture, dividing
 mixture evenly among the fillets.
 Roll the fish, securing with a
 toothpick.
4. Place in prepared baking dish.
 Dot with remaining butter. Bake,
 until fish flakes.

Note:
Juices remaining in the pan after
the fish has been cooked can be
reduced and poured over fish when
serving.

Hints:
To **grate** any **cheese** more easily, first chill it.

To **remove** fish **odor,** or any strong odor, **from hands,** wash with lemon juice or
mustard before using soap.

Caribbean Fish

Dairy • Serves 4

Chilling Time: 1 to 8 hours
Preheat oven to 200°
Oven-proof platter

FISH FILLETS

. . . .

¼ cup flour
1 teaspoon paprika
½ teaspoon salt
¼ teaspoon black pepper
4 slices fillet of flounder
¼ cup butter

1. Combine **flour, paprika, salt**, and **pepper** in a plastic bag. Shake each piece of **fish** in the bag to coat. Place fish on waxed paper lined plate and refrigerate 1 to 8 hours.
2. Twenty minutes before serving, preheat oven to 200°. Melt **butter** in a large skillet over medium high heat. Sauté fillets 3 minutes on each side. Remove with slotted spatula to an oven-proof platter. Place in the oven.

SAUCE

. . . .

2 bananas, sliced
1 cup dry white wine
1 teaspoon ground ginger
¼ cup lemon juice
½ cup sliced almonds
¼ cup firmly packed dark brown
    sugar

1. Slice **bananas** in half lengthwise and then in ½-inch slices.
2. Add **wine, ginger, lemon juice, almonds**, and **brown sugar** to remaining butter in skillet and boil 2 minutes. Reduce heat and add bananas, stir until glazed. Cook 2 minutes more. Remove fish from oven and top with banana sauce.

Cayman Island Fillets

Dairy • 8 servings

Cooking Time: 10 minutes
Large heavy skillet

FISH

1 tablespoon butter
1 tablespoon oil
1 egg
½ cup milk
salt and pepper to taste
1 cup flour
8 (6-ounce) red snapper fillets

1. In skillet, melt **butter** with **oil** over medium heat.
2. Beat **egg** with **milk**, season with **salt** and **pepper**.
3. Dip **fillets** in **flour**, egg mixture, and flour once again.
4. Sauté fish 5 minutes on each side, or until it flakes.
5. Keep warm.

SAUCE

1 tablespoon butter
½ cup spicy mango chutney
1 banana, sliced
1 mango, sliced
½ cup banana liqueur
¼ cup water
salt and pepper, to taste

1. Melt **butter**. Chop **chutney** and add to butter.
2. Add **banana** and **mango**. Sauté 3 minutes.
3. Add **liqueur** and **water**. Bring to a boil. Remove from heat and add **salt** and **pepper** to taste.
4. Spoon sauce over fish on individual plates.

Variation:
Any white, firm-fleshed, mild fish may be used.

Greek Sole

Dairy • 4 servings

Preheat oven to 400°
Cooking Time: 20-25 minutes
9 x 9-inch pan, greased

1⅓ pounds fillet of sole or flounder
½ cup bread crumbs
1 large tomato, chopped
½ medium onion, chopped
10 sliced, black olives, drained
½ cup basil-tomato spiced feta cheese
paprika
2 tablespoons white wine
1 tablespoon lemon juice

1. Dredge **fillets** in **bread crumbs**.
2. Combine **tomato, onion, olives**, and **feta cheese**.
3. Place a tablespoon of this mixture on each fillet and roll up. Use a toothpick to hold fillet closed. Place seam side down in casserole.
4. Sprinkle with **paprika**.
5. Combine **wine** and **lemon juice** and baste fillets.
6. Bake until fish flakes.

Crunchy Fish

Parve • 3 servings

Preheat oven to 375°
Cooking Time: 6 to 8 minutes
15½ x 10½ x 1-inch pan with
rack

. . . .

1 cup bread crumbs
1 teaspoon fresh chives
2 teaspoons fresh parsley
2 teaspoons minced garlic
½ teaspoon paprika
salt and pepper to taste
¼ cup oil
1 teaspoon mustard
2 teaspoons lemon juice
1 pound sole fish fillets

1. Combine **crumbs, herbs,** and **seasonings**. Mix well.
2. In a separate plate, combine **oil, mustard**, and **lemon juice**.
3. Dip **fish** in oil mixture, then in crumbs. Press crumbs into fish.
4. Place fish on rack in pan and bake until fish flakes.

Note:
Any mild white fish may be used. A cookie cooling rack works nicely. Placing the fish on the rack allows the fish to get crunchy.

Hint:
Frozen fish improves in flavor when defrosted in milk before preparation. This will change the kosher designation to dairy.

❖ Asian Steamed Fish

Parve • 4 to 6 servings

Cooking Time: 30 minutes
Wok

. . . .

2 pounds red snapper
2 tablespoons sherry or rice wine
1 tablespoon chopped scallion
2 tablespoons oil
1 thick slice ginger root, minced
4-6 dried Chinese mushrooms,
    soaked and thinly sliced
½ cup shredded carrots
¼ cup shredded green bell
    pepper
¼ cup shredded bamboo shoots
½ cup shredded red bell pepper
½ cup fresh or frozen green peas

S A U C E

3 tablespoons sugar
3 tablespoons white vinegar
2 tablespoons soy sauce
3 tablespoons ketchup
salt to taste
pepper to taste
2 tablespoons sherry or rice wine
1 teaspoon sesame oil
¼ cup water
2 tablespoons cornstarch
4 tablespoons cold water

1. Place **fish** in dish or rack above water in wok.
2. Sprinkle with **sherry** and **scallion**.
3. Steam on high heat for 20 to 25 minutes. Place fish on serving platter. Keep covered. Discard any left over water from steaming.
4. Heat **oil** in wok. Add **ginger** and stir fry 1 to 2 minutes.
5. Add **vegetables**. Stir fry 2 to 3 minutes.
6. Mix all **sauce ingredients** except cornstarch and water.
7. Add sauce to vegetable mixture. Stir one minute to blend.
8. Mix **cornstarch** with **water**. Add to vegetable mixture to thicken.
9. Pour sauce over fish.

Variation:
Scrod or grouper fillets may be used.

Salmon with Mustard

Parve • 4 servings

Cooking Time: 10 to 15 minutes
Grill or broiler

. . . .

4 salmon fillets, 6 to 8 ounces
  each
6 tablespoons Dijon mustard
2 teaspoons dried dill weed

1. Rinse and pat dry **salmon
   fillets**. Spread one side with
   mustard to desired thickness.
2. Sprinkle **dill weed** on top.
3. On grill, place fish, mustard side
   up. Grill for 15 minutes, or broil
   in oven on lower rack 10
   minutes, until fish is lightly
   browned.

Note:
Do not turn during cooking.

Salmon Dijon

Dairy • 4 servings

Cooking Time: 7 minutes each
                    side
Grill or broiler

. . . .

4 salmon steaks
4 tablespoons butter, melted

1. Brush **salmon** with **butter**.
2. Cook on outdoor grill or broil
   indoors until fish flakes.

S A U C E

. . . .

¼ cup sour cream
3 tablespoons Dijon mustard
2 teaspoons fresh lemon juice
2 tablespoons melted butter
1 clove garlic, minced
¼ teaspoon dried dill weed
fresh dill for garnish

1. Combine **sour cream, mustard,
   lemon juice, butter, garlic**, and
   dill weed. Refrigerate.
2. Serve sauce over salmon and
   garnish with fresh dill.

Hint:
Cook **fish** for 10 minutes for each 1-inch thickness; measure thickest part. Applies
to baking at 450°, grilling, broiling, or poaching.

Orange Soy Salmon

Parve • 4 servings

Marinating Time: 2-3 hours
Grill or broiler

. . . .

4 salmon steaks, 1 inch thick

M A R I N A D E

⅓ cup orange juice
⅓ cup soy sauce
2 tablespoons oil
2 tablespoons dried parsley,
   chopped
1 clove garlic, minced
½ teaspoon dried basil

1. Combine **orange juice, soy sauce**, and **oil** with **herbs**. Pour over **salmon steaks**. Marinate 2 to 3 hours in refrigerator. Turn occasionally.
2. Grill 8 minutes, basting with marinade. Turn and grill until done, about 5 minutes.

Brown Sugar Baked Salmon

Dairy • 6 servings

Marinating Time: 30 minutes to
   6 hours
Preheat oven to 400°
9 x 13-inch glass baking dish

. . . .

½ cup brown sugar
4 tablespoons melted butter
3 tablespoons soy sauce
3 tablespoons fresh lemon juice
2 tablespoons dry white wine, or
   water
6 salmon steaks, 1-inch thick or
   a 2 pound salmon fillet

1. Combine **sugar, butter, soy sauce, lemon juice**, and **wine** in baking dish.
2. Add **fish** and marinate, in refrigerator, 30 minutes to 6 hours.
3. Bake, uncovered, 10 to 15 minutes,or 5 minutes per inch of thickness. Baste frequently. Serve immediately.

Note:
Fish flakes easily when done. Do not turn fish.

Salmon with Citrus Coriander Sauce

Parve • 4 to 6 servings   Broiler, skillet

· ·

2 pounds of salmon steaks or
  fillets, 1-inch thick
3 tablespoons margarine
⅓ cup chopped, sweet onion
2 tablespoons chopped coriander
2 tablespoons white wine
  vinegar
⅓ cup grapefruit juice
¼ teaspoon Dijon mustard
⅛ teaspoon cumin

1. Broil **salmon** 5 minutes per side.
2. Heat **margarine** in a skillet.
   Sauté **onion** for 5 minutes
   stirring frequently.
3. Add **coriander**. Cook 1 minute,
   stirring constantly.
4. Add **vinegar**. Cook rapidly for 2
   minutes.
5. Remove pan from heat. Add
   grapefruit juice, mustard, and
   cumin.
6. Lower heat and cook 1 minute.
7. Pour sauce over fish.

Note:
The sauce can be made a day ahead
of time, then reheated.

Simple Salmon

Dairy • 4 to 5 servings

Preheat oven to 325°
1½-quart casserole, greased
Cooking Time: 1 hour

· ·

4 eggs
14¾ ounces canned red salmon,
  drained and boned
¾ cup cooked rice
1 small onion, grated
¾ cup milk
½ cup condensed cream of
  mushroom soup
3 tablespoons butter, melted

1. Beat **eggs**.
2. Mix with **salmon, rice, onion,
   milk, soup**, and **butter**.
3. Pour into prepared pan. Bake
   until set and brown.

❖ *Coulibiac of Salmon*

Dairy • 6 to 10 servings

Preheat oven to 400°
Cooking Time: 35 minutes
Jellyroll pan, greased and floured

. . . .

1½ pounds boneless, fresh
   salmon
2 cups dry white wine
1 tablespoon plus 2 teaspoons
   dried dill (divided)
1 bay leaf
2 whole cloves
salt and pepper
1 cup bulgur
2 cups water
3 tablespoons butter or
   margarine (divided)
1 onion, finely chopped
1 cup sliced, fresh mushrooms
2 tablespoons minced fresh
   parsley
¼ teaspoon nutmeg
¼ teaspoon lemon juice
1 pound prepared puff pastry
   dough
2 sliced, hard boiled eggs
1 egg, beaten
1 pint sour cream
½ teaspoon fresh dill or to taste

Variation:

One pound of canned salmon can be used. 6 sheets of phyllo may be substituted for puff pastry. Brush each phyllo with melted butter, and layer sheets.

1. Put **salmon** in a shallow saucepan. Cover with **wine**. Add 1 tablespoon **dill, bay leaf, cloves, salt**, and **pepper**. Simmer 5 minutes.
2. Drain salmon, reserving ¼ cup liquid. Flake into bite size pieces.
3. Combine **bulgur, water**, salt, and 1 tablespoon **butter** in saucepan. Cook rapidly, stirring for 4 minutes. Cover pan and simmer for 25 minutes. Liquid should be absorbed.
4. Cook **onion** in 2 tablespoons remaining butter until soft. Add **mushrooms** and cook for 3 minutes.
5. Add salmon, bulgur, **parsley**, remaining 2 teaspoons dill, **nutmeg, lemon juice**, and reserved salmon liquid.
6. On a floured piece of foil, roll **puff pastry** into a rectangle about 11 x 13 inches.
7. Place half of the salmon mixture in a compact mound on the pastry, leaving 4 inches on the sides and 2 inches on either end. Cover with the **hard boiled eggs**, and the rest of the salmon. Form into a loaf shape.
8. Brush edges of pastry with water. Fold long sides over filling, envelope style, and pinch all edges together to seal completely. A perfect seal is important.
9. Place pan alongside coulibiac. Lift foil and gently roll pie over on its back onto the pan, seam side down.

Coulibiac of Salmon *(continued)*

10. Make 4 diagonal slits on top for steam vents. Cut pastry trimmings into diamonds and arrange in a pattern on top of pie. Brush top with beaten **egg**.
11. Bake 15 minutes at 400°. Decrease temperature to 350° and continue to bake for 20 minutes or until pastry is a rich brown color.
12. Serve warm, cut into 1½-inch slices.
13. Season **sour cream** with ½ teaspoon **dill**. Serve in a sauce boat.

Note:
6 sprigs of fresh dill can be substituted for dried dill. Coulibiac can be covered with foil and refrigerated until 15 minutes before baking.

Sesame Fish Steaks

Parve • 4 servings

Cooking Time: 10 minutes
Broiler or grill

. . . .

¼ cup soy sauce
3 tablespoons dry sherry
1 teaspoon sugar
1 teaspoon minced ginger
1 teaspoon toasted sesame oil
4 tuna steaks

Variation:
Halibut or salmon can be used.

1. Combine **soy sauce** with **sherry, sugar, ginger**, and **oil**. Stir well and pour over **fish**. Cover and refrigerate for one hour, turning once.
2. Preheat broiler or grill.
3. Drain and reserve marinade. Place fish on the grill and cook 5 minutes per side, or until fish is flaky, basting occasionally.

Tangy Tuna with Lime Juice

Parve • 4 servings   Grill or broiler

. . . .

4 tuna steaks, 1-inch thick
2 tablespoons oil

S A U C E

3 tablespoons margarine
2 cloves garlic, minced
¾ cup chopped, sweet onion
⅓ cup fresh lime juice
¼ teaspoon soy sauce
dash of cayenne pepper

1. Brush **tuna** with **oil**. Grill 5 minutes per side.
2. Heat **margarine** in a skillet. Add **garlic** and **onion** and sauté until soft, about 5 minutes.
3. Add **lime juice, soy sauce**, and **pepper**.
4. Spoon over tuna.

Grilled Tokyo Tuna

Parve • 6 servings   Marinating Time: 4 hours
                                            Grill or broiler

M A R I N A D E   . . . .

¼ cup sesame oil
½ cup oil
¼ cup rice wine vinegar
2 tablespoons dry vermouth
1 tablespoon brown sugar
¼ cup low sodium soy sauce
2 tablespoons minced, fresh
    ginger
3 cloves garlic, minced
3½ pounds fresh tuna steak

1. Make marinade by combining **oils, vinegar, vermouth, sugar, soy sauce**, **ginger** and **garlic**.
2. Marinate **tuna** at least 4 hours in refrigerator.
3. Grill or broil fish 7 to 10 minutes per side.
4. Baste with marinade while cooking.

W A S A B I   B U T T E R (optional) . . . .

1 stick margarine
1½ teaspoons wasabi paste
3 tablespoons coriander

Variation:
May use any firm fish, or chicken.

1. Combine **margarine** and **wasabi**. Add **coriander**.
2. Dot cooked fish with 1 table-spoon butter before serving.

Tuna Provençal

Parve • 4 servings

Preheat oven to 400°
Cooking Time: 12 minutes
Oven proof non-stick skillet

S A U C E

1 tablespoon olive oil (divided)
1 red bell pepper, chopped
1 yellow bell pepper, chopped
1 small red onion, sliced
2 cloves garlic, minced
2 tomatoes, peeled, seeded and
  chopped
¼ cup water or fish stock
2 tablespoons dry red wine
2 tablespoons sliced, pitted,
  black olives
½ tablespoon chopped fresh
  rosemary
salt and pepper to taste

1. In a skillet over medium heat,
   heat 2 teaspoons **olive oil**.
2. Add **peppers, onion**, and
   garlic. Sauté 2 to 3 minutes.
3. Add **tomatoes, water** or **stock**,
   and **wine**. Bring to a boil.
4. Cook, uncovered, over high heat
   for 10 minutes, or until thickened, stirring frequently.
5. Stir in **olives** and **rosemary**.
   Season with **salt** and **pepper**.

F I S H

4 (4-ounce) tuna steaks, about
  1-inch thick
salt and pepper to taste

1. Brush both sides of the **tuna
   steaks** with remaining 1 teaspoon olive oil and season both
   sides lightly with salt and
   pepper.
2. Heat nonstick skillet over high
   heat until almost smoking. Sear
   tuna for 20 to 45 seconds per
   side, or until lightly browned.
3. Place skillet in oven and bake
   for about 10 minutes, or until
   fish flesh is opaque.
4. Place tuna on individual plates
   and spoon the tomato mixture
   on top.

Cold Sesame Noodles

Meat • 4 servings

Cooking Time: 20 minutes
2-quart saucepan

. . . .

1 pound thin Chinese lo mein
   noodles
3 tablespoons soy sauce
2 tablespoons rice vinegar
½ teaspoon dried red pepper
   flakes
2 tablespoons brown sugar
½ cup creamy peanut butter
1-2 tablespoons sesame oil
½ cup chicken broth
slivered scallion for garnish
sliced cucumber for garnish
grated carrot for garnish

Variation:
Vermicelli or capellini pasta may be
used.

1. Cook and drain **pasta** according
to package directions and set
aside.
2. In a saucepan, combine **soy
sauce** with **rice vinegar, red
pepper flakes, sugar, peanut
butter, sesame oil**, and **broth**.
3. Cook over medium heat until
mixture begins to simmer. Stir
with a whisk until mixture is
thick and smooth.
4. Remove from heat. Allow sauce
to cool to room temperature.
5. Immediately before serving,
combine sauce and pasta. Toss.
Garnish with **vegetables**.

Note:
If preparing ahead, do not combine
sauce and pasta. Refrigerate both
until 1 hour before serving. Bring to
room temperature, combine and
garnish.

Fusilli with Artichokes

Dairy • 4 servings

Cooking Time: 10 minutes
Large skillet

. . . .

8 ounces fusilli or tagliatelle
   pasta
14 ounces artichoke hearts
1 tablespoon olive oil
2 medium red or green bell
   peppers, chopped
⅓ cup finely chopped onions
2 cloves garlic, minced
1 medium tomato, seeded and
   chopped
¼ cup fresh basil, chopped
2 tablespoons grated Parmesan
   cheese

1. Cook and drain **pasta** according
to package directions.
2. Rinse, drain and quarter **artichoke hearts**.
3. Heat **oil** in skillet over medium-
high heat. Add artichokes,
peppers, onion, and **garlic**.
Cook and stir for 5 minutes, or
until tender.
4. Stir in **tomato** and **basil** and
cook and stir for 2 minutes, or
until heated through.
5. Add artichoke mixture to pasta.
Toss gently to mix.
6. Serve with **grated cheese**.

Pasta with Caramelized Onions and Mixed Greens

Meat • 6 to 8 servings

Cooking Time: 25 minutes
Heavy, large skillet

. . . .

1 tablespoon olive oil
2 tablespoons margarine
(divided)
4 medium onions, peeled, cut
into ¼-inch rings
1 teaspoon sugar
½ cup red bell pepper, thinly
sliced
½ cup mushrooms, thinly sliced
4 cups chicken broth
salt and pepper to taste
1 pound fettuccine
Your choice of two greens:
12 ounces to 1 pound fresh
spinach
1 pound bok choy
1 pound napa cabbage
1 head of bitter greens, such as
kale, rappini, or chicory

1. Heat **oil** and 1 tablespoon
   margarine in a skillet over
   medium-high heat.
2. Add **onions** and **sugar** and
   cook, stirring once or twice, until
   well browned, about 10 minutes.
3. Remove onions and add **red
   pepper** and **mushrooms**,
   adding the smallest amount of
   oil, if necessary, sautéing until
   mushrooms just start to soften.
4. Return half the onions to skillet.
5. Add **broth** and bring to a boil.
   Cook over high heat for 10
   minutes, scraping bottom of pan
   occasionally. Season to taste with
   salt and **pepper**.
6. Cook **pasta** in boiling water until
   al dente. Drain.
7. Add to broth, simmer for 2 to 3
   minutes.
8. Add **greens**, cook, covered, until
   wilted, about 1 to 3 minutes,
   depending upon greens chosen.
9. Stir in additional tablespoon
   margarine. Put in serving bowl
   and top with red pepper,
   mushroom slices and remaining
   onions. Serve immediately.

Asparagus Lemon Pasta

Dairy • 4 servings   Large skillet

. . . .

1 pound fresh asparagus
½ pound angel hair pasta
2 tablespoons unsalted butter
1 cup heavy cream
2 tablespoons olive oil
2-3 tablespoons lemon juice
freshly ground black pepper to
　　taste
Rind of 1 lemon, cut in fine
　　julienne strips
½-1 cup grated Parmesan cheese

1. Cutting on the diagonal, trim tough ends off **asparagus** and cut spears into 1½-inch pieces. Cook asparagus in lightly salted water for 2 minutes until crisp tender. Cool under cold running water, drain, and set aside.
2. Cook **pasta** until al dente. Drain. Rinse in cold water.
3. While pasta is boiling, melt **butter** in **cream** in a small saucepan over medium heat, stirring occasionally. Simmer at low heat for 10 minutes.
4. Heat **oil** in a large skillet over medium heat. Add asparagus and hot cream mixture. Gradually stir in **lemon juice**. Season with **black pepper**.
5. Add drained pasta and toss well. Heat through, stirring gently.
6. Garnish individual servings with **lemon strips**. Sprinkle with **Parmesan cheese**.

Spinach Fettuccine with Goat Cheese

Dairy • 6 to 8 servings

Cooking Time: 10 minutes
Large skillet

. . . .

¼ cup olive oil
1 cup green onion, chopped
½ cup green bell pepper, diced
½ cup red bell pepper, diced
½ cup sun-dried tomatoes, chopped
2 teaspoons basil, dried
1 teaspoon oregano, dried
3 cups tomatoes, seeded and chopped
3 medium cloves garlic, minced
¼ cup fresh parsley, minced
½ teaspoon salt
½ teaspoon black pepper
1 pound spinach fettuccine
¾ cup goat cheese, crumbled

1. Heat **olive oil** in skillet over medium heat. Add **onions, pepper, sun-dried tomatoes, basil**, and **oregano**. Sauté 5 to 6 minutes.
2. Add **tomatoes, garlic, parsley, salt**, and **pepper**. Cook an additional 3 minutes.
3. Cook and drain **fettuccine** according to package directions.
4. In a large serving dish, combine fettuccine, vegetables, and **goat cheese**. Toss well. Serve immediately.

Hint:
When using dry-packed **sun-dried tomatoes**, rehydrate by covering with hot water for thirty minutes.

Pesto Primavera

Dairy • 6 to 8 servings

Cooking Time: 10 minutes
3-quart pot

. . . .

½ pound spinach linguine
½ pound egg linguine
2 cups broccoli florets
1 cup carrots, cut into match stick pieces
1 cup snow pea pods
½ cup red bell pepper, diced
½ cup tomatoes, diced
1 cup spinach pesto
¼ cup Parmesan cheese

1. Cook **linguine** according to package directions.
2. While linguine is cooking, place **broccoli, carrots, snow pea pods**, and **red pepper** in a colander. When linguine is done, drain over vegetables in colander.
3. Transfer linguine and vegetables to a large serving dish. Add **tomatoes** and **spinach pesto**. Toss to combine.
4. Place in individual serving dishes. Sprinkle with additional grated **Parmesan** and serve.

SPINACH PESTO

2 medium cloves garlic, minced
2 cups packed fresh spinach leaves
¾ cup olive oil
½ cup fresh parsley
¼ cup pine nuts
2 tablespoons fresh basil
½ teaspoon salt
¾ cup Parmesan cheese, grated

1. Place **garlic** in a food processor. With machine running, add **spinach, oil, parsley, pine nuts, basil**, and **salt**. Purée until smooth, scraping down sides a few times with rubber spatula.
2. Transfer to a small bowl. Stir in **Parmesan** and butter.

Note:
This method results in crisp broccoli and carrots. If softer vegetables are preferred, first blanch broccoli and carrots 2 to 3 minutes, then add them at the same time as the tomatoes and pesto.

Skillet Spaghetti

Meat • 4 to 6 servings

Cooking Time: 60 minutes
Large covered skillet

. . . .

1 pound ground beef
1 cup chopped onion
2 medium cloves garlic, minced
8 ounces tomato sauce
6 ounces tomato paste
2 cups tomato juice
1½ cups water
1 teaspoon sugar
1 teaspoon dried oregano
1 tablespoon chili powder
3 teaspoons salt
dash pepper
8 ounces spaghetti
1 small onion, sliced
1 small green bell pepper, sliced

1. In skillet, brown **beef**, adding **onion** and **garlic** about half way through process. Continue until all the meat is browned.
2. Add **tomato sauce, tomato paste, tomato juice, water, sugar, oregano**, and **spices**.
3. Cover and bring to a boil. Reduce heat and simmer 30 minutes, stirring occasionally.
4. Break **spaghetti** in half. Add to skillet, stirring to separate strands.
5. Simmer 25 minutes longer, or until spaghetti is tender, stirring frequently .
6. Add rings of **onion** and **pepper**. Cook an additional 5 minutes.

Note:
This can be prepared through step 5 and refrigerated. Add onion and pepper, reheat in microwave oven approximately 12 minutes.

Eggplant Spaghetti Bake

Dairy • 4 servings

Preheat oven to 400°
Cooking Time: 40 minutes
8 x 10-inch casserole, lightly
greased

. . . .

1 teaspoon olive oil
1 medium onion, diced
4 cloves garlic, minced
1 medium eggplant, diced
12 mushrooms, sliced
½ pound angel hair or thin
spaghetti
2 cups meatless spaghetti sauce
½ cup bread crumbs
¼ cup grated Parmesan cheese
1 teaspoon margarine
½ cup grated low fat mozzarella
cheese

1. Heat **olive oil**. Sauté **onion** and **garlic** until soft. Add **eggplant** and **mushrooms**. Continue to sauté for 5 minutes.
2. In a separate pot, cook **spaghetti**, al dente. Drain and rinse with cold water.
3. Pour spaghetti in prepared casserole.
4. Pour eggplant mixture over spaghetti. Add **spaghetti sauce**.
5. Combine **bread crumbs** and **Parmesan cheese**. Sprinkle over sauce. Scatter with dots of **margarine**.
6. Bake until bubbly and cheese is browned, about 5 minutes. Before serving, sprinkle **mozzarella cheese** over the top and return casserole to the oven until cheese melts.

Herbed Tortellini

Dairy • 4 servings

Chilling Time: 2 hours

. . . .

1 pound tortellini
1 cup fresh basil
1 cup fresh parsley, finely
chopped
1 cup olive oil
1 cup grated Parmesan cheese
8 cloves garlic, minced

1. Cook **tortellini** according to package directions. Drain.
2. Blend **basil, parsley, oil, cheese**, and **garlic** in a blender or food processor.
3. Mix with tortellini and refrigerate until ready to serve.

Spinach and Bow Ties

Dairy • 4 servings   Saucepan

. . . .

3 tablespoons butter (divided)
2 small shallots, minced
10 ounces frozen chopped
  spinach, thawed, and drained
1 cup heavy cream (divided)
salt and pepper to taste
8 ounces bow tie pasta, cooked
1 cup Parmesan cheese, plus
  additional cheese to pass

1. Melt 1 tablespoon **butter** in a
   saucepan over low heat. Sauté
   shallots, stirring often so they
   do not brown.
3. Add **spinach** and mix well for
   one minute.
4. Add ¾ cup **cream, salt**, and
   pepper. Continue to stir until
   just heated through. Taste and
   adjust seasonings.
5. Raise heat just enough to bring
   cream sauce to a simmer. Add
   remaining cream and butter and
   return to simmer again.
6. Cook and drain **pasta** according
   to package directions.
7. Place pasta in a serving bowl
   and toss with sauce. When
   mixed well, toss again with
   Parmesan cheese. Serve
   immediately.

✡ *Passover Lasagna*

Dairy • 6 servings

Preheat oven to 350°
Cooking Time: 40 to 45 minutes
8 x 8 x 2-inch baking dish,
   greased

. . . .

2 eggs
16 ounces large curd cottage
   cheese
salt and pepper to taste
¼ teaspoon garlic powder
3 matzoh
12 ounces tomato sauce or
   marinara sauce (divided)
8 ounces shredded muenster
   cheese

1. Beat **eggs** and mix with **cottage cheese, salt, pepper**, and **garlic powder**.
2. Moisten **matzoh** with warm water. Do not allow to become soggy.
3. Cover the bottom of pan with one-quarter of the **sauce**.
4. Layer: matzoh, cheese mixture, sauce, **muenster cheese**.
5. Repeat, ending with muenster cheese.
6. Bake until golden.

Note:
Allow casserole to stand 5 to 10 minutes before serving.

We have an unusual tradition for Passover. Every year at the Seder, our grandfather would hide the afikomen (Matzoh) in the exact same place. Every year, the youngest kids and grandkids would look and look and look for the afikomen. After about 3 minutes the older kids would go to the usual spot and find the afikomen and get the reward.

Heavenly Veggie Lasagna

Dairy • 12 servings

Preheat oven to 350°
Cooking Time: 30 minutes
13 x 9 x 2-inch glass pan, greased

. . . .

1 pound lasagna noodles
1 teaspoon oil
1 large onion, chopped
2 medium cloves garlic, minced
10 ounces fresh mushrooms,
 sliced
28-32 ounces low fat spaghetti
 sauce
1 pound part-skim ricotta cheese
12 ounces part-skim mozzarella
 cheese
½ cup grated Parmesan cheese

Variation:
Try short tube pasta, penne, or ziti
instead of lasagna noodles.

1. Boil **noodles** until al dente in
 water which has **oil** added to it.
 Oil prevents noodles from
 sticking together. Rinse cooked
 noodles thoroughly in cold
 water.
2. Sauté **onion** and **garlic** on
 medium heat, about 5 minutes,
 or until starting to brown. Add
 mushrooms and sauté until
 tender.
3. Spread ½ cup of **sauce** on
 bottom of pan. Place 1 layer of
 overlapping noodles in dish.
 Spread 4 ounces of **ricotta
 cheese** on top. Add ¼ of
 mushroom mixture, ¼ of shredded **mozzarella cheese** and ½
 cup of sauce.
4. Repeat layers until mushroom
 mixture is used up, ending with
 4 to 5 noodles on top. Cover
 noodles with remaining sauce.
 Sprinkle with **Parmesan cheese**.
5. Cover loosely with aluminum foil
 and bake 20 minutes. Remove
 foil for last 10 minutes. Lasagna
 should be set and Parmesan
 cheese golden.

Note:
Slightly undercook noodles so they
do not overcook in the oven.
Can be frozen.

✡ *Matzoh Marinara*

Dairy • 8 servings

Preheat oven to 350°
Cooking Time: 40 minutes
13 x 9 x 2-inch, greased

. . . .

2 large onions, sliced
½ stick margarine
3 green bell peppers, sliced
½ pound mushrooms, sliced
1 pound farmer cheese
2 eggs
1 teaspoon garlic powder
1 tablespoon mixed Italian herbs
½ pound muenster cheese,
   shredded
1½ quarts marinara sauce
   (divided)
6 matzoh
1 pound mozzarella cheese,
   shredded
salt and pepper to taste

1. In a skillet, sauté **onions** in **margarine** for 3 to 4 minutes.
2. Add **peppers,** cover and steam for 4 minutes.
3. Add sliced **mushrooms**. Cover and steam 3 minutes. Recipe can be prepared to this point one day ahead and refrigerated.
4. Mix together **farmer cheese, eggs, garlic powder**, and **Italian herbs**. Add **muenster cheese** and blend well by hand.
5. Cover bottom of prepared pan with 2 cups **marinara sauce**. Cover completely with 2 dry **matzoh**, breaking pieces as evenly as possible. Do not overlap. Spread cheese mixture over matzoh.
6. Add another layer of matzoh, cover with half of the remaining sauce. Top with sautéed **vegetables, salt**, and **pepper** to taste.
7. Cover with left over matzoh and remaining sauce. Top with **mozzarella cheese**.
8. Bake 20 minutes. At this time, if top is nicely browned, cover with foil and bake 20 minutes more.

Note:
Can be frozen.

Beyond Carrots

VEGETABLES

"Grate" Carrot Pudding

Parve • 12 servings

Preheat oven to 350°
Cooking Time: 40 to 45 minutes
11 x 7 x 2-inch baking pan,
  greased

. . . .

¾ cup oil
1 cup brown sugar
2 eggs
1 tablespoon water
2 cups grated carrots
½ cup matzoh meal
3 tablespoons potato starch
¼ teaspoon salt (optional)

1. Mix **oil, sugar, eggs, water, carrots, matzoh meal, potato starch**, and **salt** until well blended.
2. Pour into prepared pan and bake until set.

Variation:
¾ cup honey can be substituted for
1 cup brown sugar.

✡ Passover Carrot Mold

Parve • 8 servings

Preheat oven to 350°
Cooking Time: 1 hour
1½ quart casserole, greased

. . . .

3 pounds carrots, sliced
1 cup cake meal
1 teaspoon salt
¾ cup sugar
¼ teaspoon nutmeg
¼ teaspoon cinnamon
1 stick margarine, melted
3 eggs, separated

1. Cook **carrots**, covered, in a small amount of water until tender, about 20 minutes. Mash carrots.
2. Mix **cake meal** and **salt** in a large bowl.
3. Add **carrots, sugar, nutmeg, cinnamon, margarine**, and **egg yolks**, blending well.
4. Beat **egg whites** until stiff but not dry.
5. Fold egg whites into carrot mixture.
6. Pour into prepared pan and bake until set.

Julienne Carrots

Dairy • 4 servings

Preheat oven to 350°
Cooking Time: 1½ hours
9-inch square baking pan, lightly
greased

. . . .

18 small carrots, pared
5⅓ tablespoons butter
½ cup granulated sugar
1 teaspoon salt
⅓ teaspoon cinnamon
⅓ cup boiling water

1. Cut **carrots** into strips, approximately ¼ by 3-inches. Put carrots into prepared pan.
2. Cream **butter, sugar, salt, cinnamon**, and **water** until blended. Pour over peeled carrots. Cover and bake until carrots are tender and glazed.

Carrot Bundles

Parve • 6 servings

Chilling Time: 2 hours
Large covered skillet

. . . .

4 large carrots
1 tablespoon olive oil
1 teaspoon lemon juice
1 teaspoon minced garlic
1 tablespoon fresh parsley,
 minced
½ teaspoon pepper
salt to taste
2 tablespoons wine vinegar
1½ teaspoons sugar
1 bunch chives

1. Cut **carrots** into ¼-inch sticks. Cook 5 minutes until al dente. Plunge into ice water. Drain.
2. Make marinade by combining **olive oil, lemon juice, herbs, spices, vinegar**, and **sugar**. Pour over carrots. Refrigerate several hours.
3. Drop **chives** in boiling water for 2 minutes to make them pliable.
4. To make a bundle, tie 4 carrot sticks with 2 or 3 chives. Repeat until all carrots are bundled.
5. Refrigerate until ready to use.

Variation:
1. Blanch some sugar snap peas, cut lengthwise and add 2 halves to each bundle along with carrot sticks. 2. Blanch green part of scallion and use one scallion per bundle in place of chives.

Dilled Carrots

Meat • 6 to 8 servings

Preheat oven to 400°
Cooking Time: 10 minutes
9-inch square pan, ungreased

. . . .

1 pound carrots
½ cup water or chicken broth
salt and pepper to taste
3 tablespoons margarine
2-3 tablespoons lemon juice
3 tablespoons fresh dill

1. Peel **carrots** and slice in long diagonals. Cover and cook in **broth** for 5 minutes or until just tender. Drain and season with **salt** and **pepper**.
2. Melt **margarine**. Combine with **lemon juice**. Pour over carrots.
3. Place carrot mixture in pan and bake for 5 minutes or heat for 1 minute in microwave.
4. Sprinkle with **dill** before serving.

Glazed Carrots and Apples

Parve • 4 servings

Cooking Time: 25 minutes
Covered skillet

. . . .

4 tablespoons margarine
2 tablespoons water
1½ cups baby carrots cut in half lengthwise
1½ cups pared and thinly sliced apples
1 tablespoon brown sugar
¼ teaspoon salt
⅛ teaspoon nutmeg
⅛ teaspoon dried marjoram

1. Melt **margarine** in skillet, add **water** and **carrots**.
2. Cover and cook over low heat for 20 minutes.
3. Add **apples** and sprinkle with **brown sugar, salt, nutmeg**, and **marjoram**.
4. Cover and cook until apples are tender, approximately 5 minutes.

❖ *Ginger Glazed Baby Carrots*

Parve • 6 servings

Cooking Time: 15 minutes
Large Skillet

. . . .

1 inch fresh ginger
1½ pounds baby carrots, peeled
1 tablespoon margarine
1 tablespoon brown sugar
1 teaspoon cornstarch
½ teaspoon grated orange zest
½ cup orange juice
1 tablespoon soy sauce
¼ cup finely chopped green bell
   pepper
orange slices for garnish
green pepper rings for garnish

1. Peel and slice **ginger** and cut into matchstick size pieces.
2. Cook **carrots** in small amount of lightly salted water until tender, 7 to 9 minutes. Drain and keep warm.
3. Sauté ginger in **margarine** for 2 minutes.
4. Stir in **brown sugar, cornstarch**, and **orange zest** and mix until well blended.
5. Add **orange juice** and **soy sauce**.
6. Cook and stir constantly until mixture boils and thickens.
7. Cook and stir an additional 1 minute.
8. Add chopped **green pepper** and cook and stir 1 minute.
9. Add ginger mixture to carrots. Reheat.
10. Edge platter with **orange slices** and **pepper rings**.
11. Spoon carrots into center.

Hint:
Fresh ginger can be refrigerated, tightly wrapped, for up to three weeks, or frozen in a jar up to one year.

Zesty Carrots

Dairy • 6 servings

Preheat oven to 375°
Cooking Time: 15 minutes
8-inch square pan, greased

. . . .

1 pound carrots
¼ teaspoon salt
2 tablespoons grated onion
2 tablespoons horseradish
½ cup light mayonnaise
½ teaspoon salt
¼ teaspoon freshly ground
   pepper
¼ cup water
¼ cup bread crumbs
1 tablespoon melted butter

1. Cut **carrots** into thin strips.
2. Cook carrots in salted water until tender, 5 to 8 minutes.
3. Place carrots in prepared pan.
4. Mix together **onion, horseradish, mayonnaise, salt, pepper**, and **water**.
5. Pour over carrots.
6. Sauté **bread crumbs** in **butter**.
7. Sprinkle carrots with buttered crumbs.
8. Bake until heated through and topping starts to brown.

Note:
Serve immediately.

Baked Carrot Ring

Parve • 8 to 10 servings

Preheat oven to 375°
Cooking Time: 1 hour
6 cup mold, greased

. . . .

2 pounds carrots, sliced
1 stick margarine, softened
⅔ cup flour
½ cup sugar
green peas (optional)

1. Cook **carrots**, covered, in a small mount of water until tender, about 20 minutes. Mash carrots.
2. Add **margarine, flour**, and **sugar** and mix until well blended.
3. Pour into prepared mold. Bake until set.
4. Invert the mold. Fill the center with heated **green peas**.

Note:
Serve immediately.

✡ *Baked Artichoke Hearts*

Dairy • 4 servings

Preheat oven to 350°
Cooking Time: 20 minutes
9-inch square pan

. . . .

12 artichoke hearts, drained
3 teaspoons olive oil (divided)
1 cup matzoh meal
⅛ teaspoon dried basil
⅛ teaspoon garlic powder
⅛ teaspoon dried oregano
⅛ teaspoon dried fennel
⅛ teaspoon black pepper
⅛ teaspoon onion powder
¼ pound grated cheddar cheese

1. Cut **artichoke hearts** in half.
   Place in pan.
2. Drizzle with 2 tablespoons **olive
   oil**.
3. Sprinkle with **matzoh meal**.
4. Season with **herbs** and **spices**.
5. Drizzle with remaining olive oil.
6. Sprinkle the **grated cheese** on
   top. Bake until cheese is melted
   and bubbly.

Green Beans Lyonnaise

Dairy • 4 to 6 servings

Cooking Time: 10 minutes
2 quart covered pot

. . . .

1 pound green beans
½ teaspoon salt (optional)
½ cup boiling water
1 tablespoon butter
1 cup thinly sliced onion
¼ teaspoon pepper
¼ teaspoon nutmeg
1 tablespoon lemon juice
1 tablespoon fresh parsley,
   minced

1. Drop **beans** into **salted boiling
   water**. Cover and cook 5
   minutes. Rinse with cold water.
   Drain.
2. Melt **butter** in skillet, add
   onions. Cook until onions are
   transparent.
3. Add beans, **pepper**, and **nut
   meg**. Sauté 5 minutes.
4. Add **lemon juice** and **parsley**.
   Serve.

Festive Green Beans

Parve • 8 servings

Preheat oven to 375°
Cooking Time: 7 to 10 minutes
8 x 8-inch casserole, greased

. . . .

1 pound fresh green beans,
  trimmed
8 scallions with long green stems
1 red bell pepper, cut into
  ¼-inch strips
1 clove garlic, minced
4 tablespoons margarine, melted
½ teaspoon fresh thyme
¼ teaspoon salt
¼ teaspoon white pepper

1. Cook **beans** in salted water to cover for 3 minutes. Plunge into ice water to stop cooking process. Drain.
2. Cook **scallions** in boiling water for 15 seconds. Pat dry and cut off the white onion bulb. Set aside.
3. Divide beans into 8 portions. Make bundles by tying a scallion stem around each bundle, placing several **red pepper strips** under each knot.
4. Place the bundles in prepared casserole.
5. Slice onion bulbs. Sauté with **garlic** for 3 minutes in **margarine**.
6. Add **thyme, salt**, and **pepper**. Pour over beans.
7. Bake until heated through.

Note:
Can be prepared one day ahead before baking. Cover and refrigerate. Bring to room temperature and bake as directed.

Grilled Eggplant Parmesan

Dairy • 4 servings

Cooking Time: 30 minutes
Grill or broiler

. . . .

1 large eggplant
2 cloves garlic
1 teaspoon salt
¼ teaspoon dried oregano
3 tablespoons olive oil
1 tablespoon wine vinegar
1 large tomato
fresh basil to taste (optional)
pepper to taste
4 teaspoons grated Parmesan
   cheese (divided)
4 ounces mozzarella cheese,
   thinly sliced (divided)

1. Remove stem end from **eggplant**. Slice eggplant lengthwise into 4 equal slabs. Trim peel from outer slices.
2. Crush **garlic** with **salt**.
3. Add **oregano, oil**, and **vinegar** to garlic.
4. Brush both sides of eggplant with garlic mixture.
5. Grill over slow coals 15 to 20 minutes. Turn frequently and brush with remaining oil.
6. Slice **tomato** into 4 thick slices. Top each eggplant piece with slice of tomato.
7. Sprinkle each tomato slice with **basil, pepper**, 1 teaspoon **Parmesan** and ¼ of the **mozzarella**. Repeat with remaining 3 slices.
8. Lower grill hood or cover with a pot lid. Cook several more minutes until cheese melts.

Eggplant Melt Down

Dairy • 15 to 18 slices

Preheat oven to 350°
Cooking Time: 25 to 30 minutes
Jelly roll pan, ungreased

. . . .

1 medium eggplant
1 medium tomato, thinly sliced
1 medium onion, thinly sliced
½ cup mayonnaise (divided)
½ cup grated white cheddar
   cheese (divided)

Note:
Can be served hot or cold.

1. Slice unpeeled **eggplant** into ½ inch thickness. Place on pan.
2. Quarter **tomato** slices.
3. Layer a slice of **onion** and a slice of tomato on each piece of eggplant.
4. Spread 1 teaspoon **mayonnaise** on top of tomato, covering completely.
5. Sprinkle with **cheese**.
6. Bake until cheese is bubbly and eggplant is soft.

Rochester Ratatouille

Parve • 8 servings

Cooking Time: 40 minutes
Large covered skillet

. . . .

¼ cup vegetable oil
4 garlic cloves, minced
1 bay leaf
1 onion, chopped
2 teaspoons salt, (divided)
1 small eggplant, cut in chunks
3 tablespoons dry red wine
1 teaspoon dried basil
1 teaspoon dried marjoram
½ teaspoon dried oregano
2 medium zucchini, cut into
    chunks
2 green bell peppers, cut in
    pieces
½ teaspoon pepper
2 tomatoes, cut in chunks
2 tablespoons tomato paste
¼ cup grated Parmesan cheese
    (optional)
½ cup black olives (optional)

1. Heat **oil** in skillet.
2. Add minced **garlic, bay leaf**, and **onion**.
3. **Salt** lightly. Sauté over medium heat until onion is transparent.
4. Add **eggplant, wine, basil, marjoram**, and **oregano**. Mix well.
5. Cover and simmer until eggplant is tender enough to be pierced by a fork.
6. Add **zucchini** and **peppers**. Cover and simmer 10 minutes.
7. Add salt, **pepper, tomatoes**, and **tomato paste**. Mix well and continue to simmer until vegetables reach desired tenderness.
8. Top with **Parmesan cheese** and **black olives**.

Hint:
How to cook vegetables: If it grows beneath the ground, start in cold water and cover with a lid. If it grows above the ground, start in boiling water and cook uncovered.

❖ *Ratatouille Pie*

Dairy • 6 servings

Preheat oven to 400°
Cooking Time: 45 minutes
10-inch pie plate, greased

. . . .

1 medium eggplant, peeled and
  cubed
2 medium zucchini, cubed
1 large onion, chopped
¼ cup olive oil
4 medium tomatoes, peeled,
  seeded and chopped
3 eggs
¾ cup grated Parmesan cheese
  (divided)
1 teaspoon minced fresh parsley
½ teaspoon fresh basil
½ teaspoon fresh oregano
salt and pepper to taste
¼ pound mozzarella cheese,
  sliced

1. In a large frying pan, sauté the
   eggplant, zucchini, and **onion**
   in **olive oil** for 10 minutes.
2. Add the **tomatoes** and cook
   over moderate heat for 20
   minutes. Vegetables should be
   very soft.
3. Increase heat to high. Cook,
   uncovered, stirring until the
   liquid has evaporated.
4. Transfer mixture to a large bowl
   and cool.
5. Whisk **eggs** with ¼ cup **Parmesan cheese, parsley, basil**,
   and **oregano**.
6. Combine this with the vegetable
   mixture and season with **salt**
   and **pepper**.
7. Pour ½ of this mixture into the
   prepared pie pan.
8. Sprinkle with ¼ cup Parmesan
   cheese.
9. Add remaining vegetable
   mixture. Sprinkle with remaining ¼ cup Parmesan cheese.
   Top with **mozzarella cheese**.
10. Bake until cheese is bubbly and
    golden brown.

Pepper Petals

Parve • 8 to 10 servings   Round platter

. . . .

1 green bell pepper
1 red bell pepper
1 yellow pepper
1 orange pepper
10 ounces pitted black olives,
    drained

1. Roast **peppers** by placing them
   under the broiler. Keep turning
   until all sides are charred.
2. Place in paper bag until cool
   enough to touch, about 15 to 20
   minutes.
3. Remove charred skin and cut in
   half. Discard seeds and membranes.
4. Cut into 1-inch strips.
5. Place strips (petals) around the
   outside circumference of platter,
   alternating colors. Roll under the
   sides of the strips to shape so
   that the narrower end points to
   the center. When the first circle
   is complete, continue to make
   concentric overlapping circles
   until pepper pieces are used up.
6. In the center, place a small
   round bowl of **pitted black
   olives** to complete the flower.

Red and White Stuffed Peppers

Dairy • 6 servings

Preheat oven to 350°
Cooking Time: 1 hour 30 minutes
13 x 9 x 2-inch baking pan,
    greased

. . . .

6 medium red bell peppers
1 pound farmers cheese
15 ounces ricotta cheese
salt and pepper, to taste
1 egg
5 mushrooms, sliced
2 onions, diced
2 ounces prepared spaghetti
    sauce
2 ounces water
paprika

Note:
To reduce cooking time, microwave
unfilled peppers for 8 minutes.
Reduce baking time to 35 minutes.

1. Cut **peppers** in half and core.
2. Combine **cheeses, salt, pepper**,
   and **egg**.
3. Fill each half of pepper with
   cheese mixture.
4. Sauté **mushrooms** with **onions**
   until onions are translucent.
   Place over filled peppers.
5. Mix **spaghetti sauce** with **water**
   and spoon over filled peppers.
6. Sprinkle **paprika** over filled
   peppers.
7. Bake until peppers start to
   shrivel.

Spinach Pie with Muenster Crust

Dairy • 6 servings

Preheat oven to 350°
Cooking Time: 60 minutes
10-inch pie plate, ungreased

. . . .

¾ pound thick sliced muenster
   cheese
30 ounces chopped frozen
   spinach
1 cup cottage cheese
⅓ cup Parmesan cheese
3 eggs, beaten
1 medium onion, finely chopped
½ teaspoon dried dill weed
salt and pepper to taste

1. Line pie plate with overlapping slices of **muenster cheese**. Be sure to cover the bottom and three-quarters of the way up the side of the pie plate.
2. Cook **spinach** according to package directions. Drain well.
3. Combine spinach, **cheeses, eggs, onion, dill weed, salt**, and **pepper**. Pour into pie plate, covering cheese.
3. Bake until top is lightly browned and filling is set. Allow to stand for 5 minutes before slicing.

Note:
Excellent as a side dish or as an hors d'oeuvre. Serve hot or cold.

✡ Spinach 'n' Cheese

Dairy • 4 to 6 servings

Preheat oven to 350°
Cooking Time: 40 minutes
9 x 9-inch pan, greased

. . . .

3 eggs
2 cups cottage cheese
1 cup grated Swiss cheese
1 cup grated cheddar cheese
6 tablespoons flour
1 teaspoon garlic powder
1 teaspoon salt
10 ounces frozen chopped
   spinach, thawed and drained
1 tablespoon minced onion
   (optional)
½ cup wheat germ

1. Mix together **eggs, cheeses, flour, garlic powder**, and **salt** until well blended.
2. Fold in **spinach** and **onion**.
3. Pour mixture into prepared pan.
4. Sprinkle **wheat germ** on top.
5. Bake until firm.

Note:
For Passover, substitute matzoh meal for flour and farfel for wheat germ.

✡ *Vegetable Soufflé*

Dairy • 9 servings

Preheat oven to 350°
Cooking Time: 50 minutes
9-inch square pan, lightly greased

. . . .

20 ounces frozen chopped
   spinach or broccoli
1 cup mayonnaise
10.5 ounces condensed
   mushroom soup
4 eggs

1. Cook and drain **spinach** or **broccoli** according to package directions.
2. Add **mayonnaise, soup**, and **eggs**, mixing well.
3. Bake in uncovered pan until bubbly.

Note:
1. Do not freeze. 2. Suitable for Passover.

❖ *Tomatoes Provençal*

Parve • 4 servings

Preheat oven to 450°
Cooking Time: 10 minutes
9 x 9 x 2-inch pan, greased

. . . .

½ cup finely chopped fresh
   parsley
1 cup loosely packed fresh basil
   leaves, finely chopped
1 tablespoon minced garlic
3 large tomatoes, cored, and
   thickly sliced
salt and pepper to taste
¼ cup fine bread crumbs
½ cup olive oil

1. Combine **parsley, basil**, and **garlic**.
2. Arrange **tomatoes** in prepared baking dish in single layer.
3. Sprinkle with **salt** and **pepper**.
4. Top with herb mixture.
5. Sprinkle tomato with **bread crumbs**. Drizzle with **oil**.
6. Bake until tops are golden.

Baked Summer Squash

Dairy • 6 servings

Preheat oven to 375°
13 x 9 x 2-inch pan, ungreased
Cooking Time: 1 hour

. . . .

3 pounds yellow summer squash
½ cup chopped onion
2 eggs
1 stick butter (divided)
1 tablespoon sugar
salt and pepper to taste
½ cup bread crumbs

1. Wash, cut, and peel **squash**.
2. Simmer the squash, covered, until tender, for about 6 to 8 minutes. Drain thoroughly and mash.
3. Add **onion, eggs**, 4 tablespoons **butter**, **sugar,** and **salt** and **pepper** to taste.
4. Melt remaining 4 tablespoons butter.
5. Place mixture in pan. Pour melted butter over the top and sprinkle with **bread crumbs**. Bake until brown.

Italian Zucchini Pie

Dairy • 6 servings

Preheat oven to 375°
Cooking Time: 18 to 20 minutes
9-inch pie plate

. . . .

4 cups thinly sliced, unpeeled zucchini
1 cup coarsely chopped onion
4-8 tablespoons butter or margarine
¼-½ cup chopped fresh parsley
¼ teaspoon fresh basil leaves
¼ teaspoon garlic powder
¼ teaspoon fresh oregano
½ teaspoon salt
½ teaspoon pepper
2 eggs, well beaten
8 ounces shredded muenster cheese
1 unbaked 9-inch pie crust

1. In a skillet, sauté **zucchini** and **onion** in **margarine** until tender, about 10 minutes. Stir in **parsley, herbs, salt,** and **pepper**.
2. In a large bowl, blend **eggs** and **cheese**. Stir in vegetable mixture.
3. Pour into **pie crust**. Bake until knife inserted near center comes out clean. Let stand 10 minutes before serving.

Note:
This recipe can be frozen and reheated.

Hint:
If **pie crust** becomes brown before dish is ready, cover crust with foil and continue baking until pie filling is done.

Zucchini with Balsamic Vinegar

Parve • 4 to 6 servings

Cooking Time: 5 minutes in
microwave
1½ to 2-quart microwave safe
casserole

. . . .

2 zucchini (approximately 1
pound)
2 scallions, minced
2 teaspoons oil
2 tablespoons balsamic vinegar
2 tablespoons chopped fresh
mint
2 teaspoons chopped fresh
parsley
½ teaspoon salt
¼ teaspoon pepper
2 tablespoons roasted pine nuts

1. Cut **zucchini** into 1½-inch long
strips.
2. Toss the zucchini with **scallions**
and **oil** and spread in casserole.
3. Cover with plastic wrap, poke
holes, and microwave on HIGH
about 5 minutes.
4. Toss with **vinegar, herbs**, and
spices.
5. Sprinkle with **pine nuts** and
serve warm or at room
temperature.

Roasted Root Vegetables

Meat • 12 servings

Preheat oven to 350°
Cooking Time: 1 to 1½ hours
Roasting pan

. . . .

3 tablespoons olive oil
12 shallots, peeled
12 baby turnips, peeled and
quartered
6-8 peeled carrots, cut into 2-
inch pieces
6 potatoes, quartered
2 acorn squash, peeled, seeded,
and cut into 2-inch cubes
6 leeks cut into 2-inch pieces,
white part only
1 bunch kohlrabi, peeled and
quartered
12 peeled garlic cloves
1½ cups chicken or vegetable
stock
1 tablespoon pepper
salt to taste

1. In a large sauce pan, heat **olive
oil**. Add prepared **vegetables**
and **garlic** in batches to brown,
adding more oil as needed.
2. Place browned vegetables in
roasting pan, add **stock**, and
roast, uncovered, 1 to 1½ hours.
Check periodically to see if more
stock is needed to prevent
vegetables from drying out.
3. When vegetables are soft and
tender, season with **salt** and
pepper and serve.

Note:
This can also be served at room
temperature.

Ghivetch

Parve • 8 to 10 servings

Preheat oven to 350°
Cooking Time: 45 minutes
6 to 8-quart covered casserole

. . . .

2 sliced carrots
1 small cauliflower, cut into
  small flowerets
3 medium diced potatoes
½ pound green beans cut into
  2-inch pieces
2 green bell peppers cut into
  strips
3 medium sliced zucchini
2 stalks sliced celery
1 medium butternut squash
  peeled and cubed
1 small cabbage, sliced
4-5 fresh tomatoes, peeled and
  sliced
4 tablespoons margarine
2 large onions, sliced
2 cloves of garlic, minced
½ cup white wine
½ cup water
3 tablespoons vinegar
¼ cup parsley, chopped
2 teaspoons dried thyme
1 tablespoon fresh basil or 1
  teaspoon dried
2 teaspoons salt
½ teaspoon pepper
½ cup olive oil

1. Place **carrots** and next nine
   vegetables in casserole.
2. Heat **margarine** in a skillet and
   sauté **onions** and **garlic** until
   lightly browned.
3. Add **wine, water, vinegar,
   herbs**, and **spices**. Bring to a
   boil.
4. Add **olive oil** and bring to a
   simmer.
5. Pour hot liquid over vegetables.
6. Cover casserole tightly and bake
   until most of the liquid has
   evaporated.
7. Remove from oven and let cool.

Note:
This can be served hot, warm, or at
room temperature. Serve with
slotted spoon.

Hints:
You can **store roasted vegetables** in the refrigerator for up to 4 days. When ready
to serve, reheat in the microwave or oven, or eat at room temperature. When
refrigerated, they do not lose their flavor.

Leftover raw vegetables can be used as a "rack" for roasting meats. Toss them in a
pan with fresh herbs and place meat on top. Only delicate vegetables, like snap peas
or tender greens, do not take well to roasting.

Beyond Kugel

SIDE DISHES

Fantastic Family Potato Kugel

Parve • 12 to 16 servings

Preheat oven to 350°
Cooking Time: 1½ hours
13 x 9 x 2-inch pan, greased

. . . .

5 pounds potatoes, peeled, and
  quartered
2 large onions, quartered
5 tablespoons matzoh meal
4 eggs
¾ teaspoon salt
pepper to taste
⅛ teaspoon garlic powder
1 stick margarine, melted

1. Using a food processor, with
   metal blade attached, grate
   potatoes and **onions**.
2. Combine **matzoh meal, eggs**,
   and **spices**. Add to potatoes and
   onions. Mix by hand.
3. Add **margarine** and mix again.
4. Spread mixture in prepared pan.
   Bake until top is browned.

Note:
If greased pan is hot before adding
mixture, bottom will crisp.
Can be frozen.

Individual Potato Kugels

Parve • 12 to 16 servings

Preheat oven to 375°
Cooking Time: 35 to 45 minutes
14-inch by 16-inch baking sheet,
  greased

. . . .

6 large potatoes
2 eggs
⅓ cup oil
⅓-½ cup flour
1 teaspoon salt
¼ teaspoon pepper

Variation:
One small onion, grated, may be
added to potato mixture.

1. Peel and shred **potatoes** (do not
   grate). Strain.
2. Beat **eggs** and combine with **oil**,
   and enough **flour** so that
   mixture just holds together. Add
   salt and **pepper**.
3. Using hands, form into balls,
   using ¼ cup mixture for each
   kugel.
4. Bake on prepared baking sheet
   until lightly browned.

Note:
1. Wet hands for ease in handling.
2. For Passover use matzoh meal
instead of flour. 3. Can be made
ahead and frozen.

Knishes

Meat or Parve • 64 knishes

Preheat oven to 425°
Cooking Time: 20 minutes
Baking sheet, ungreased

DOUGH

2 cups flour
2 teaspoons baking powder
1 tablespoon sugar
¾ cup shortening
1 beaten egg, chilled
4 tablespoons water (divided)
1 egg yolk

CHICKEN FILLING

2 cups cooked chicken, chopped
½ cup bread crumbs or matzoh meal
1 cup chicken broth
salt and pepper to taste

MEAT FILLING

2 cups cooked meat, chopped
½ cup mashed potatoes
1 small onion, chopped
1 beaten egg
salt and pepper to taste
2 tablespoons oil

POTATO FILLING

3 large potatoes, peeled and quartered
3 tablespoons margarine, melted
3 tablespoons vegetable oil
2 large onions, chopped
¼ cup chopped fresh parsley
½ teaspoon salt
¼ teaspoon cracked pepper
2 eggs lightly beaten

1. Mix together **flour, baking powder**, and **sugar**. Cut in **shortening** with a pastry blender.
2. Add egg and up to 3 tablespoons **water**, to form a dough. This is enough dough for one filling.
3. Chill the dough for 15 minutes. Divide dough into 8 balls. Remove 1 ball of dough from the refrigerator.
4. Roll into a rectangle about 8-inches by 3-inches.
5. Spread one-eighth of the filling, about ¼ cup, down center length of the rectangle. Pinch the open ends shut.
6. Cut each strip into 8 pieces. Place cut side down on baking sheet.
7. Mix **egg yolk** with remaining 1 tablespoon water. Brush tops of knishes with the glaze.
8. Bake until golden brown, about 20 minutes.

FILLINGS

1. For chicken filling: Mix **chicken** with **crumbs**, **broth**, and **seasonings** until well blended.
2. For meat filling: Mix **meat** with **potatoes, onions, egg, seasoning**, and **oil** until well blended
3. For potato filling: Cook **potatoes** in boiling, salted water, to cover, for 25 minutes. Drain and mash potatoes. In a large skillet, combine **margarine** and **oil**. Add **onions** and fry until golden. Combine potatoes, onions, **parsley**, and **eggs**. Mix until well blended.

Good For You Noodle Pudding

Dairy • 6 servings

Preheat oven to 375°
Cooking Time: 50 minutes
8-inch baking pan, lightly greased

. . . .

¼ cup melted margarine
8 ounces no-yolk broad noodles,
   cooked and drained
3 egg whites
8 ounces low fat cottage cheese
8 ounces low fat sour cream
¼ cup sugar
1 teaspoon vanilla
¾ cup raisins

1. Combine **margarine** with
   **noodles, egg whites, cottage
   cheese, sour cream, sugar,
   vanilla**, and **raisins**.
2. Spoon into prepared pan.
3. Sprinkle topping over noodle
   mixture. Dot with **margarine**.
4. Bake until pudding is set.

T O P P I N G

2 teaspoons cinnamon
2 teaspoons brown sugar
¼ cup corn flake crumbs
1 tablespoon margarine
   (optional)

. . . .

1. Combine **cinnamon, brown
   sugar**, and **cornflake crumbs**.
2. Set aside.

No Boil Noodle Kugel

Dairy • 12 servings

Preheat oven to 350°
Cooking Time: 1 hour,
   15 minutes
13 x 9 x 2-inch pan, greased

. . . .

½ pound medium egg noodles,
   uncooked
1 quart skim milk
5 heaping tablespoons sugar
8 ounces sour cream
4 eggs
½ cup white raisins
1 tablespoon cinnamon
¼ cup sugar

1. Spread **noodles** in bottom of
   prepared pan.
2. With an electric mixer, mix
   together **milk,** 5 heaping tablespoons **sugar, sour cream**, and
   eggs. Pour over noodles.
3. Mix **cinnamon** and ¼ cup
   sugar together. Sprinkle over
   noodle mixture.
4. Top with **raisins**.
5. Cover with foil and bake ½ hour.
   Uncover, and continue baking
   until golden.

Golden Kugel

Parve • 12 servings

Preheat oven to 350°
Cooking Time: 1 hour
13 x 9 x 2-inch pan, greased

. . . .

12 ounces egg noodles
1 stick margarine, melted
2 eggs, beaten
1 large apple, unpeeled, cored,
and chopped
¾ cup seedless golden raisins
¼ cup brown sugar
3 tablespoons lemon juice
⅛ teaspoon cinnamon

1. Cook and drain **noodles** according to package directions.
2. In a large bowl, toss hot noodles with **margarine**.
3. Stir in **eggs, fruits, sugar, lemon juice**, and **cinnamon**.
4. Spoon into prepared pan. Cover with foil.
5. Bake for 50 minutes. Remove foil. Bake for 10 minutes more, or until lightly browned.

Kluski Noodle Pudding

Dairy • 10 to 12 servings

Cooking Time: 40 minutes
Preheat oven to 350°
13 x 9 x 2-inch pan, greased

. . . .

16 ounces kluski noodles
2 sticks butter, melted
6 eggs, beaten
1 pint non-dairy creamer
2 envelopes dried onion soup
mix, approximately 2.3 ounces
total
20 ounces frozen, chopped
spinach, cooked and drained

1. Cook and drain **noodles** according to package directions. Pour **butter** over cooked noodles.
2. Beat **eggs** lightly in a separate bowl.
3. Add **non-dairy creamer** and **soup mix** to eggs.
4. Blend egg mixture into noodles.
5. Gently fold in **spinach** and mix until all ingredients are well blended. Pour into prepared pan and bake.

Note:
Can be frozen.

Apricot Noodle Kugel

Dairy • 12 to 16 servings

Preheat oven to 350°
Cooking Time: 60 minutes
13 x 9 x 2-inch pan, lightly
  greased

. . . .

12 ounces medium egg noodles
1 stick butter, melted
¼ cup sugar
3 eggs, beaten
1 cup milk
4 ounces cream cheese
16 ounces apricot halves,
  including juice

1. Cook and drain **noodles** according to package directions.
2. Using an electric mixer, mix **butter, sugar, eggs, milk**, and **cream cheese** until well blended. Fold into noodles.
3. Add **apricots** and **juice** to noodle mixture.
4. Pour into prepared pan.
5. Sprinkle topping over noodle mixture.
6. Bake until kugel is set and noodles are golden.

TOPPING

. . . .

3-4 cups corn flakes, crushed
¼ cup sugar
1 stick butter, melted
1 teaspoon cinnamon

1. Combine **corn flakes, sugar, butter**, and **cinnamon**.
2. Set aside.

The Ultimate Noodle Kugel

Dairy • 12 to 15 servings

Preheat oven to 375°
Cooking Time: 40 minutes
13 x 9 x 2-inch pan, greased

FILLING

8 ounces medium egg noodles, cooked and drained
8 ounces crushed pineapple, drained
2 eggs
½ cup sugar
1 teaspoon vanilla
4 tablespoons butter, melted
1 cup milk
8 ounces creamed cottage cheese
½ pint sour cream
3 ounces cream cheese

1. Combine **noodles** and **pineapple**. Set aside.
2. In a large bowl of an electric mixer beat **eggs, sugar, vanilla, butter**, and **milk**.
3. Add **cottage cheese, sour cream**, and **cream cheese**, mixing until well blended.
4. Fold in noodle and pineapple mixture.
5. Pour into prepared pan and sprinkle topping over noodle mixture.
6. Bake until knife inserted into center of kugel comes out clean.

TOPPING

¾ cup graham cracker crumbs
½ cup cornflake crumbs
½ cup sugar
6 tablespoons melted butter
1 teaspoon cinnamon

1. Combine **graham cracker crumbs** and **cornflake crumbs**.
2. Add **sugar, butter**, and **cinnamon**. Mix well.

Note:
Can be made ahead and frozen. To reheat, defrost and warm in microwave oven, covered.

Hint:
If you don't have **sour cream**, you can use one of these as a substitution. For 1 cup, use 1 cup plain yogurt or 1 cup evaporated milk plus 1 tablespoon vinegar, or use 1 cup cottage cheese mixed in a blender with 2 tablespoons milk and 1 teaspoon lemon juice.

Vegetable Kugel

Dairy • 16 to 20 servings

Preheat oven to 350°
Cooking Time: 30 to 40 minutes
13 x 9 x 2-inch pan, greased

. . . .

8 ounces egg noodles
1 onion, diced
1 clove garlic, minced
8 ounces sliced mushrooms
2 tablespoons margarine or oil
2 cups coarsely chopped raw
　broccoli
2 cups coarsely chopped raw
　cauliflower
2 cups low fat cottage cheese
6 ounces cheddar cheese, grated
　(divided)
1½ teaspoons dried tarragon
½ teaspoon dry mustard
salt and pepper to taste

1. Cook **noodles** al dente as
directed on package. Drain.
2. Sauté **onion, garlic**, and **mushrooms** in **margarine** until onion
is translucent. Add to noodles.
3. Toss noodles with **broccoli,
cauliflower, cottage cheese**, 3
ounces of **cheddar cheese**, and
seasonings.
4. Spoon into prepared pan,
sprinkle with reserved cheddar
cheese and bake until set and
light golden brown.

Variations:
Use frozen vegetables, or fresh
zucchini and peppers.

✡ *Passover Apple Kugel*

Parve • 6 to 8 servings

Preheat oven to 350°
Cooking Time: 45 minutes
1½-quart casserole, well greased

KUGEL

3 cups matzoh farfel
6 eggs
½ cup sugar
¼ teaspoon cinnamon
½ teaspoon salt
⅓ cup chopped almonds
½ cup golden raisins
4 tart apples, peeled and
    coarsely grated
grated zest of one orange

1. Rinse **farfel** in colander under water until just soft. Drain all excess moisture. Set aside.
2. Beat **eggs**. Add **sugar, cinnamon**, and **salt**. Continue beating until well blended.
3. Stir in farfel, **almonds, raisins, apples**, and **orange zest**.
4. Place mixture in prepared casserole.

TOPPING

¼ teaspoon cinnamon
1 tablespoon sugar
¼ cup melted margarine

1. Combine **cinnamon, sugar**, and melted **margarine** to make topping. Sprinkle on top of farfel mixture.
2. Bake until firm and evenly browned.

✡ *Matzoh Farfel Pudding*

Parve • 12 to 16 servings

Preheat oven to 350°
Cooking Time: 1 hour
13 x 9 x 2-inch pan, greased

1 pound matzoh farfel
5 eggs
½ cup oil
2 cups sugar
1 cup sweet red wine
½ cup nuts, coarsely chopped
2 pounds tart apples cored,
    peeled, and sliced
2-3 tablespoons lemon juice
1 teaspoon cinnamon

1. Pour boiling water over **farfel** in a colander. Squeeze out excess water.
2. Beat **eggs** with **oil** and **sugar**.
3. Add **wine, nuts, apples, lemon juice**, and **cinnamon**.
4. Combine with softened farfel until well blended. Pour into prepared pan.
5. Bake until top is browned.

✡ *Passover Apple Pudding*

Parve • 8 servings

Preheat oven to 350°
Cooking Time: 45 minutes
13 x 9 x 2-inch pan, greased

. . . .

3 matzoh
4 apples cored, peeled and
    sliced
½ cup sugar
¾ cup raisins
2 tablespoons oil
3 eggs
¼ teaspoon grated lemon zest
¼ teaspoon cinnamon

1. Soak the **matzoh** in a small
   amount of water.
2. When soft, drain and break into
   pieces. Place in a medium size
   bowl.
3. Add **apples, sugar, raisins, oil,
   eggs, lemon zest**, and **cinnamon**. Mix until well blended.
4. Place mixture in prepared pan
   and bake until golden and
   apples are soft.

Note:
This freezes well.

✡ *Pineapple Farfel Kugel*

Parve • 8 servings

Preheat oven to 350°
Cooking Time: 30 to 45 minutes
13 x 9 x 2-inch pan, greased

. . . .

3 cups matzoh farfel
5 eggs, separated
1 teaspoon salt
6 tablespoons sugar (divided)
1 stick margarine, melted
2 teaspoons cinnamon (divided)
2 cups applesauce
8 ounces crushed pineapple,
    drained

1. Pour hot water over **farfel** in a
   colander. Drain well.
2. Beat **egg yolks, salt**, 4 tablespoons **sugar**, and melted
   margarine.
3. Stir in farfel.
4. Add 1 teaspoon **cinnamon,
   applesauce**, and **pineapple**.
5. Beat **egg whites** until stiff. Fold
   into farfel mixture.
6. Pour into prepared pan. Mix
   remaining cinnamon and sugar
   and sprinkle over farfel mixture.
7. Bake until firm.

Note:
Can be frozen.

Rice and Noodle Medley

Meat • 6 cups

Cooking Time: 25 minutes
2-quart covered pan

. . . .

2 tablespoons olive oil
½ cup whole grain rice
2 medium onions, coarsely
   chopped
1½ cups medium egg noodles,
   uncooked
2 cups boiling water
2 chicken bouillon cubes
1 cup seedless red and green
   grapes, cut in half

1. Heat **oil** in pan.
2. Sauté **rice** and **onions** until rice
   is lightly browned and onions
   are translucent. Stir occasionally.
3. Add **noodles** and sauté about 2
   more minutes.
4. Add **water** and **bouillon cubes**,
   stirring until cubes are dissolved
   and all ingredients are mixed.
   Cover and turn heat to low.
   Cook 20 minutes or until all
   water is absorbed.
5. Add **grapes** and mix well.

Note:
1. Cut grapes with a scissors.
2. Stays warm for 10 to 15 minutes
as long as it is covered.

How hard can it be to make rice? Well, my husband was trying to help me cook dinner. He asked what he could do, so I suggested he make the rice. He never read the instructions to know that the rice is measured by the cup not by the box like some prepared rices. He poured the whole box of rice into the pot. We ended up with 18 cups of cooked rice for 2 people.

Baked Rice with Pine Nuts

Meat • 4 servings

Preheat oven to 400°
Cooking Time: 30 minutes
1-quart covered casserole dish

. . . .

2 tablespoons margarine
¼ cup onion, minced
1 clove garlic, minced
1 cup uncooked rice
1½ cups chicken broth
¼ cup water
1 tablespoon dried parsley
⅛ teaspoon dried thyme
½ bay leaf
⅛ teaspoon cayenne pepper
⅛ teaspoon black pepper
¼ cup toasted pine nuts

1. Melt **margarine** in a skillet.
   Sauté **onion** and **garlic** in butter
   until translucent. Add **rice**. Stir
   until rice is coated with butter.
2. Stir in **broth** and **water**. Add
   herbs and **spices**.
3. Put in a covered casserole and
   bake until rice is soft.
4. Remove bay leaf. Stir in **pine
   nuts**.

So Easy Rice Pilaf

Meat • 4 to 5 servings

Cooking Time: 30 minutes
2-quart covered sauce pan

. . . .

4 tablespoons margarine
½ cup fine egg noodles
1 cup long grain rice
2 cups chicken broth
4 ounces sliced water chestnuts
parsley for garnish

1. Melt **margarine** over medium
   heat.
2. Add uncooked **noodles** and stir
   until lightly browned.
3. Stir in uncooked **rice** and
   chicken broth.
4. Cover pan and cook over very
   low heat until liquid is absorbed.
   Stir well.
5. Add **water chestnuts**. Stir again.
6. Garnish with **parsley**. Serve hot.

Porcini Mushroom Risotto

Dairy • 4 servings

Cooking Time: 45 minutes
Soup pot with a heavy bottom

. . . .

¼ cup dried porcini mushrooms, diced
4 cups vegetable broth (divided)
1 tablespoon olive oil
½ cup onion, chopped fine
1 cup Arborio rice
½ cup white wine or cooking sherry
½ pound white mushrooms, coarsely chopped
salt and freshly ground black pepper to taste
½-1 cup grated Parmesan cheese

Suggestion:
This makes a tasty appetizer.

1. Place **dried mushrooms** in a small bowl and cover with boiling water. Soak 10 minutes. Reserve soaking liquid.
2. Heat **broth** in a large sauce pan. Keep warm.
3. Heat **oil** in pot. Sauté **onions** in oil until lightly brown.
4. Add **rice** to onions and stir to coat.
5. Add **wine** and stir until absorbed. Add the soaking liquid from the mushrooms and cook until it is absorbed.
6. Add about a cup of simmering broth to the rice and cook over high heat, stirring often with a wooden spoon, until the broth is completely absorbed. Add another cup of broth, as well as **white** and dried **mushrooms**, and repeat. Continue to add broth about ½ cup at a time, stirring each time until it is absorbed. It should take about 4 cups of broth to get to the point where the rice appears to be creamy, and firm. If there is not enough broth, you can substitute boiling water.
7. When rice seems done, add a small amount of liquid so that it appears creamy. Stir in **salt, pepper**, and **cheese**. Serve at once.

Note:
This dish will not taste the same made with other types of rice.

Crunchy Barley Pilaf

Meat • 5 to 8 servings

Cooking Time: 50 minutes
2-quart saucepan

. . . .

1 tablespoon oil
½ cup finely chopped onion
1 teaspoon curry powder
14 ounces chicken broth
¾ cup water
½ teaspoon salt
1 cup pearl barley
1 cup shredded carrots
1 cup shredded zucchini

1. Heat **oil** over medium high heat. Add **onions** and **curry powder**. Cook and stir for 3 minutes.
2. Add **broth, water**, and **salt**. Bring to a boil.
3. Stir in **barley** and return to a boil. Cover and simmer over low heat until barley is tender.
4. Stir in **carrots** and **zucchini**. Cook 1 to 2 minutes more.

Hint:
To **change a recipe to parve** that is designated meat because it uses a meat based broth, substitute vegetable broth.

Turkish Pilaf

Parve • 6 servings

Cooking Time: 20 minutes
1-quart saucepan

. . . .

3 tablespoons margarine
2 onions, chopped
1 cup rice
¼ cup raisins
¼ cup chopped walnuts, or
   blanched and sliced almonds
½ teaspoon cardamon
3 bay leaves
3 garlic cloves
1 cinnamon stick
salt and pepper to taste
pinch of saffron, soaked in 2
   tablespoons hot water
2 cups boiling water

1. Melt **margarine**. Add **onions** and sauté for 10 minutes, being careful not to brown onions.
2. Add **rice** and sauté for another 5 minutes.
3. Add **raisins** and **nuts** and sauté for a few more minutes.
4. Add **herbs, spices**, and **saffron water**.
5. Cover with boiling water and cook, covered, until rice is soft.

Mediterranean Couscous

Parve • 8 to 10 servings   Chilling Time: 2 hours

. . . .

1½ cups water
1 cup orange juice
¼ cup olive oil
3 tablespoons rice vinegar
   (divided)
2 teaspoons grated ginger
1 tablespoon golden raisins
1 tablespoon dried currants
8 dried apricots, thinly sliced
¼ teaspoon salt
½ cup red onion, finely diced
1 cup cooked couscous
2 tablespoons toasted pine nuts

1. In a saucepan, combine **water, juice, olive oil**, and 2 tablespoons **rice vinegar**. Bring to a boil.
2. Stir in **ginger, raisins, currants, apricots**, and **salt**. Pour into a bowl.
3. Cool, cover, and allow to stand for 20 minutes.
4. Boil enough water to cover **onion**. Put onion in boiling water for 15 seconds. Drain. Splash with ½ tablespoon vinegar.
5. Combine onion with sauce in bowl.
6. Add sauce to **couscous**. Add **pine nuts** and the rest of the vinegar. Chill and serve.

Fresh Tomato Risotto

Meat • 4 servings

Preheat oven to 375°
Cooking Time: 1 hour
1½-quart covered casserole,
   greased

. . . .

1 cup peeled and chopped
   tomatoes
¾ cup rice
½ cup finely chopped onions
1 clove garlic, minced
½ teaspoon dried oregano
⅓ teaspoon salt
1¾ cups chicken broth

1. Combine **tomato, rice, onions, garlic, oregano**, and **salt** in casserole.
2. Pour boiling **broth** over tomato-rice mixture.
3. Cover and bake, stirring occasionally, until rice is tender.

Potato Latkes

Parve • 27 latkes

Large skillet

. . . .

6 medium potatoes, unpeeled
1 medium onion, grated
2 eggs, beaten slightly
3 tablespoons flour
¼ teaspoon pepper
1 teaspoon salt
½ teaspoon baking powder
vegetable oil for frying
sugar (optional)
sour cream (optional)
apple sauce (optional)

1. Grate **potatoes**.
2. Drain and squeeze out as much liquid as possible.
3. Add **onion, eggs, flour, salt, pepper**, and **baking powder** to potatoes.
4. Mix until well blended.
5. Heat **oil** until very hot.
6. Carefully drop heaping tablespoons of potato mixture into pan. Fry until brown on both sides.
7. Drain on paper towels. Serve with **sugar, sour cream**, or **apple sauce**.

Note:
Can be frozen. To reheat, do not defrost. Preheat oven to 425°. Place latkes on baking sheet. Bake 15 to 20 minutes, or until sizzling.

Garlic Mashed Potatoes

Dairy • 4 servings

Cooking Time: 20 minutes
Microwave oven

. . . .

4 medium potatoes
1 cup skim milk
2 tablespoons butter or
    margarine
3 medium cloves garlic, minced
salt and pepper to taste

1. Scrub **potatoes** and pierce with a fork. Microwave about 13 minutes or until potatoes are tender.
2. Peel and discard skins of potatoes. Mash potatoes.
3. Pour **milk, butter**, and **garlic** into a glass measuring cup. Microwave about 2 minutes. Mix liquid into potatoes. Add additional milk, if desired, for thinner consistency. Add **salt** and **pepper** to taste. Microwave 1 or 2 minutes or until thoroughly heated before serving.

Crispy Roasted Potatoes

Meat • 8 servings

Preheat oven to 350°
Cooking Time: 2 hours
13 x 9 x 2-inch pan

. . . .

1 stick margarine
8 large baking potatoes, peeled
1 teaspoon salt
½ cup clear condensed chicken
  soup

1. Melt **margarine** in pan.
2. Roll **potatoes** in margarine until well coated.
3. Sprinkle with **salt**.
4. Bake uncovered for 1 hour. Turn.
5. Add **soup** and bake one hour longer, basting, and turning as needed until browned evenly.

Roasted Potatoes and Onions

Parve • 6 to 8 servings

Preheat oven to 450°
Cooking Time: 45 minutes
Jelly roll pan, lightly greased

. . . .

2½ pounds potatoes
½ teaspoon salt
½-1 teaspoon freshly ground
  pepper
½ cup oil
2¾ cups onions, peeled
1 clove garlic, minced

1. Peel **potatoes**, cut into eighths, sprinkle with **salt** and **pepper**.
2. Toss potatoes with **oil**.
3. Arrange in a single layer on pan. Bake 20 minutes. Remove from oven.
4. Cut **onions** into thin wedges. Combine with potatoes. Sprinkle with **garlic**.
5. Roast for another 25 minutes or until browned and crisp. Stir occasionally so potatoes bake and brown evenly.

Dilled Potato and Spinach Bake

Dairy • 4 to 6 servings

Preheat oven to 350°
Cooking Time: 20 minutes
1½-quart casserole, greased

. . . .

10 ounces frozen chopped
   spinach
6-8 large potatoes
¾ cup light cream
1 stick margarine, melted
2 teaspoons salt
¼ teaspoon pepper
2½ tablespoons chopped fresh
   dill
2 tablespoons chopped chives

1. Cook **spinach** per package instructions. Drain, squeeze dry, and set aside.
2. Boil **potatoes** until soft. Remove skins and mash.
3. Heat **cream** until warm.
4. Add cream, **margarine, salt**, and **pepper** to potatoes. Beat until light and fluffy.
5. Add **dill, chives**, and cooked spinach to the potato mixture. Beat until well blended.
6. Place in prepared casserole. Bake until set and lightly browned.

✡ Vegetarian Low Fat Tzimmes

Parve • 8 to 10 servings

Preheat oven to 350°
Cooking Time: 2 hours,
   15 minutes
13 x 9 x 2-inch pan, greased

. . . .

3 pounds sweet potatoes
3 pounds white potatoes
3 medium onions
8 large carrots
1 cup pitted prunes
1½ cups vegetarian broth
1 cup orange juice
1 unpeeled orange cut into
   chunks or thinly sliced
   (optional)
4 tablespoons brown sugar

Variation:
Use 1 tablespoon grated orange zest
for orange slices.

1. Cut **potatoes, onions**, and **carrots** into small chunks. Combine and place in prepared pan.
2. Add **prunes, broth, orange juice**, and **orange**. Sprinkle top with **brown sugar**.
3. Cover with foil and bake 1½ hours, or until all vegetables are tender. Uncover and spoon juices evenly around vegetables.
4. Bake an additional 45 minutes or until all vegetables are golden brown and liquid is thickened. Add more broth or orange juice as needed.

Roasted Roots

Parve • 6 servings

Preheat oven to 350°
Cooking Time: 1¼ hours
17 x 11½ x 2-inch roasting pan

. . . .

1½ pounds sweet potatoes,
   unpeeled and scrubbed
1 pound turnips or rutabaga,
   peeled
¾ pound small red potatoes,
   unpeeled
3 tablespoons oil (divided)
1 medium onion, diced
½ teaspoon salt

1. Cut each **sweet potato** lengthwise into 1-inch slices. Cut
   turnips into ¾-inch chunks. Cut
   each **red potato** in half.
2. In a large bowl, toss sweet
   potatoes with 1 tablespoon **oil**
   and arrange them at one end of
   the roasting pan.
3. Toss turnips, in same bowl, with
   1 tablespoon oil and place them
   in pan next to sweet potatoes.
4. Repeat with red potatoes and
   remaining 1 tablespoon oil.
5. Sprinkle **onions** and **salt** over
   vegetables.
6. Roast vegetables on lower oven
   rack until tender and browned.
   Turn vegetables once with
   spatula during roasting.

Yams à la Madeline

Parve • 4 servings

Preheat oven to 350°
Cooking Time: 30 minutes.
8-inch square pan, lightly greased

. . . .

16 ounces canned yams or sweet
   potatoes, drained
1 cup pitted prunes
4 tablespoons margarine,
   softened
½ cup corn syrup
¼ cup maple syrup
¾ cup pecans

1. Place **potatoes** and **prunes** in
   prepared pan.
2. Mix **margarine, corn syrup**,
   and **maple syrup**. Pour over
   potatoes.
3. Bake 20 minutes.
4. Sprinkle with **pecans** and bake
   10 minutes more or until glazed.

Variation:
¼ cup brown sugar can be
substituted for maple syrup.

Candied Yams with Apples and Chestnuts

Dairy • 8 servings

Preheat oven to 350°
Cooking Time: 55 minutes
13 x 9 x 2-inch baking pan,
greased

. . . .

6 sweet potatoes, peeled and cut
   in 1-inch cubes
1 stick butter or margarine,
   melted
½ cup brown sugar
¼ cup orange juice
½ teaspoon cinnamon
⅛ teaspoon salt
dash of pepper
4 tart apples, peeled and cut in
   1-inch cubes
2 dozen chestnuts

1. Arrange **sweet potatoes** in
   prepared pan.
2. Mix together **butter, brown
   sugar, orange juice, cinnamon, salt**, and **pepper**. Pour
   over sweet potatoes.
3. Bake, basting with the glaze.
4. Add **apples** and **chestnuts** and
   mix in with potatoes. Bake an
   additional 15 minutes, or until
   apples are tender.

*PREPARATION OF
CHESTNUTS*

. . . .

1. **Baking method**: With a sharp
   knife cut an X on the round side
   of each chestnut. Spread chestnuts in one layer in a baking pan
   and add ¼ cup water. Bake in a
   preheated 450° oven for 15
   minutes or until the shells open.
   Shell and peel while hot.
2. **Boiling method**: Place chestnuts in a single layer in a large
   frying pan. Add water to cover.
   Simmer 15 to 25 minutes, or until
   tender. Drain, pat dry, and peel.

Hint:
To **change a recipe to parve** that is designated dairy because butter is used,
substitute margarine.

Sweet Potato Casserole

Dairy • 8 servings

Preheat oven to 325°
Cooking Time: 30 to 45 minutes
1½-quart casserole, greased

. . . .

3 cups cooked mashed sweet
  potatoes
¾-1 cup sugar
1½ sticks butter (divided)
2 eggs, beaten
1 teaspoon vanilla
⅓ cup milk
½-1 cup light brown sugar
½ cup flour
1 cup chopped nuts

1. Blend together **sweet potatoes,
   sugar**, 1 stick **butter, eggs,
   vanilla**, and **milk**. Place in
   prepared casserole.
2. Mix together **brown sugar,
   flour**, remaining ½ stick butter,
   and **nuts**. Sprinkle over potato
   mixture.
3. Bake until very hot.

Hot Fruit Compote

Dairy • 12 servings

Preheat oven to 325°
Cooking Time: 60 minutes
3-quart casserole, lightly greased

. . . .

29 ounces sliced peaches,
  drained
29 ounces apricots, drained
29 ounces pineapple chunks,
  drained
29 ounces sliced pears, drained
29 ounces bing cherries, drained
10 ounces frozen raspberries,
  thawed and drained (reserve
  juice)
1 teaspoon cinnamon
1 tablespoon brown sugar
1 tablespoon lemon juice
1 tablespoon orange flavored
  liqueur
1 tablespoon butter (divided)
1 tablespoon cornstarch

1. Combine **peaches** with all **fruits**
   except **raspberries**.
2. Combine **cinnamon** and **sugar**.
3. Combine **lemon juice** and
   liqueur.
4. Make three or four layers of each
   ingredient in this order: raspberries, fruit mixture, ⅓ of
   sugar/cinnamon mixture, 2
   teaspoons lemon juice liqueur
   mixture, and 1 teaspoon **butter**.
5. Bake, uncovered, for 45 minutes.
   Mixture will be bubbly and juicy.
6. Mix **raspberry juice** with
   cornstarch.
7. Add raspberry juice to casserole
   and bake 15 minutes more.

✡ *Fruit Tzimmes*

Parve • 10 to 12 servings

Chilling Time: Overnight
Large covered pot

. . . .

22 ounces dried fruit
1 cup dry white wine
3 inch cinnamon stick
1 cup orange juice
¼ teaspoon ground cinnamon
8 ounces dried pitted prunes
1 cup raisins

1. Combine **dried fruit, wine**, and **cinnamon sticks** with enough water to barely cover fruit. Cook, over low heat, in a covered pot until fruit is tender, 30-40 minutes.
2. Add **orange juice, cinnamon, prunes**, and **raisins**.
3. Cool to room temperature. Refrigerate, covered, overnight or until ready to serve.
4. Drain and serve at room temperature.

Note:
1. Prunes and raisins should not be included in original dried fruit mixture. 2. A crockpot can be used.

Cheddar -n- Chunks

Dairy • 6 servings

Preheat oven to 350°
Cooking Time: 20 minutes
1-quart casserole, greased

. . . .

20 ounces pineapple chunks, including juice
3 tablespoons flour
½ cup sugar
3 tablespoons pineapple juice
1 cup grated cheddar cheese
1 cup crushed butter-flavored crackers
4 tablespoons margarine, melted

1. Drain **pineapple**, reserving 3 tablespoons of drained juice.
2. Mix **flour** and **sugar** together. Add **juice**, blending to make a smooth mixture.
3. Put pineapple chunks into casserole.
4. Mix in **cheddar cheese**. Pour juice mixture over all. Mix lightly.
5. Mix **crackers** with **margarine**. Sprinkle over pineapple mixture.
6. Bake until golden and bubbly.

Note:
Has to be tasted to be believed. This dish can be reheated in a microwave oven.

Poached Fruit Medley

Parve • 6 to 8 servings

Chilling Time: 2 hours
2-quart covered pan

. . . .

2 cups apple juice
1 cup cranberry juice
2 tablespoons lemon juice
1 cup water
1 teaspoon vanilla extract
1 teaspoon cinnamon
3 cups peeled, sliced, seasonal
    fruit

Variation:
Almond or maple extract, nutmeg or
clove can be used for flavoring.

1. Combine **juices** and **water**.
2. Add one or more teaspoons of
   extracts and/or **spices**. Bring to
   a boil.
3. Poach **fruit** in juices, 20 minutes
   for hard fruits like apples and
   pears, or 10 minutes for soft
   fruits like plums.
4. Cool. Remove fruit from liquid.
5. Place liquid in pan and reduce to
   half to thicken. Serve over fruit,
   warm or chilled.

Suggestion:
Try a combination of apples, pears,
plums, peaches and/or oranges.

Hints:
To **chop** raisins or other **sticky fruit,** first heat the knife or chopping blade with very
hot water.

To **enhance** the **flavor** of combined fruits or vegetables, refrigerate at least 24
hours before serving.

Beyond Strudel

DESSERTS

DESSERTS

Strudel

Parve • 30 to 36 slices

Preheat oven to 325°
Cooking Time: 60 minutes
Baking sheet, greased

DOUGH

3 eggs
½ cup oil
¼ cup water
2 tablespoons sugar
2 cups flour

1. In a large bowl, mix **eggs, oil, water, sugar**, and **flour** with a wooden spoon.
2. Knead dough on floured board and divide into 3 parts.

FILLING

4 apples cored, peeled, and diced
⅔ cup raisins
⅔ cup walnuts
1 cup jam of choice (divided)
1 cup bread crumbs (divided)
½ cup sugar
2 tablespoons cinnamon
oil for brushing

1. Coarsely chop **apples, raisins**, and **walnuts** together.
2. Roll out ⅓ dough into a 11 x 14-inch rectangle.
3. Spread ⅓ cup **jam** over dough. Sprinkle with ⅓ cup **bread crumbs**.
4. Spread with ⅓ of apple mixture.
5. Roll into a 14-inch jelly roll, tucking in ends. Place lengthwise on baking sheet. Repeat with remaining dough.
6. Combine **sugar** with **cinnamon**.
7. When all three rolls are done, brush with **oil** and sprinkle generously with sugar and cinnamon mixture. Mark for slicing with a sharp knife about 1-inch apart and about ¼-inch deep.
8. Bake until dough is flaky and golden. Remove from oven. Cool and slice at markings, cutting through to bottom. Separate slices and return to oven for 5 minutes.

Baked Ice Cream Strudel

Dairy • 36 slices

Chilling Time: Overnight
Preheat oven to 350°
Baking sheet, greased

. . . .

2 sticks butter, softened
1 cup vanilla ice cream
2 cups flour
6 ounces apricot jam
1½ cups white raisins
1¼ cups chopped nuts

1. Mix **butter** with **ice cream**. Blend in **flour**.
2. Refrigerate overnight, covered.
3. Dust board lightly with flour. Divide dough in half. Roll each half into a 6 x 14-inch rectangular strip.
4. Spread each half with half of the **jam**. Sprinkle with half of the **raisins** and half of the **nuts**, leaving a 1 inch border on all sides.
5. Roll up rectangles, starting with long side. Pinch ends together and seal seams.
6. Bake for 30 minutes or until bottom is lightly browned.
7. Cool and cut into ¾ inch slices.

Note:
These can be frozen after baking.

Mandel Bread

Parve • 70 slices

Preheat oven to 350°
Cooking Time: 35 minutes
2 baking sheets, greased

. . . .

3 eggs
1 cup sugar
½ teaspoon salt
1 cup oil
1 cup chopped nuts
1 teaspoon vanilla extract
½ teaspoon lemon extract
½ teaspoon almond extract
3½ cups flour
2 teaspoons baking powder
1 tablespoon cinnamon
¼ cup sugar

1. Beat **eggs, sugar**, and **salt** until well blended.
2. Blend in **oil, nuts**, and **extracts**.
3. Mix in **flour** and **baking powder**.
4. Shape into 4 loaves, 12-inches long by 2-inches wide, on prepared baking sheets.
5. Mix **cinnamon** and **sugar** together. Sprinkle half of this mixture on the loaves.
6. Bake 30 minutes. Remove and slice into approximately ¾-inch slices. Put back on baking sheets, placing cut sides up. Sprinkle with remaining cinnamon and sugar mixture. Bake 5 mintues longer.

Chocolate Chip Mandel Brot

Dairy • 48 slices

Preheat oven 375°
Cooking Time: 30 minutes
2 baking sheets, greased

. . . .

3 eggs
1 cup sugar
¾ cup oil
2 teaspoons vanilla
1 teaspoon baking soda
1 teaspoon baking powder
pinch of salt
3 cups flour
1 cup nuts chopped
½ cup mini chocolate chips
¼ cup sesame seeds

1. Mix together **eggs, sugar, oil**, and **vanilla**.
2. Sift **dry ingredients** together. Blend into batter.
3. Fold in **nuts, chocolate chips**, and **sesame seeds**.
4. Divide dough into 4 parts.
5. Form each into a strip, 2 inches x 12 inches, on prepared baking sheets.
6. Bake 25 minutes. Remove from oven. Cut into 1-inch diagonal slices. Put back on cookie sheets, placing cut sides up. Bake 5 minutes longer, until crisp and golden.

Apple Floden

Parve • 20 servings

Preheat oven to 350°
Cooking Time: 50 to 60 minutes
Baking sheet, greased

DOUGH

2 cups flour
1 egg
¼ teaspoon salt
2 tablespoons oil
scant ½ cup warm water

1. Place **flour** in a large bowl and make a well in center. Place **egg, salt,** and **oil** in the well. Knead together, adding drops of warm water as needed, until dough holds together. Place dough in a clean bowl and cover with a warm, moist towel. Set in a warm place for 1 hour.
2. Divide the dough in half. Knead each half a few times or until silky and pliable. Place back in the bowl to rest for another 20 minutes.
3. Roll out half of the dough on a floured pastry cloth, shaping it into a 12-inch diameter circle.
4. Lift circle of dough carefully on back of hands with fingers curled inward, pulling your hands apart from center to further stretch the dough. Move hands to different areas of center and stretch as much as possible without tearing the dough. Small holes will not matter.
5. When dough is stretched, return to pastry cloth and stretch the thick outer edges by pulling. The circle should measure about 24-inches in diameter and resemble parchment. Trim the remaining thick edges with a knife.
6. Repeat the procedure with the other half of the dough.

Apple Floden (continued)

FILLING . . . .

1 cup plus 1 tablespoon sugar
  (divided)
1 tablespoon cinnamon
½ cup water
2 cups plain bread crumbs
16 ounces pitted prunes
8 ounces dark raisins
½ cup oil (divided)
12 ounces finely chopped
  walnuts
6 peeled apples, thinly sliced

Variation:
Mix 1 stick of melted **margarine** with
½ cup **oil**. Brush 4 sheets of **phyllo
dough** with some of this mixture. Fill
and roll as directed for stretched
dough recipe. Brush top of roll with
some of the oil mixture. With a sharp
knife, make shallow cuts in the
dough every 1½ inches. Bake
as above.

1. Mix 1 cup **sugar** with
   cinnamon.
2. Mix 1 tablespoon **sugar** with
   water. Add **bread crumbs**.
3. Purée **prunes** with **raisins** in a
   food processor.
4. Divide filling in half to use for
   the two pieces of dough.
   Sprinkle each circle lightly with
   3 tablespoons **oil**, one-third cup
   cinnamon and sugar mixture,
   and half of bread crumbs
   and **walnuts**.
5. Distribute prune and raisin
   mixture on circles by half
   teaspoons.
6. Spread **apples** evenly on top.
7. To roll up the filled dough,
   grasp two ends of the cloth
   nearest you and begin to roll up
   the dough away from you. The
   finished roll should be about
   4 inches wide. Pinch the edges
   together tightly.
8. Transfer rolls from the pastry
   cloth to baking sheet by
   shaping the cloth into a small
   hammock. The rolls can be
   curved into a horseshoe shape
   if necessary to fit baking sheet.
9. Sprinkle tops with remaining
   oil, cinnamon, and sugar
   mixture.
10. Bake until golden brown.

Note:
Flip dough circle over to prevent
curling and avoid folds in the dough.
Do not freeze.

Almond Biscotti

Dairy • 60 cookies

Preheat oven to 375°
Cooking Time: 50 minutes
Baking sheet

. . . .

2 eggs
½ cup sugar
1 teaspoon vanilla
½ teaspoon almond extract
1½ cups flour
1 teaspoon baking powder
¼ teaspoon salt
½ cup almonds, finely chopped
½ cup miniature chocolate chips
  (optional)
1 teaspoon grated orange zest
  (optional)

1. Line baking sheet with heavy duty foil.
2. Beat **eggs** and **sugar** at medium speed of electric mixer until well blended. Add **vanilla** and **almond extracts**.
3. Combine **flour, baking powder, salt, nuts, chips**, and **zest**. Add to creamed mixture.
4. Divide dough and form two 8 x 4-inch rectangles on prepared baking sheet. Bake for 20 minutes at 375°. Decrease oven temperature to 350° and bake for 20 minutes. Remove from oven.
5. Immediately cut rectangles into ¼-inch slices. Cut each slice in half crosswise and place back on baking sheet cut side down. Bake for an additional 10 minutes or until crisp and golden brown. Cool on wire racks.

Note:
Batter will be very thick. These can be frozen.

Hint:
If you don't have **baking powder**, you can mix together 2 tablespoons cream of tartar, 1 tablespoon bicarbonate of soda (baking soda), and 1 tablespoon cornstarch. Use the same amount as you would if you were using regular baking powder.

Hazelnut Biscotti With Bittersweet Chocolate

Parve • 2 dozen cookies

Preheat oven to 350°
Cooking Time: 50 minutes
1 baking sheet, greased

. . . .

1¾ cups flour
½ teaspoon baking powder
⅛ teaspoon salt
3 eggs, at room temperature
  (divided)
1 egg yolk, at room temperature
1 cup sugar
1 teaspoon vanilla
1 cup bittersweet chocolate,
  chopped
2 cups hazelnuts, toasted,
  skinned and coarsely chopped

Variation:
1 cup mini semi-sweet chocolate chips can be used in place of chopped chocolate.

1. Combine **flour, baking powder**, and **salt** in a bowl.
2. Place 2 **eggs, egg yolk, sugar**, and **vanilla** in a large bowl. Mix until blended.
3. Gradually add flour mixture to egg mixture until blended. Fold in **chocolate** and **hazelnuts**.
4. Divide dough in half. Wet hands and, on baking sheet, shape dough into 2 logs, each 2½-inches wide and 12-inches long.
5. Lightly beat the remaining egg. Brush the top of each log with beaten egg.
6. Bake 35 minutes. Remove from oven. Reduce temperature to 325°. Cut logs into 1-inch slices crosswise and place them cut side down on the baking sheet.
7. Return logs to oven and continue baking for another 15 minutes, or until golden. Cool on racks.

Note:
Using a serrated knife makes cutting easier.

Rugelach

Dairy • 30 to 36 pieces

Preheat oven to 350°
Cooking Time: 30 to 35 minutes
Large baking sheet, greased

. . . .

2 sticks butter
2 cups flour
1 scant cup sour cream
1 teaspoon salt
1 cup sugar (divided)
1 tablespoon cinnamon (divided)
12-15 ounces apricot jam
  (divided)
1 cup chopped walnuts (divided)
1 cup golden raisins (divided)
1 egg white, beaten

1. In a medium bowl, cut **butter** into **flour**. Add **sour cream** and **salt**. Mix until blended.
2. Roll into a ball (it will be sticky). Chill 30 minutes. Divide dough into 4 balls.
3. On a well-floured board, or pastry cloth, roll each ball into an 8 x 12-inch rectangle, ⅛-inch thick.
4. Sprinkle with ¼ cup **sugar** and a dusting of **cinnamon**. Spread ¼ of **jam** on rectangle. Sprinkle with ¼ cup **nuts** and ¼ cup **raisins**.
5. Carefully roll rectangle, length-wise, into a 12 x 3-inch roll. Transfer to prepared baking sheet using spatulas or pastry scrapers.
6. Repeat process with remaining dough and ingredients.
7. Brush top with **egg white**. Bake until golden brown. Cool and cut into 1-inch slices.

When we were growing up, my aunt and uncle owned a Jewish bakery. We would always go there for Shabbat and other holidays to pick up baked goods. They eventually sold their bakery and moved out of town. Every year at Purim, they would still treat all of us to their delicious homemade hamantashen. They would wrap it up and mail it to our families to enjoy. Now they are in their 80's, and they have stopped sending hamantashen care packages, but we will always remember them at Purim.

✡ *Raisin Hamantashen*

Dairy • 48 cookies

Preheat oven to 350°
Chilling Time: 2 to 3 hours
Baking sheet, greased

. . . .

DOUGH

1 stick margarine
1 cup sugar
1 egg
½ teaspoon vanilla
½ cup sour cream
2½ cups flour
1 teaspoon baking powder
½ teaspoon baking soda
¼ teaspoon salt

1. Blend **margarine, sugar, egg**, and **vanilla**. Beat until fluffy. Blend in **sour cream**.
2. Mix **flour** with **baking powder, baking soda**, and **salt**. Add a little at a time to sour cream mixture. Work by hand. If dough is too soft, add more flour until dough is not sticky.
3. Refrigerate, covered, for 2 to 3 hours.
4. Roll one fourth of the dough on a lightly floured board until ⅛-inch thick. Cut into 3-inch circles. With your finger, brush water around the rim of the circles.
5. Place a rounded teaspoon of filling in the center of each circle. Bring the edges up to form a triangle, pressing the 3 edges together to hold triangle shape. Some of the filling will be visible in the center of the cookies.
6. Place filled cookies an inch apart on prepared baking sheet. Bake until edges and bottoms are golden, 8 to 10 minutes.

FILLING

. . . .

8 ounces raisins
⅓ cup sugar
1½-2 teaspoons cornstarch
1½-2 teaspoons water

1. Simmer **raisins**, uncovered, in just enough water to cover, 20 to 30 minutes, or until soft. Make sure raisins are always covered with water. Drain and reserve water.
2. Add **sugar**. Mix.
3. Dissolve **cornstarch** in an equal amount of **water**. Add 2 tablespoons raisin water and return mixture to the pot. Continue to heat and stir until raisin filling is thickened. Cool before filling cookies.

Note:
Do not make in humid weather as dough gets sticky too fast.

Lemon Tea Cookies

Dairy • 48 cookies

Preheat oven to 350°
Cooking Time: 12 to 14 minutes
Baking sheet, ungreased

. . . .

1½ teaspoons vinegar
½ cup milk
1 stick butter or margarine
¾ cup sugar
1 egg
1 teaspoon grated lemon zest
1¾ cups sifted flour
1 teaspoon baking powder
¼ teaspoon baking soda
¼ teaspoon salt

G L A Z E

¾ cup sugar
¼ cup lemon juice

1. Stir **vinegar** into **milk**.
2. Cream **butter** and **sugar** until fluffy. Add **egg** and **lemon zest**. Beat well.
3. Sift together **flour, baking powder, baking soda**, and **salt**.
4. Alternately add dry ingredients and milk mixture to creamed mixture, beating until smooth after each addition.
5. Drop by teaspoonful, 2 inches apart, onto baking sheet. Bake until edges just start to brown.
6. Prepare glaze by mixing **sugar** with **lemon juice**.
7. Remove cookies from pan at once and brush with lemon glaze.

Very British Shortbread

Dairy • 8 to 16 pieces

Preheat oven to 325°
Cooking Time: 40 minutes
8-inch pan, greased

. . . .

1 stick butter
¼ cup sugar
1¼ cups flour
3 tablespoons cream of wheat
superfine sugar

Variation:
Semolina can be used.

1. Cream **butter** and **sugar**
2. Blend in **flour** and **cream of wheat**.
3. Form into a ball and press into prepared pan. Prick with a fork.
4. Bake until lightly golden.
5. Cut into pieces while warm and sprinkle with **superfine sugar**.

Note:
Do not use instant cereal.

Forgotten Cookies

Dairy • 36 cookies

Preheat oven to 350°
Cooking Time: 8 hours
2 cookie sheets, greased

. . . .

2 egg whites
¾ cup sugar
1 cup semi-sweet chocolate
 chips
1 cup chopped pecans

1. Beat **egg whites** and **sugar** until shiny.
2. Stir in **chocolate chips** and **pecans**.
3. Drop about 2 teaspoons of batter for each cookie onto prepared cookie sheets, approximately 1-inch apart.
4. Place in oven. TURN OVEN OFF. Do not open for 8 hours.

Note:
Store in covered container.

Overnight Chocolate Cookies

Parve • 48 cookies

Chilling Time: Overnight
Preheat oven to 350°
Baking sheet, ungreased

. . . .

2 cups sugar
4 ounces unsweetened
 chocolate, melted
½ cup oil
2 teaspoons vanilla
4 eggs
2¼ cups flour
2 teaspoons baking powder
¼ teaspoon salt
¼ cup powdered sugar

1. Mix together **sugar, chocolate**, and **oil**.
2. Add **vanilla** and mix.
3. Add **eggs** and mix thoroughly.
4. Add **flour**, mixed with **baking powder** and **salt**.
5. Chill overnight, covered.
6. Roll batter into walnut size balls and roll each ball in **powdered sugar**. Place cookies on pan 2-inches apart. Bake 10 minutes. Cookies will crinkle but remain soft.

Note:
Do not overbake.

✡ *Chocolate Cloud Meringues*

Dairy • 36 to 48 cookies

Preheat oven to 225°
Cooking Time: 1 hour
Baking sheet, lined with wax
    paper

. . . .

3 egg whites
⅛ teaspoon salt
1 teaspoon vanilla
2 teaspoons water
1 cup sugar
3 tablespoons unsweetened
    cocoa powder
1 cup chocolate chips

1. Beat **egg whites** with **salt** until
   frothy. Mix **vanilla** and water.
   Add **sugar** and vanilla, mix,
   alternately, and beat until stiff.
2. Mix in **cocoa** and **chips**.
3. Drop by level teaspoonsful onto
   prepared baking sheet.
4. Bake until very dry.

Note:
Store in a tightly covered container.

Hint:
When egg whites are to be beaten make sure they do not contain any yolk.
Separate eggs when cold, allow to come to room temperature before beating.

Low Fat Chip Cookies

Dairy • 50 cookies

Preheat oven to 350°
Cooking Time: 9 to 12 minutes
2 baking sheets, greased

. . . .

½ cup sugar
1 cup dark brown sugar
1-1¼ cups applesauce
1 tablespoon vanilla
1 egg (or 2 egg whites)
1 cup flour
½ teaspoon baking soda
¼ teaspoon salt (optional)
3 cups oatmeal, uncooked
½ cup chocolate chips (optional)
½ cup butterscotch chips
    (optional)
½ cup raisins (optional)

1. In a large bowl, cream **sugars,
   applesauce, vanilla**, and **egg**.
2. In separate bowl, combine
   flour, baking soda, and **salt**.
   Add to creamed mixture.
3. Stir in **oatmeal**. Add **chips** and
   raisins.
4. Drop by teaspoonsful onto
   prepared baking sheets. Bake
   until brown around edges.

Note:
Quick oats can be used. Cookies
baked nine minutes will be chewy
and soft.

Devil's Food Cookies

Dairy • 54 cookies

Preheat oven to 350°
Cooking Time: 10 minutes
Baking sheet, greased

COOKIES

. . . .

2 ounces unsweetened chocolate
1 stick butter or margarine
1 cup brown sugar
1 egg
1 teaspoon vanilla
2 cups flour, sifted
½ teaspoon baking soda
¼ teaspoon salt
¾ cup sour cream
1 cup chopped nuts

1. Melt **chocolate**, cool.
2. Cream **butter** and **brown sugar** until fluffy.
3. Beat in **egg** and **vanilla**. Stir in chocolate.
4. Sift together **flour, baking soda**, and **salt**.
5. Alternately add dry ingredients and **sour cream** to chocolate mixture, blending well.
6. Stir in **nuts**.
7. Drop by teaspoonsful 2-inches apart, onto prepared baking sheet.
8. Bake until cookies rise lightly and form a thin crust. Remove from baking sheet.
9. Cool before frosting.

FROSTING

. . . .

4 tablespoons soft butter or margarine
2 tablespoons cocoa
2 teaspoons instant coffee granules
dash of salt
3 cups powdered sugar (divided)
3 tablespoons milk
1½ teaspoons vanilla

1. Cream together **butter, cocoa, coffee**, and **salt**.
2. Slowly blend in 1 cup of the **powdered sugar**.
3. Add remaining sugar, **milk**, and **vanilla**.
4. Beat until smooth.

Hints:

If you don't have **unsweetened chocolate**, you can substitute 3 tablespoons unsweetened powdered cocoa plus 1 tablespoon shortening, butter, or oil for each 1-ounce square.

Always pack down **brown sugar** when measuring.

Glazed Pumpkin Cookies

Dairy • 36 cookies

Preheat oven to 350°
Cooking Time: 15 minutes
Baking sheet, greased

COOKIE

2½ cups flour
1 teaspoon baking powder
1 teaspoon baking soda
1 teaspoon cinnamon
½ teaspoon nutmeg
½ teaspoon salt
1 stick butter, softened
1½ cups sugar
1 cup canned pumpkin
1 egg
1 teaspoon vanilla

1. Combine **flour, baking powder, baking soda, cinnamon, nutmeg**, and **salt** in a medium bowl.
2. Cream **butter** and **sugar** in large mixer bowl. Add **pumpkin, egg**, and **vanilla**. Beat until light and creamy.
3. Mix in dry ingredients until well blended.
4. Drop by a rounded tablespoonful onto prepared baking sheet. Bake until cookie springs back when lightly touched. Cool on wire racks.

GLAZE

2 cups powdered sugar, sifted
3 tablespoons milk
1 tablespoon melted butter
1 teaspoon vanilla

1. Combine **sugar, milk, butter**, and **vanilla** in a small bowl. Beat until smooth.
2. Drizzle glaze over top of cookies.

Note:
Can be frozen before glazing.

Hazelnut Chocolate Chip Cookies

Dairy • 60 to 72 cookies

Preheat oven to 325°
Cooking Time: 16 minutes
Baking sheet, greased

. . . .

2 sticks unsalted butter, softened
¾ cup sugar
¾ cup brown sugar
1 tablespoon hazelnut liqueur
1 tablespoon coffee liqueur
2 eggs
2½ cups flour
1 teaspoon baking soda
½ teaspoon salt
4 cups milk chocolate chips
1 cup chopped walnuts
1 cup chopped pecans

1. In a large bowl, beat **butter, sugars**, and **liqueurs** until light and fluffy.
2. Add **eggs**. Beat well.
3. Mix **flour, baking soda**, and **salt** in a small bowl.
4. Stir flour mixture into butter mixture.
5. Mix in **chocolate chips** and **nuts**.
6. Drop batter by rounded teaspoonfuls onto prepared baking sheet, 1-inch apart.
7. Bake until golden brown.

✡ Passover Coconut Chip Cookies

Dairy • 36 cookies

Preheat oven to 350°
Cooking Time: 20 minutes
Baking sheet, greased

. . . .

3 eggs
1 cup sugar
⅔ cup oil
1 cup matzoh meal
1¼ cups chopped walnuts
½ cup raisins
1 cup chocolate chips
3 ounces shredded coconut

1. Beat **eggs** and **sugar** together until well blended.
2. Add **oil** and mix thoroughly.
3. Add **matzoh meal, walnuts, raisins, chocolate chips**, and **coconut**. Mix until blended.
4. Drop by rounded teaspoonsful onto prepared baking sheet.
5. Bake until just golden. Loosen when slightly cooled. Cool cookies completely before removing from pan.

Hint:
Cookies will retain their shape better if you allow baking sheets to cool between batches.

Mega Chocolate Chip Cookies

Dairy • 60 cookies

Preheat oven to 350°
Cooking Time: 8 to 10 minutes
Baking sheet, greased

COOKIES

2 sticks margarine, softened
1 cup brown sugar
¾ cup sugar
1½ teaspoons vanilla
2 eggs
3 cups flour
¾ teaspoon salt
¾ teaspoon baking soda
2 cups chocolate chips
½ cup coarsely chopped
   chocolate wafers or candy bar
1 cup coarsely chopped pecans
   or walnuts

1. Cream **margarine** with **sugars**.
   Add **vanilla** and **eggs**. Beat for 4
   minutes.
2. Combine **flour, salt**, and
   baking soda. Add to margarine
   mixture.
3. Add **chocolate chips, chocolate pieces**, and **coarse nuts**.
   Blend just until mixed. Batter
   will be thick.
4. Drop batter by tablespoonsful
   onto prepared baking sheet.
   Bake until edges just start to
   brown. Cool before removing
   from pan.

GLAZE

1 cup semi-sweet chocolate
   chips
4 tablespoons margarine
2 teaspoons vegetable oil
½ cup shredded coconut
¼ cup multi-colored sprinkles
½ cup finely chopped nuts

Variation:
Toppings can be used in any
combination.

1. In top of a double boiler, melt
   chocolate chips with **margarine** and **oil**, stirring until
   smooth.
2. When cookies are cool, dip half
   of each cookie into glaze.
   Sprinkle with **coconut,
   sprinkles**, or **nuts**.
3. Rest cookies on cooling rack
   until glaze hardens and decora-
   tions set.
4. After glaze is hardened, store in
   tightly covered container.

Note:
These can be frozen.

Sinful Chocolate Cookies

Dairy • 72 cookies

Preheat oven to 375°
Cooking Time: 10 to 12 minutes
Baking sheet lined with waxed
paper

. . . .

3⅓ cups semi-sweet chocolate
chips (20-ounces) (divided)
4 ounces unsweetened chocolate
2 sticks salted butter
1½ cups sugar
4 jumbo eggs
4 teaspoons vanilla
3 cups flour
1½ cups white chocolate chips
(10-ounces)
2 cups milk chocolate chips
(11-ounces)
1½ cups butterscotch or mint
chocolate chips (10-ounces)

1. Melt 1⅔ cups **semi-sweet chocolate chips** and **unsweetened chocolate** in a double boiler placed over simmering water. Stir to blend.
2. Pour the melted chocolate into a large mixing bowl. Allow the chocolate to cool.
3. Add the **butter** and beat.
4. Add **sugar, eggs**, and **vanilla**. Beat well.
5. Add the **flour** and mix until well blended.
6. Add the remaining semi-sweet chocolate chips, **white, milk, butterscotch** or **mint chocolate chips**, distributing evenly.
7. Place heaping tablespoons of dough, 1½-inches apart on prepared baking sheet.
8. Bake until a thin crust forms. Cool 5 minutes, then place cookies on a flat surface.
9 Store in an airtight container.

Note:
These freeze well and they are even great eaten directly out of the freezer. They are very sweet and rich.

Hint:
In any recipe calling for egg yolks alone, whole **eggs** can be substituted. Simply use 1 whole egg for each 2 egg yolks. The opposite also holds true, use 2 egg yolks for each whole egg. Use leftover egg whites for scrambled eggs, with a little food coloring, the way commercial egg substitutes do.

Classic Walnut Balls

Parve • 42 cookies

Preheat oven to 300°
Cooking Time: 20 minutes
Baking sheet, ungreased

. . . .

5 tablespoons sugar
2 sticks margarine, softened
2 teaspoons vanilla
1 tablespoon water
2 cups flour
pinch of salt
2 cups finely chopped walnuts
½ cup powdered sugar

1. Mix **sugar** and **margarine** together.
2. Add **vanilla, water**, and **flour**. Mix well.
3. Add **salt** and **walnuts**. Mix well.
4. Roll into walnut size balls and place on pan.
5. Bake for 10 minutes on bottom shelf of oven. Bake 10 minutes on top shelf of oven.
6. Remove from pan and place on paper towels. Roll in **powdered sugar**.

Note:
These freeze well in a covered container.

✡ Passover Toffee Squares

Dairy • 36 to 40 pieces

Preheat oven to 350°
Cooking Time: 20 minutes
Jelly roll pan, greased

. . . .

2 sticks butter or margarine
1 cup sugar
1 egg
1 teaspoon vanilla
¼ teaspoon salt
1 cup matzoh cake meal
12 ounces sweet chocolate, melted
1 cup walnuts (optional)

1. Cream **butter** and **sugar** until smooth.
2. Add **egg** and beat well.
3. Blend in **vanilla, salt**, and **matzoh cake meal**, mixing well.
4. Spread dough in prepared pan. Bake until lightly browned.
5. Remove from oven, spread at once with **chocolate**.
6. Sprinkle **walnuts** on top of chocolate.
7. Cool and cut into squares.

Sour Lemon Bars

Dairy • 32 bars

Preheat oven to 350°
Chilling Time: 4 hours
9 x 9 x 2-inch pan

CRUST

. . . .

1½ cups flour
¼ cup powdered sugar
pinch of salt
1 stick chilled, unsalted, butter,
  cut into pieces
½ teaspoon vanilla

1. Position rack in center of oven.
2. Line the pan with foil extending
   1-inch above two sides of pan.
3. Grease the other two (uncovered) sides of pan.
4. Combine **flour, powdered
   sugar**, and **salt** in a food
   processor.
5. Add **butter** and cut in using
   on/off turns until mixture
   appears sandy.
6. Add **vanilla** and process until
   dough begins to come together.
7. Press dough evenly on bottom of
   prepared baking pan. Bake crust
   28 minutes or until golden
   brown.

TOPPING

. . . .

5 eggs, at room temperature
2 cups sugar
1 cup strained, fresh lemon juice
3 tablespoons flour
1 tablespoon grated lemon zest
powdered sugar for garnish

Variation:
To add tartness, use up to an
additional 1½ tablespoons of lemon
zest.

1. Reduce oven temperature to
   325°.
2. Whisk **eggs** and **sugar** in a
   medium bowl to blend.
3. Whisk in **lemon juice** and
   flour.
4. Mix in **lemon zest**.
5. Spread topping evenly over
   crust.
6. Bake 22 minutes, or until sides
   are set and filling no longer
   moves in center when pan is
   shaken.
7. Cool on rack.
8. Cover and chill at least 4 hours.
9. Using foil sides as an aid, lift
   dessert from pan. Fold down foil
   sides. Cut 16 squares, cut each
   square diagonally, forming
   triangles. Sift **powdered sugar**
   on top just before serving.

Note:
Can be prepared 1 day ahead.
Refrigerate in airtight container.

✡ *Passover Brownies*

Dairy • 16 to 20 brownies

Preheat oven to 350°
Cooking Time: 20 to 30 minutes
13 x 9 x 2-inch pan, greased and
  floured

. . . .

9 ounces semi-sweet chocolate
2 sticks butter or margarine
4 eggs
1⅓ cups sugar
1 cup matzoh cake meal
½ teaspoon salt
1 cup chopped walnuts

1. Melt **chocolate** and **butter**
   together. Set aside.
2. Add **eggs** to **sugar**, beating well
   after each egg.
3. Stir in chocolate mixture. Blend
   in **matzoh cake meal** and **salt**.
   Stir in **nuts**. Pour into
   prepared pan.
4. Bake until toothpick inserted in
   center comes out clean.

First Date Bars

Dairy • 30 bars

Preheat oven to 300°
Cooking Time: 30 minutes
13 x 9 x 2-inch pan, ungreased

D A T E   M I X T U R E

8 ounces pitted dates, cut up
¾ cup sugar
1 cup water
1 teaspoon lemon juice
½ teaspoon almond extract

1. In a medium saucepan, combine
   **dates, sugar, water, lemon
   juice**, and **almond extract**.
2. Cook, stirring occasionally, until
   thick, 10 to 12 minutes.

C R U M B   M I X T U R E

1½ cups flour
1 cup quick oats
1 cup brown sugar
1 stick butter or margarine
1 teaspoon baking soda
½ teaspoon salt
powdered sugar for garnish

1. Mix **flour, oats, brown sugar,
   butter, baking soda**, and **salt**
   until well blended.
2. Firmly pat down a generous half
   of this mixture on the bottom of
   the pan.
3. Spread date mixture on top.
4. Sprinkle with remaining crumbs.
5. Bake until golden and somewhat
   firm. When baked, remove from
   oven and cool slightly. Sprinkle
   with **powdered sugar**. Cut into
   squares. Leave in pan until cold.

Jammin' Jam

Dairy • 16 to 20 bars

Preheat oven to 375°
Cooking Time: 25 minutes
11 x 7 x 2-inch pan, greased

. . . .

1½ cups sifted flour
1 teaspoon baking powder
¼ teaspoon salt
1½ cups rolled oats
1 cup brown sugar
1½ sticks butter
¾ cup apricot jam

Variation:
Your favorite flavor of jam can be
substituted for apricot jam.

1. Sift together **flour, baking powder**, and **salt**. Stir in **oats** and **sugar**.
2. Cut in **butter** until dough is the size of small peas.
3. Press two-thirds of the dough into the prepared pan.
4. Spread **jam** evenly over dough. Sprinkle the remaining dough over the jam.
5. Bake until the top is browned and fruit is bubbly.
6. Cut into bars when cooled.

Chocolate Chip Delight Bars

Dairy • 12 to 14 bars

Preheat oven to 350°
Cooking Time: 40 minutes
9-inch square pan, greased

B A R S

1 stick margarine
1 egg yolk
2 tablespoons water
1¼ cups flour
1 teaspoon sugar
1 teaspoon baking powder
2 cups chocolate chips

1. Mix together **margarine, egg yolk, water, flour, sugar**, and **baking powder**.
2. Pat into prepared pan.
3. Bake 10 minutes. Remove from oven.
4. Sprinkle **chocolate chips** on top and return to oven until chips are melted, approximately 2 minutes. Remove from oven, spread chocolate evenly.

T O P P I N G

2 eggs
¾ cup sugar
6 tablespoons margarine, melted
2 teaspoons vanilla
2 cups chopped walnuts

1. Beat **eggs, sugar, margarine, vanilla**, and **nuts**, until blended.
2. Spread on top of melted chocolate. Bake 30 minutes longer, or until the top is golden in color.
3. Cut into bars when completely cooled.

1-2-3-4 Peanut Butter Bars

Dairy • 24 to 30 bars

Preheat oven to 350°
Cooking Time: 20 to 25 minutes
13 x 9 x 2-inch pan, greased

. . . .

18 ounces peanut butter, smooth
  or chunky
1 egg
1 scant cup sugar
½ cup mini chocolate chips

1. Combine **peanut butter** with
   egg and **sugar** until well
   blended. Mix in **chips**.
2. Spread in prepared pan.
3. Bake until edges are lightly
   browned.
4. Cool and cut into bars.

Chocolate Peanut Butter Bar

Dairy • 96 squares

Chilling Time: 60 minutes
13 x 9 x 2-inch pan, greased

. . . .

1 cup crunchy peanut butter
1 cup softened margarine
1 pound powdered sugar
1½ cups of graham cracker
  crumbs
6 ounces chocolate chips, melted

1. Combine **peanut butter** with
   margarine, sugar, and **crumbs**.
   Press into prepared pan.
2. Spread **chocolate** over peanut
   butter mixture.
3. Refrigerate until firm. Cut into
   1 x 1-inch squares.

Note:
Bring to room temperature before
cutting or chocolate top will crack.

✡ *Chocolate Covered Matzoh*

Dairy • 12 to 16 servings

Chilling Time: overnight

. . . .

5 matzoh
12 ounces chocolate chips
⅓ cup milk
5 tablespoons sweet wine

1. Lightly dampen **matzoh** on both sides with water. Set aside.
2. Melt **chocolate chips** with **milk** over simmering water. Stir until consistency of sour cream.
3. Place one dampened matzoh on large sheet of aluminum foil. Sprinkle with **wine**. Spread a thin layer of chocolate mixture over entire matzoh.
4. Place second matzoh over first, repeating procedure with wine and chocolate. Continue until all matzoh are covered.
5. Allow chocolate to set at room temperature.
6. Fold aluminum foil over layered matzoh and place in refrigerator to chill.
7. To serve, cut into squares with a sharp knife.

Cranberry Bog Bark

Dairy • 2 pounds

Chilling Time: 30 minutes
Foil lined baking sheet

. . . .

1 cup craisins (dried cranberries)
24 ounces white chocolate
2 cups broken walnuts

1. Place **craisins** in a vegetable steamer. Cover and steam 2 to 3 minutes, or until softened. Place on paper towel, blot and cool.
2. Melt **chocolate** in double boiler. Remove from heat.
3. Stir in craisins and **walnuts**.
4. Spread evenly over prepared baking sheet. Refrigerate 30 minutes or until candy is hard. Break into 2-inch pieces.

Teiglach

Parve • 60 pieces

Cooking Time: 45 minutes
2-quart covered sauce pan

DOUGH

3 eggs
2 tablespoons oil
1½ cups flour
½ teaspoon salt
¼ cup boiling water

. . . .

1. In bowl of electric mixer, beat **eggs** and **oil** until creamy. Slowly add **flour** and **salt**. The batter will be soft.
2. Divide the dough into 4 equal parts. Flour your hands to handle the dough. Roll the dough between your palms to make ½-inch ropes. Cut the ropes into 1½-inch pieces.
3. Drop pieces of individual dough into the boiling syrup. Cover and simmer for 15 minutes, then stir.
4. Cover and continue to simmer 30 minutes, stirring occasionally, until pieces are rich amber color and feel hollow to the touch.
5. Remove from heat and add **boiling water** to pan.
6. Lightly grease 2 large sheets of aluminum foil. Sprinkle **currants** on one sheet and **walnuts** on the other sheet.
7. Carefully remove the individual teiglach with a slotted spoon and drop on the nuts or currants and roll to coat.
8. Once cool, store separately in airtight plastic containers at room temperature.

SYRUP

1 cup buckwheat honey
1 cup sugar
1 teaspoon ground ginger

. . . .

1. Combine **honey, sugar**, and **ginger** in pan.
2. Bring to a boil.

COATING

½ cup currants
½ cup chopped walnuts

. . . .

Note:
Can be frozen.

Upstate Apple Cake

Parve • 12 servings

Preheat oven to 350°
Cooking Time: 1 hour
13 x 9 x 2-inch pan, ungreased

. . . .

3 eggs
1¾ cups sugar
1 cup oil
1 teaspoon vanilla
2 cups flour
¼ teaspoon salt
1 teaspoon baking soda
¾ teaspoon cinnamon
¼ teaspoon nutmeg
¼ teaspoon allspice
6 medium apples, cored and
  pared
½ cup chopped walnuts
¼ cup powdered sugar

1. In an electric mixer on high
   speed, beat **eggs**. Add **sugar** and
   beat until pale and thickened.
2. Add **oil, vanilla, flour, salt,
   baking soda**, and **spices**.
3. Slice **apples** into ½-inch slices.
   Fold apples and **nuts** into batter.
4. Pour into pan. Bake 1 hour or
   until cake is slightly brown.
5. Sprinkle with **powdered sugar**.
   Cool before slicing.

Everybody's Favorite Apple Cake

Parve • 12 to 16 servings

Preheat oven to 325°
Cooking Time: 1 hour 15 minutes
10-inch Bundt pan, greased and
  floured

. . . .

3 cups peeled, cored and diced
  apples
3 teaspoons cinnamon
5 tablespoons sugar plus 2 cups
  (divided)
3 cups flour
3 teaspoons baking powder
1 teaspoon salt
1 cup oil
4 eggs, beaten
¼ cup orange juice
1 teaspoon vanilla

1. In a 1 quart bowl, mix **apples**,
   cinnamon, and 5 tablespoons
   of the **sugar**.
2. In a large bowl, mix **flour**,
   remaining sugar, **baking powder**, and **salt**.
3. Make a well in the dry ingredients and add **oil, eggs, orange
   juice**, and **vanilla**.
4. Mix with a spoon until well
   blended.
5. Pour ½ of the batter into the
   prepared pan. Add all of the
   apple mixture. Pour in the
   remaining batter.
6. Bake until the top is firm and
   golden and a cake tester inserted
   in the center comes out dry.

Swedish Apple Cake

Dairy • 12 to 15 servings

Preheat oven to 325°
Cooking Time: 55 minutes
13 x 9 x 2-inch pan, greased

CRUST

2 sticks butter or margarine
½ cup brown sugar
1¾ cups flour
½ cup bread crumbs or corn
   flake crumbs
1 teaspoon salt

1. Mix **butter, brown sugar, flour, bread crumbs**, and **salt** together.
2. Press ⅓ of mixture into a prepared pan. Reserve rest of the mixture. Bake for 5 minutes.
3. Remove pan from oven. Increase oven temperature to 350°.

FILLING

⅓ cup brown sugar
1 tablespoon cornstarch
1 teaspoon cinnamon
4 cups apples, peeled and thinly
   sliced
1 teaspoon grated lemon zest
2 egg yolks

1. Mix **brown sugar, cornstarch, cinnamon, apples, lemon zest**, and **egg yolks**. Spread evenly over crust.
2. Top with reserved flour mixture. Bake at 350° for 40 minutes or until top is lightly browned.
3. Remove pan from oven. Decrease oven temperature to 325°.

MERINGUE

4 egg whites
½ teaspoon salt
⅔ cup brown sugar
1 cup chopped, toasted pecans
   for garnish

1. Beat **egg whites, salt**, and **sugar** until stiff.
2. Spread the meringue over the baked cake. Use a metal spoon to make little peaks.
3. Sprinkle with **pecans**.
4. Bake at 325° for 10 minutes or until the tips and ridges are golden.
5. Serve warm.

✡ *Passover Apple Cake*

Parve • 12 servings

Preheat oven to 350°
Cooking Time: 1 hour
13 x 9 x 2-inch pan, greased

C A K E

. . . .

6 eggs
1 cup oil
2 cups sugar
2 cups cake meal
2 tablespoons potato starch

1. Beat **eggs**. Add **oil, sugar, cake meal**, and **potato starch**. Mix until well blended.
2. Spread half of batter in prepared pan.

A P P L E   F I L L I N G

. . . .

3 pounds apples, sliced
4 tablespoons lemon juice
¾ cup sugar
2 teaspoons cinnamon

1. Combine **apples, lemon juice, sugar**, and **cinnamon**. Distribute evenly over batter.
2. Spread remaining batter on top of the apple filling.

T O P P I N G

. . . .

½ cup chopped nuts
1 tablespoon cinnamon
¼ cup sugar

1. Combine **nuts** with **cinnamon** and **sugar**.
2. Sprinkle sweetened nuts over the batter.
3. Bake until toothpick inserted in the center comes out clean.

Date Cake in a Can

Dairy • 8 servings

Preheat oven to 350°
Cooking Time: 1 hour
8 x 4 x 2½-inch loaf pan, greased

. . . .

8 ounces dates, cut in pieces
1 teaspoon baking soda
1 cup boiling water
1 tablespoon margarine
½ cup sugar
1 egg
1 teaspoon vanilla
1½ cups flour
½ cup walnuts, chopped
   (optional)
cream cheese (optional)

1. Combine cut-up **dates, baking soda**, and boiling **water** in bowl.
2. Add **margarine, sugar, egg, vanilla, flour**, and **nuts**. Blend thoroughly.
3. Pour into prepared pan. Bake until cake tester inserted in center comes out clean. Cool before removing from pan.

Note:
Two 15 ounce white lined cans, greased, can be used. Fill cans half full. Batter will rise. Can be frozen.

Carrot Cake

Dairy • 12 to 16 servings

Preheat oven to 350°
Cooking Time: 45 minutes
10 x 3½-inch Bundt pan,
   greased

. . . .

2 cups flour
2 cups sugar
2 teaspoons baking soda
1 teaspoon salt
1 teaspoon cinnamon
4 eggs
½ cup oil
½ cup non-fat vanilla yogurt
½ cup flaked coconut
2 cups grated carrots
8 ounces crushed pineapple,
   drained
½ cup walnut pieces

FROSTING

8 ounces cream cheese
2 teaspoons milk
3½ cups powdered sugar
½ teaspoon vanilla

1. Mix **flour** with **sugar, baking soda, salt**, and **cinnamon**.
2. Beat **eggs**, mix with **oil** and **yogurt**. Add to dry ingredients.
3. Add **coconut, carrots, pineapple**, and **walnuts**.
4. Bake in prepared pan until a cake tester inserted in the center comes out clean.
5. Prepare frosting by mixing **cream cheese** with **milk, sugar**, and **vanilla** until fluffy. Frost cake when cool.

Hints:

To **store** a **frosted cake** that has been sliced, pat plastic wrap against the **cut surfaces**. The wrap sticks to the frosting, keeping the cake moist. Keep it under a cake dome, or any large inverted bowl.

Refrigerate any cake with a **dairy frosting**. Bring it to room temperature before serving it again.

Tropical Carrot Cake

Dairy • 8 to 12 servings

Preheat oven to 350°
Cooking Time: 40 to 55 minutes
13 x 9 x 2-inch, or 3 (9-inch)
   round pans, greased and
   floured

CAKE

2 cups flour
2 teaspoons baking powder
1 teaspoon baking soda
1 teaspoon cinnamon
½ teaspoon salt
½ teaspoon nutmeg
½ teaspoon allspice
4 eggs, slightly beaten
2 cups sugar
1¼ cups oil
2 cups shredded raw carrots
   (about 6 carrots)
1 cup chopped pecans
1 cup crushed pineapple,
   drained
½ cup flaked coconut

1. Mix together **flour, baking powder, baking soda, cinnamon, salt, nutmeg**, and **allspice**.
2. Add **eggs**.
3. Gradually add **sugar** and beat. Stir in **oil**.
4. Stir in **carrots, pecans, pineapple**, and **coconut**.
5. Bake until cake tester inserted in the center comes out clean.
6. Cool cake in pan for 10 minutes. Remove from pan and cool completely.
7. Frost with Tropical Butter Frosting.

TROPICAL BUTTER FROSTING

4 tablespoons butter or
   margarine
1 pound powdered sugar
¼ cup lightly drained crushed
   pineapple
2 tablespoons sour cream
1 teaspoon vanilla
¼ teaspoon salt
¾ cup flaked coconut
2 teaspoons grated orange zest

1. Beat **butter** until light.
2. Add **sugar, pineapple, sour cream, vanilla, salt, coconut**, and **orange zest**. Mix until well blended.

Note:
Can be frozen.

Hint:
Applesauce can be used for up to one-third of the **oil**, margarine, or shortening in cookies, muffins, or cakes. Substitute an equivalent amount of applesauce for each amount of oil replaced.

90's Carrot-Apricot Cake

Parve • 12 to 16 servings

Preheat oven to 350°
Cooking Time: 1½ hours
10 x 3½-inch Bundt pan, lightly
    greased

· ·

3 cups flour
2 teaspoons baking soda
2 teaspoons baking powder
2 teaspoons ground cinnamon
¼ teaspoon ground mace
¼ teaspoon ground allspice
1 cup sugar
¼ teaspoon salt
½ cup oil
1 cup applesauce
5 egg whites
1 teaspoon vanilla
3 cups shredded carrots
1 cup raisins
1 cup chopped walnuts
1 cup chopped dried apricots

1. In a large bowl, sift **flour**
   together with **baking soda,
   baking powder, cinnamon,
   mace, allspice, sugar**, and **salt**.
2. In a medium bowl, mix **oil,
   applesauce, egg whites**, and
   vanilla.
3. Add **carrots, raisins, walnuts**,
   and **apricots**. Blend well and
   add to the flour mixture.
4. Pour the batter into prepared
   pan. Bake until a toothpick
   inserted in the center of the cake
   comes out clean.

Berry Meringue Cake

Dairy • 9 servings

Preheat oven to 450°
Cooking Time: Overnight
8 x 10-inch pan, ungreased

· ·

5 egg whites
¼ teaspoon cream of tartar
¼ teaspoon salt
1½ cups sugar
½ teaspoon vanilla
½ pint heavy cream, chilled
1 pint fresh strawberries or 10
    ounces frozen berries

Variation:
Raspberries or blueberries or a
combination of berries can be used.

1. Mix **egg whites** with **cream of
   tartar** and **salt**.
2. Blend in **sugar**. Beat with
   electric mixer 15 minutes, or
   until whites are almost stiff. Add
   vanilla and continue beating
   until egg whites hold stiff peaks.
3. Spread egg white mixture in pan.
   Place in oven and shut the door.
   Turn off oven. Leave overnight.
4. The next day, whip **heavy
   cream**. Cover meringue with
   whipped cream. Leave in
   refrigerator 6 hours.
5. To serve, cut into squares. Pass
   berries or put berries over
   whipped cream just before
   serving.

Fresh Fruit Bundt Cake

Parve • 12 to 16 servings

Preheat oven to 350°
Cooking Time: 1 hour and
  15 minutes
10 x 3½-inch Bundt pan, greased

FILLING

6 large cooking apples
⅓ cup sugar
1½ teaspoons cinnamon
¾ teaspoon nutmeg (optional)

1. Pare, core and thickly slice **apples**.
2. Combine with **sugar, cinnamon**, and **nutmeg**. Set aside.

BATTER

3 cups flour
2 cups sugar
3 teaspoons baking powder
1 teaspoon salt
1 cup oil
4 eggs
¼ cup orange juice
1 tablespoon vanilla
powdered sugar for garnish

Variation:
Can be made with fresh peaches or plums.

1. Sift together **flour, sugar, baking powder**, and **salt** in a large bowl.
2. Make a well in the center of dry ingredients and pour in **oil, eggs, orange juice**, and **vanilla**.
3. Beat until thick and well blended.
4. Spoon into pan, alternating layers of batter, with layers of apple filling ending with batter.
5. Bake until the top is firm and golden and a cake tester inserted at the cake's highest point comes out dry. Cool to lukewarm before removing from pan.
6. Sprinkle **powdered sugar** on top.

"You have to beat the eggs just right," is what my aunt said. "That's what makes my sponge cake higher and better tasting than my sisters'." Each year my mother and her six sisters would have a competition to see who would bake the best sponge cake. Since all seven sisters used the same recipe, all the cakes looked and tasted the same. Each cousin would, of course, vote his/her mother's cake the best. After many years all the sisters used different variations making the competition much more fun.

✡ *I Love You Honey Cake*

Parve • 10 to 12 servings

Preheat oven to 350°
Cooking Time: 40 to 45 minutes
10 x 4-inch tube pan, greased and
    bottom lined with waxed paper

. . . .

1½ cups sugar
1 cup honey
½ cup oil
3 eggs
2½ cups flour
2 teaspoons baking powder
1 teaspoon baking soda
½ teaspoon ground cloves
1½ teaspoons allspice
¼ teaspoon nutmeg
2 teaspoons cinnamon
½ teaspoon ground ginger
1 cup coffee
¾ cup chopped walnuts or
    almonds
anise seed and slivered almonds
    to taste

1. Combine **sugar, honey**, and **oil**.
2. Add **eggs** one at a time, mixing
   well after each addition.
3. In a separate bowl, mix **flour,
   baking powder, baking soda**,
   and **spices**.
4. Alternately add dry ingredients
   and **coffee** to batter. Mix well.
5. Stir in **chopped nuts**.
6. Pour into prepared pan. Sprinkle
   with **anise** and **almonds**.
7. Bake until toothpick inserted
   near the center comes out clean.

✡ *Passover Chiffon Cake*

Parve • 12 to 16 servings

Preheat oven to 325°
Cooking Time: 50 minutes
10 x 4-inch tube pan, ungreased

. . . .

8 eggs, separated
½ cup potato starch (divided)
1 cup matzoh cake meal
1½ cups sugar
1 teaspoon salt
½ cup oil
¾ cup orange juice
grated zest of 1 orange or
    1 lemon

1. In a large bowl of an electric
   mixer beat **egg whites** until
   foamy.
2. Add ½ teaspoon of **potato
   starch**. Beat until very stiff. Set
   aside.
3. Sift **matzoh cake meal**, remaining potato starch, **sugar**, and
   salt into a small electric mixer
   bowl. Make a well in the center.
4. Add **oil, unbeaten egg yolks,
   orange juice**, and **zest**. Beat
   1 minute.
5. Carefully fold this mixture into
   egg whites until well blended.
6. Pour into pan. Bake until cake
   springs back when lightly
   touched. Cool cake completely
   before removing from pan.

Poppy Seed Cake

Dairy • 14 servings

Preheat oven to 325°
Cooking Time: 55 minutes
10 x 3½-inch Bundt pan, greased
and floured

. . . .

2 sticks unsalted butter
1¾ cups sugar (divided)
5 eggs, separated
2⅔ cups sifted flour
1¼ teaspoons baking powder
1¼ teaspoons baking soda
½ teaspoon salt
1 cup buttermilk
⅓ cup poppy seeds
1 tablespoon grated lemon zest
¼ cup powdered sugar
    (optional)

1. In a large bowl, beat **butter** and 1½ cups of the **sugar** until light and fluffy.
2. Beat in **yolks**, one at a time.
3. Add **sifted flour, baking powder, baking soda**, and **salt**, alternately with **buttermilk** to yolk mixture, starting and ending with dry ingredients. Beat well after each addition. Beat until smooth.
4. Beat in **poppy seeds** and **lemon zest**. Set aside.
5. Beat **egg whites** until foamy. Gradually beat in remaining ¼ cup of sugar until egg whites form soft peaks.
6. Fold into batter carefully.
7. Pour into prepared pan.
8. Bake until top springs back when lightly touched with fingertip. Let stand 5 minutes. Loosen cake around sides with spatula or knife. Invert onto wire rack. Cool completely. Just before serving, sprinkle with **powdered sugar**.

Hint:
When beating **egg whites**, always have them at room temperature. Beat only to the stiff shiny stage. If beaten longer, they become granular.

Orange Ripple Cake

Dairy • 12 to 16 servings

Preheat oven to 350°
Cooking Time: 50 to 60 minutes
10 x 3½-inch Bundt pan, greased
and floured

. . . .

1 stick margarine, softened
1 stick butter, softened
1½ cups sugar (divided)
3 eggs
1¾ cups flour
1 teaspoon baking powder
1 teaspoon baking soda
1 cup sour cream
1 tablespoon grated orange zest
2 tablespoons cocoa
1 teaspoon cinnamon
powdered sugar for decorating

1. In a large mixing bowl, cream **margarine, butter**, and 1 cup **sugar** at medium speed until light and fluffy. Add **eggs** and beat one minute at low speed.
2. Sift **flour, baking powder**, and **baking soda**. Alternately add flour mixture and **sour cream** to batter.
3. Add **orange zest** and blend thoroughly.
4. Spoon half of the mixture into prepared pan.
5. Mix together remaining ½ cup sugar, **cocoa**, and **cinnamon**. Sprinkle half over batter in pan.
6. Repeat with remaining batter and sugar mixture. Swirl through with knife.
7. Bake until toothpick inserted in the center comes out clean. Cool in pan for 10 minutes. Invert onto serving plate.
8. Sprinkle with **powdered sugar** before serving.

Hint:
Do not use **"lite" butter** or **"lite" margarine** for baking as they are high in water content.

✡ *Flourless Orange Cake*

Parve • 12 servings

Preheat oven to 350°
Cooking Time: 1 hour
9½-inch springform pan, greased

. . . .

¼ cup matzoh meal
2 thin-skinned juice oranges
1½ cups blanched almonds
1 cup sugar (divided)
6 eggs, separated
powdered sugar for garnish

1. Dust prepared pan with **matzoh meal**.
2. Scrub the **oranges** well. Place in a covered pot with a few inches of water and cook over medium heat for about 1 hour, or until oranges are soft.
3. Remove oranges and let them cool. Cut open and remove seeds.
4. In a food processor, mince oranges, including peel. Set aside in a large bowl.
5. In processor, finely grind **almonds** with ½ cup **sugar** until consistency of coarse flour. Add to oranges.
6. Mix in remaining sugar and **egg yolks**.
7. In a clean bowl, beat **egg whites** until stiff and fold into orange mixture.
8. Pour into pan and bake 60 minutes, or until top is lightly browned and cake feels firm to the touch.
9. Cool on rack and dust with **powdered sugar** before serving.

Note:
Oranges may be prepared in advance.

Light and Layered Bundt Cake

Dairy • 12 servings

Preheat oven to 350°
Cooking Time: 50 minutes
10 x 3½-inch Bundt pan, greased
and floured

. . . .

4 ounces semi sweet chocolate
1 stick margarine plus 2
  tablespoons margarine
  (divided)
1 tablespoon cocoa
1 cup egg whites (8 eggs)
½ teaspoon cream of tartar
1¼ cups plus 2 tablespoons
  sugar (divided)
2 egg yolks
2 tablespoons flour plus ¾ cup
  flour (divided)
1¼ teaspoons baking powder
  (divided)

1. Melt **semi-sweet chocolate**,
   1 stick **margarine**, and **cocoa**.
   Mix until smooth. Cool.
2. With an electric mixer, beat **egg
   whites** and **cream of tartar**
   until frothy. Gradually add 1¼
   cups **sugar** and continue beating
   until mixture forms very stiff
   peaks.
3. Set aside three heaping tablespoons stiffened egg white
   mixture.
4. With electric mixer, beat remaining 2 tablespoons margarine and
   remaining 2 tablespoons sugar.
   Add **yolks**, 2 tablespoons **flour**,
   and ¼ teaspoon **baking pow-
   der**. Fold in reserved 3 tablespoons of egg whites.
5. Gently fold cooled chocolate
   into egg whites.
6. Mix remaining ¾ cup flour with
   remaining 1 teaspoon baking
   powder. Add to egg
   white/chocolate mixture.
7. Layer chocolate mixture and yolk
   mixture alternately.
8. Bake in prepared pan, until cake
   pulls away from sides of pan.

✡ *Chocolate Mousse Cake*

Dairy • 10 servings

Preheat oven to 350°
Cooking Time: 40 to 50 minutes
9-inch spring form pan, greased

. . . .

10 ounces semi-sweet chocolate
1 teaspoon instant coffee
  granules
1¼ cups sugar
2½ sticks unsalted margarine,
  softened
10 eggs, separated

1. Melt **chocolate** with **coffee** in top of double boiler. Stir until smooth. Set aside to cool.
2. Using an electric mixer, cream **sugar** and **margarine** in a large bowl. Add chocolate mixture and blend well.
3. Add **yolks**, one at a time, continually beating at low speed for 15 minutes.
4. At high speed, in a clean bowl, beat **egg whites** until stiff. Fold into chocolate mixture.
5. Pour ¾ of batter into prepared pan. Bake until cake rises. Center of cake will drop. Cool completely.
6. Spread remaining uncooked batter on top of cake. Cover and chill overnight.

Note:
This recipe contains uncooked egg yolks and egg whites.

✡ *Chocolate Nut Decadence*

Dairy • 12 servings

Preheat oven to 375°
Cooking Time: 25 minutes
8-inch round cake pan, greased

C A K E

4 ounces semi-sweet chocolate
1¾ cups walnuts
2 tablespoons plus ½ cup sugar
  (divided)
1 stick unsalted butter or
  margarine
3 eggs
1 tablespoon rum

1. Cover bottom of greased pan
   with waxed paper and grease
   paper.
2. Melt **chocolate**. Cool slightly.
3. In a food processor, pulse
   walnuts and 2 tablespoons of
   sugar, until finely ground.
   Remove from processor.
4. Place **butter** and remaining
   ½ cup sugar in food processor.
   Mix until well blended. Pour in
   chocolate and mix until smooth.
5. Add **eggs** and **rum**. Pulse to
   mix. Mix in sugared ground nuts.
6. Pour into prepared pan. Bake.
   Cake will be soft. It firms as it
   cools.
7. Cool in pan for 20 minutes on
   wire rack. Remove from pan and
   cool completely before glazing.

G L A Z E

1 cup semi-sweet chocolate
  chips
6 tablespoons unsalted butter or
  margarine
2 dozen walnuts halves for
  garnish

Note:
If this is to be used for Passover,
substitute a flavoring of your choice
for the rum.

1. Melt **chocolate chips** and
   butter in a heavy saucepan,
   stirring until smooth.
2. Dip ½ of each **walnut** into
   glaze. Refrigerate walnuts until
   glaze is set.
3. Cool remainder of glaze until
   thickened but soft enough to
   pour.
4. Pour glaze onto middle of cake
   and spread with a spatula. Allow
   glaze to drip randomly down
   sides of cake.
5. Decorate with glazed walnuts.

Note:
This is a very rich cake. Keep at
room temperature for up to 2 days,
or freeze in tightly sealed freezer
paper.

❖ Mascarpone Cake with Raspberry Sauce

Dairy • 6 servings

Chilling Time: Overnight
9 x 5 x 3-inch loaf pan

R A S P B E R R Y   S A U C E . . . .

20 ounces frozen raspberries in
   syrup, thawed
1 teaspoon cornstarch
2 tablespoons water
1 teaspoon fresh lemon juice

1. In a food processor, with metal blade, purée the thawed **raspberries**. To remove seeds, force the raspberries through a fine sieve over a pan.
2. In a small pan, bring purée to a simmer. Combine **cornstarch** with **water** and **lemon juice**, add to pan. Boil and stir for 1 minute.
3. Cool and chill, covered. This can be prepared 2 days in advance.

M A S C A R P O N E   C A K E . . . .

3 eggs separated, at room
   temperature
⅓ cup sugar
½ pound mascarpone cheese
1½ teaspoons vanilla
½ teaspoon grated lemon zest
2 ounces semi-sweet chocolate,
   grated
fresh raspberries for garnish
   (optional)

1. Line pan with plastic wrap. Leave a 2-inch overhang on the ends. Chill pan in freezer.
2. Beat the **egg yolks** and **sugar** together until mixture is thick and pale. Beat in the **mascarpone, vanilla**, and **lemon zest**.
3. In another bowl, beat the **egg whites** until they hold stiff peaks.
4. Gently fold the whites into the yolk mixture.
5. Spoon half of the mascarpone mixture into prepared pan. Sprinkle with the **chocolate** and spoon on the rest of the mascarpone mixture, carefully smoothing the top.
6. Freeze, covered with the plastic wrap, for 8 hours or overnight.
7. Unmold onto a serving dish. Arrange fresh **raspberries** on top.
8. Slice and serve with the raspberry sauce.

❖ Strawberries 'n' Cream Cheesecake

Dairy • 10 to 12 servings

Preheat oven to 325°
Cooking Time: 50 minutes
9-inch springform pan, ungreased

. . . .

1⅓ cups chocolate cookie
    crumbs
½ teaspoon cinnamon
5 tablespoons butter or
    margarine, melted
24 ounces cream cheese,
    softened
1 cup sour cream
2 tablespoons cream or milk
1 cup sugar
3 eggs
8 ounces white chocolate
½ cup strawberry cream liqueur
2 teaspoons vanilla
strawberries for garnish

Variation:
Your favorite fruit and cream liqueur
can be substituted.

1. Mix **cookie crumbs** with
   cinnamon and **butter** until
   blended. Press onto bottom and
   partly up sides of pan.
2. Mix **cream cheese** with **sour
   cream** until fluffy. Add **cream**
   and blend.
3. Add **sugar**. Beat until fluffy.
4. Add **eggs** 1 at a time. Beat on
   low speed until blended.
5. Melt **chocolate**. Add **liqueur** to
   chocolate and blend.
6. Add chocolate mixture to cheese
   mixture.
7. Add **vanilla** and blend.
8. Pour into crust. Bake 50 minutes.
   Turn off heat and leave cake in
   oven for an additional hour with
   door slightly open.
9. Garnish with **strawberries**.

Mint Lady Finger Torte

Dairy • 12 to 15 servings

Chilling Time: 4 hours
9-inch springform pan, ungreased

. . . .

21 ounces lady fingers
2 cups chocolate chips
3 tablespoons margarine
¼ cup water
¼ teaspoon peppermint extract
12 ounces whipped topping
¼ cup ground walnuts for
   garnish

Variations:
If lady fingers are not available, use
a sliced pound cake, sponge cake, or
angel food cake to line the
springform pan.

For a change, prepare a mousse,
pudding, or custard for the filling.

1. Layer bottom and sides of the pan with **lady fingers**.
2. Melt together **chocolate chips** and **margarine**. Add **water** and **peppermint extract**. Fold two-thirds of the **whipped topping** into chocolate mixture.
3. Pour half of the chocolate mixture onto the bottom layer of lady fingers. Add a layer of lady fingers. Repeat this pattern one more time ending with a layer of lady fingers.
4. Using the remaining whipped topping, frost cake. Garnish with **walnuts** in the center. Refrigerate or freeze. If freezing, defrost in refrigerator 1 hour before serving.

Cranberry Swirl Ice Cream Cake

Dairy • 8 to 10 servings

Chilling Time: 6½ hours
8-inch spring form pan, lightly
greased

CRUST

1½ cups ground chocolate
  cookies
4 tablespoons unsalted butter,
  melted

1. In a bowl, stir together **crumbs**
   and **butter** until mixture is well
   combined.
2. Pat mixture on bottom and
   1-inch up the side of prepared
   pan. Freeze for 30 minutes or
   until firm.

CRANBERRY PURÉE

1½ cups cranberries
½ cup light corn syrup
⅓ cup sugar
⅓ cup water

1. In a covered saucepan, simmer
   **cranberries, corn syrup,
   sugar**, and **water** for 10 minutes, or until cranberries are soft.
2. In a food processor, purée the
   cranberry mixture.
3. Pour mixture into a small bowl,
   cover and chill for 1 hour or
   until cold, stir until smooth.

FILLING

1½ pints vanilla ice cream,
  softened
½ cup shelled pistachio nuts,
  chopped fine
1 tablespoon butter
¼ teaspoon salt
1 cup heavy cream, chilled
3 tablespoons powdered sugar
1 teaspoon vanilla
Chocolate curls or grated
  bittersweet chocolate for
  garnish

1. Spread half the **ice cream** over
   the crust. Drizzle with all but ⅓
   cup of cranberry purée.
2. Spread remaining ice cream on
   top. Draw a knife through ice
   cream mixture in loops to
   marbleize. Smooth the top.
3. Freeze cake for 30 minutes, or
   until purée is firm.
4. Spread remaining ⅓ cup cranberry purée evenly over the top
   and freeze the cake for 15
   minutes, or until the purée is
   firm.
5. In a small skillet, melt **butter**,
   add **pistachio nuts** and **salt**,
   and sauté over moderate heat.
   Let cool.
6. Pour **heavy cream** into a bowl
   and beat with an electric mixer
   until it holds soft peaks. Add
   powdered sugar and **vanilla**,
   and beat mixture until it holds
   stiff peaks.

Cranberry Swirl Ice Cream Cake *(continued)*

7. Fold in **pistachios**. Spread mixture over the cake and freeze cake for 30 minutes or until top is firm.
8. Cover cake with plastic wrap and foil and freeze for 4 hours.
9. Just before serving, wrap a warm, dampened kitchen towel around side of pan, remove the side and transfer cake to serving plate.
10. Garnish with **chocolate curls** or **grated chocolate**. Cut wedges with a knife dipped in warm water.

Note:
Can be made 5 days in advance, kept tightly covered and frozen.

Miniature Cheesecakes

Dairy • Serves 24

Preheat oven to 375°
Cooking Time: 15 to 20 minutes
24 cup mini muffin pan, lined with muffin papers

. . . .

24 vanilla wafers
6 ounces cream cheese, softened
¾ cup sugar
2 eggs
1 tablespoon lemon juice
1 teaspoon vanilla
20 ounces canned pie filling (blueberry, cherry, or peach)
½ cup sliced nuts (optional)

1. Place a **vanilla wafer** in bottom of each liner.
2. In a small bowl, beat **cream cheese** , **sugar**, **eggs**, **lemon juice**, and **vanilla** until light and fluffy.
3. Fill liners ⅔ full with cheese mixture.
4. Bake until set.
5. Remove from oven. Top each cake with a spoonful of **pie filling** and 1 teaspoon **nuts**.
6. Chill until ready to serve.

Pineapple Meringue Torte

Dairy • 8 servings

Preheat oven to 325°
Cooking Time: 25 minutes
Two 8-inch layer cake pans,
  greased and floured

BATTER

1 stick butter
½ cup sugar
4 eggs, separated
⅔ cup flour
4 tablespoons milk
2 tablespoons flour
1 teaspoon baking powder
¼ teaspoon salt

1. Cream **butter** and **sugar** together.
2. Add well-beaten **egg yolks** and mix thoroughly.
3. Add **flour** alternately with **milk**.
4. Sift **flour** with **baking powder** and **salt**. Add to batter.
5. Pour batter into prepared pans.

MERINGUE

1 teaspoon vanilla
¾ cup sugar
¾ chopped nuts

1. Beat **egg whites** until frothy. Add **vanilla**.
2. Add **sugar** gradually. Beat until stiff.
3. Spread on unbaked batter. Sprinkle with **nuts**.
4. Bake until meringue is golden. Cool.

FILLING

1 cup heavy cream, chilled
1½ tablespoons powdered sugar
1 cup crushed pineapple, well drained
½ teaspoon vanilla

1. Place one layer, meringue side down, on plate.
2. Whip the **cream**, add **sugar, pineapple**, and **vanilla**.
3. Spread filling on first layer. Place remaining layer on top of filling, meringue side up.

Hint:
To keep a **meringue** from shrinking when cut, sprinkle a little granulated sugar over it before cutting.

Apple Torte Supreme

Dairy • 8 to 10 servings

Preheat oven to 350°
Cooking Time: 1 hour,
    15 minutes
9-inch springform pan, greased
    and floured

C R U S T

½ cup sugar
2 sticks unsalted butter
1½ cups flour
1 egg
¼ cup bread crumbs

1. Combine **sugar, butter, flour**, and **egg** in a food processor with steel blade attached. Pulse until dough is crumbly. Refrigerate dough for 30 minutes.
2. Press dough into prepared pan, covering bottom and halfway up sides.
3. Sprinkle crust with a thin layer of **bread crumbs**.

F I L L I N G

4 large apples
½ cup heavy cream
2-3 tablespoons lemon juice
2 eggs
1 cup sour cream
½ cup sugar
½ teaspoon vanilla
¼ cup apricot jam

1. Pare and core **apples**. Cut in half, vertically. Score rounded sides at ¾ inch intervals, about ¼ inch deep.
2. Place apples in pan, rounded sides up, in a circle, starting from outside and working inward. Fill in spaces with extra apple slices.
3. Mix together **heavy cream, lemon juice, eggs, sour cream, sugar**, and **vanilla**. Pour over apples.
4. Place pan on baking sheet on low shelf of oven. Bake until apples are tender and filling is set. Cool 10 minutes.
5. Melt **jam** over low heat. Brush over apples with a pastry brush.

Note:
Apples will open up where scored, creating an attractive pattern.

❖ Cranberry Surprise Pie

Dairy • 6 servings

Preheat oven to 325°
Cooking Time: 40-50 minutes
8-inch pie pan, greased

. . . .

2 cups cranberries
½ cup chopped walnuts
1½ cups sugar (divided)
2 eggs
1 cup flour
4 tablespoons melted shortening
½ cup melted butter or
　margarine
ice cream (optional)
frozen yogurt (optional)

1. Spread **cranberries** over bottom of prepared pan.
2. Sprinkle with **nuts** and ½ cup **sugar**.
3. Beat **eggs** well. Add remaining sugar gradually. Beat until thoroughly mixed.
4. Add **flour, shortening**, and **butter**. Beat well.
5. Pour batter over cranberries.
6. Bake until crust is golden.
7. Serve warm or cold.
8. Serve topped with **ice cream** or **frozen yogurt**.

Hint:
Cranberries are a good source of vitamin C and potassium. They can be frozen in their original plastic package for several months. Because foods frozen at their peak quality taste best, be sure to stock up on cranberries in the fall.

Berrytime Glaze Pie

Parve • 6 to 8 servings

Preheat oven to 450°
Cooking Time: 12 to 15 minutes
9-inch pie plate

CRUST (MAKES 2 CRUSTS) . . . .

2 cups flour
1 teaspoon salt
5 tablespoons shortening
5 tablespoons margarine
⅓ cup cold water
⅛ teaspoon vinegar

1. Mix **flour** and **salt**.
2. Cut in **shortening** until size of small peas.
3. Cut in **margarine** until size of small peas.
4. Mix **water** and **vinegar** together.
5. Add to flour mixture, a little at a time.
6. Form into a ball and chill ½ hour.
7. Roll out half of dough. Turn into pan and bake 12-15 minutes, until lightly browned. Cool. Freeze remaining dough for later use.

FILLING   . . . .

1 quart raspberries or blueberries divided
3 tablespoons cornstarch
1 cup sugar
1 teaspoon lemon juice
whipped cream (optional)

1. Wash and drain **berries**.
2. Line cooled pastry with layer of berries. In a small pot, set aside 1 cup for glaze.
3. Combine **cornstarch** and **sugar**. Add to reserved fruit for glaze.
4. Cook glaze over medium heat, stirring constantly, until thick and clear.
5. Add **lemon juice**. Cool.
6. Pour over berries in shell. Chill.
7. Serve with whipped cream, if desired.

❖ Strawberry Rhubarb Pie

Parve • 6 to 8 servings

Chilling Time: 30 minutes
Preheat oven to 450°
9-inch pie plate

SHELL

2⅓ cups flour
½ teaspoon salt
½ cup cold shortening
1 large egg lightly beaten
2 teaspoons fresh lemon juice or
   vinegar
1½-2 tablespoons ice water

1. In a bowl, combine **flour** and **salt**. Add **shortening**. Blend until it resembles course meal.
2. Stir in **egg, lemon juice**, or **vinegar**, and enough **ice water** to form a soft ball.
3. Knead the dough lightly to combine.
4. Wrap dough, in waxed paper and chill for 30 minutes or overnight.
5. Roll dough ⅛-inch thick on lightly floured surface. Drape it over pie plate, trim edge, leaving 2-inch overhang.

FILLING

2 cups fresh rhubarb
1 pint fresh strawberries, halved
4 tablespoons cornstarch
3 tablespoons fresh lemon juice
   or to taste
½ teaspoon cinnamon
pinch of ground cloves or
   allspice
1 cup sugar

1. Cut **rhubarb** into 1-inch pieces. In a large bowl combine rhubarb and **strawberries**.
2. In a small bowl whisk together **cornstarch, lemon juice, cinnamon**, and **cloves**. Combine with fruit.
3. Add **sugar**. Let stand for 15 minutes.
4. Spoon filling into the shell and bring the dough over the filling, forming a natural ruffle.
5. Bake the pie for 10 minutes at 450°. Reduce the heat to 350° and bake for 35 to 40 minutes, or until the crust is golden and the filling bubbles.
6. Cool pie for 30 minutes.

Recipe continues on page 257.

Strawberry Rhubarb Pie *(continued)*

GLAZE

¼ cup strawberry preserves, melted
1 tablespoon powdered sugar
whipped cream or ice cream (optional)

Substitution:
1 pound of frozen rhubarb, thawed and drained, can be used in place of fresh rhubarb.

1. Brush crust with **preserves** and sift **powdered sugar** over the crust.
2. Serve with **whipped cream** or **ice cream**.

Note:
Do not use a metal pie plate.

Orange Chiffon Pie

Dairy • 6 servings

Chilling Time: 4 hours
9-inch pie plate

3 ounces lady fingers
1 envelope unflavored gelatin
½ cup sugar
2 eggs, separated
1 cup water
1 6-ounce frozen orange juice, unthawed
¼ teaspoon cream of tartar
2 cups frozen whipped topping, thawed

Variations:
1. One cup heavy cream, whipped, can be substituted for whipped topping.
2. Sponge cake can be used to line the pie plate.

1. Line sides and bottom of pie plate with split **lady fingers**.
2. Combine **gelatin** and **sugar** in a small saucepan. Add **egg yolks** and **water**. Cook over medium heat until gelatin dissolves, stirring occasionally.
3. Remove from heat; add **orange juice**, stirring to dissolve.
4. Place in refrigerator for 15-25 minutes or until orange mixture begins to mound when dropped from a spoon.
5. Beat **egg whites** until frothy. Add **cream of tartar**. Beat until stiff peaks form.
6. Fold egg whites and **whipped topping** into orange mixture.
7. Spoon chiffon mixture into pie plate. Chill.

Pumpkin Cheese Marble Tart

Dairy • 10 to 12 servings

Preheat oven to 400°
Cooking Time: 35 minutes
10-inch springform, ungreased

CRUST . . . .

1 cup flour
¼ cup ground pecans or walnuts
¼ teaspoon salt
4 tablespoons cold butter or
   margarine
1 tablespoon shortening
1 egg yolk
2 tablespoons water

1. In a medium bowl combine
   flour, nuts, and **salt**. Cut in
   butter and **shortening** until
   mixture resembles coarse
   crumbs. Make a well in the
   center.
2. Beat together **egg yolk** and
   water. Add to flour mixture.
   Stir until dough forms a ball.
3. Turn onto a floured surface and
   knead 3 or 4 times. Roll out and
   fit into pan.
4. Prick with a fork. Bake for 10
   minutes at 400°. Cool.

FILLING . . . .

8 ounces cream cheese, softened
½ teaspoon vanilla
⅓ cup sugar
1 tablespoon flour
dash of salt
1 egg
2 tablespoons plus ¼ cup milk
   (divided)
1 cup canned or mashed
   pumpkin (not pie filling)
⅓ cup packed brown sugar
1 teaspoon pumpkin pie spice
½ cup chilled heavy cream,
   whipped, for garnish
½ cup whole pecans or walnuts,
   for garnish

1. Decrease oven temperature to
   375°.
2. Beat **cream cheese** and
   vanilla until fluffy.
3. Add **sugar, flour**, and **salt**.
   Beat until smooth.
4. Add **egg**. Mix until just combined.
5. Stir in 2 tablespoons **milk**.
6. Set aside ½ cup of filling
   mixture.
7. Combine **pumpkin, brown
   sugar**, and **spice** with the ½
   cup filling mixture and remaining ¼ cup milk.
8. Alternately spoon pumpkin
   mixture and cream cheese
   mixture into crust. Swirl with a
   spatula.
9. Bake until top is set.
10. Garnish with **whipped cream**
    and **nuts**.

❖ *Lemon-Layered Alaska Pie*

Dairy • 6 to 8 servings

Chilling Time: Overnight
Preheat oven to 500°
9-inch pie plate

P I E

1 baked shell, pastry or graham
  cracker
6 tablespoons butter
1 teaspoon grated lemon zest
⅓ cup fresh lemon juice
⅛ teaspoon salt
1 cup sugar
2 eggs
2 egg yolks
1 quart vanilla ice cream
  (divided)

1. Melt **butter** in top of double
   boiler. Add **lemon zest, juice,
   salt**, and **sugar**.
2. Combine **eggs** and **egg yolks**.
   Beat lightly.
3. Stir into butter mixture and cook
   over boiling water. Beat constantly with whisk until thick and
   smooth. Cool.
4. Spread half of the **ice cream**
   over the bottom of the cooled
   pie shell. Freeze until firm.
5. Spread half of cooled lemon
   mixture over ice cream. Freeze
   until firm.
6. Cover with remaining ice cream.
   Freeze until firm.
7. Cover with remaining lemon
   mixture and freeze overnight.
8. Spread meringue on pie completely covering the filling. Make
   sure the meringue extends to the
   edge. Pie may be frozen or
   baked at this time.
9. Place pie on baking sheet in very
   hot oven. Bake 3 to 5 minutes
   until meringue is lightly
   browned. Serve immediately.

M E R I N G U E

3 egg whites
¼ cup sugar

1. Beat **egg whites** until they begin
   to hold shape.
2. Add **sugar** 1 tablespoon at a
   time. Continue beating until
   satiny and peaked.

Rich Silky Pie

Dairy • 8 servings

Chilling Time: 3 hours
9-inch pie pan, lightly greased

. . . .

2 cups crushed chocolate
  cookies
6 tablespoons margarine, melted
2 cups heavy cream, chilled
  (divided)
1 egg yolk
12 ounces mini semi-sweet or
  bittersweet chocolate chips
  (divided)

1. Combine **cookie crumbs** with
   margarine. Press into bottom
   and sides of prepared pie pan.
2. In a 2-quart saucepan, combine
   1½ cups of **cream** with **egg
   yolk**. Cook over low heat,
   stirring constantly, just until
   cream comes to a simmer.
   Remove from heat .
3. Add 1½ cups of **chips** and stir
   until smooth.
4. Sprinkle ¼ cup of chips over
   bottom of crust.
5. Pour chocolate mixture over
   crust. Sprinkle remaining chips
   over top of pie, and around
   edge, if desired.
6. Cover and refrigerate until firm.
7. Beat remaining ¼ cup of cream
   until stiff, and decorate top of
   pie.
8. Refrigerate until ready to serve.

Note:
Very rich.

❖ *French Silk Pie*

Dairy • 6 to 8 servings

Preheat oven to 275°
Chilling Time: 4 hours
9-inch pie pan, greased

SHELL

2 egg whites
¼ teaspoon cream of tartar
pinch of salt
½ cup sugar
3 tablespoons finely chopped
  walnuts

1. Beat **egg whites** with **cream of tartar** and **salt** until soft peaks form. When you have soft peaks, gradually add **sugar**. Beat until you have stiff peaks.
2. Spread meringue in prepared pan. Sprinkle with **walnuts**.
3. Bake for 1 hour. Cool on rack.

FILLING

1 stick unsalted margarine,
  softened
¾ cup sugar (divided)
1½ ounces unsweetened
  chocolate, melted and cooled
1 teaspoon vanilla
2 eggs

1. Cream **margarine**. Beat in **sugar**, ¼ cup at a time. Beat this mixture until it is fluffy.
2. Beat in **chocolate** and **vanilla**.
3. Add **eggs**, beating for 5 minutes after each egg.
4. Pour mixture into shell.

TOPPING

1 cup heavy cream, chilled
1 tablespoon coffee flavored
  liqueur
½ ounce semisweet chocolate,
  shaved

1. Beat **cream** until it holds stiff peaks.
2. Fold in **liqueur**.
3. Spread cream on top of pie. Sprinkle with **chocolate**.
4. Chill at least 4 hours.

Note:
This recipe contains uncooked eggs and /or whites.

❖ Chocolate Double Mousse Pie

Dairy • 12 servings

Chilling Time: Overnight
10-inch springform pan,
   ungreased

CRUST

3 cups chocolate cookie crumbs
1 stick unsalted butter, melted

1. Combine **crumbs** and **butter**. Press on bottom and completely up sides of pan.
2. Refrigerate 30 minutes.

FILLING

16 ounces semi-sweet chocolate
2 eggs
4 eggs, separated
2 cups heavy cream, chilled
6 tablespoons powdered sugar

1. Soften **chocolate** in top of a double boiler over simmering water. Let cool to lukewarm. Add whole **eggs** and mix well. Add **yolks** and mix until thoroughly blended.
2. Whip **cream** with **powdered sugar** until soft peaks form. Beat **egg whites** until stiff but not dry.
3. Stir a little of the cream and whites into the chocolate mixture to lighten. Fold in remaining cream and whites until completely blended.
4. Turn into crust and chill at least 6 hours or, preferably, overnight.

TOPPING

1 cup heavy cream, chilled
sugar to taste
8 ounces semi-sweet chocolate
1 tablespoon shortening
waxy leaves

1. Whip **cream** with **sugar** until stiff.
2. Melt **chocolate** and **shortening** in top of double boiler. Using spoon, generously coat underside of **leaves**.
3. Chill or freeze until firm.

Note:
This recipe contains uncooked egg yolks and whites.

Chocolate Double Mousse Pie *(continued)*

1. Loosen crust on all sides using a sharp knife. Remove springform.
2. Spread all but ½ cup whipped cream over top of mousse. Pipe remaining cream into rosettes in center of pie.
3. Separate chocolate from leaves, starting at stem end of leaf. Arrange in pattern around rosettes. Cut pie into wedges with a thin sharp knife.

Note:
This pie can be prepared ahead, frozen, and then thawed overnight in the refrigerator. This is a very rich dessert.

Hint:
To make **chocolate curls**, first warm a square of chocolate in your hand. Then, using a vegetable peeler which has been heated in very hot water, peel shavings from the flat side of the chocolate. If the chocolate begins to flake, repeat warming process.

Baklava Pie

Dairy • 8 to 12 servings

Preheat oven to 300°
Cooking Time: 1 hour, 5 minutes
9-inch pie plate, ungreased

. . . .

C R U S T

12 phyllo leaves (divided)
½ cup melted butter

F I L L I N G

1 cup honey
½ cup sugar
1 tablespoon melted butter
1 tablespoon flour
2 eggs
1 teaspoon vanilla
½ teaspoon cinnamon
¼ teaspoon salt
1¼ cups chopped walnuts

G L A Z E

1 tablespoon melted butter
1 tablespoon honey

Note:
Keep 8 phyllo leaves covered while making crust. See hint.

1. Brush 4 **phyllo leaves**, one at a time, with melted **butter**. Place one leaf into pie plate, extending over rim of plate. Trim excess with a scissors, removing 4 to 5 inches. About an inch should be left extending over the rim. Use the leftover for the next layer, adding a new leaf to complete the layer. Continue until the 4 leaves are used. Tuck all edges under.
2. Beat **honey, sugar, butter, flour, eggs,** and **spices** together. Stir in **walnuts**. Pour into pie plate.
3. Uncover remaining leaves. Brush the top one with butter. Starting at the longer side, fold leaf over by one-third. Roll into a thin rope and twist into a coil. Place in center of nut mixture.
4. Brush second leaf with butter. Fold and roll as first leaf. Place end of rope where coil left off, enlarging coil covering the filling. Continue with remaining leaves until entire nut mixture is covered with the coil.
5. Score coiled leaves with sharp knife one inch from center to one inch from edge, designating serving portion.
6. Bake 1 hour at 300°. Remove pie from oven. Raise oven temperature to 550°.
7. Combine melted **butter** and **honey**. Brush pie with this mixture to glaze.
8. Return pie to oven. Bake until brown, 5 to 6 minutes. Cool before serving.

Hint:
When working with **phyllo**, thaw according to package directions. Unroll the dough onto a sheet of plastic wrap, cover with another sheet of plastic wrap, and then top with a slightly dampened towel. Keep the phyllo covered at all times to prevent drying out.

Blueberry Chill

Dairy • 8 servings

Chilling Time: 2½ hours
Glass bowl

- -

6 ounces raspberry gelatin
1 cup water
15 ounces blueberries
8 ounces crushed pineapple
1 cup finely chopped pecans or
   walnuts
8 ounces frozen whipped
   topping, defrosted

1. Dissolve **gelatin** in boiling
   water. Cool.
2. Add undrained **fruits** and mix.
3. Refrigerate until almost set,
   about 1 hour.
4. Add **nuts**. Fold in **whipped
   topping**.
5. Spoon into brandy snifter or
   glass bowl. Refrigerate until set,
   about 1 hour and 30 minutes.

✡ Strawberry Whip

Dairy • 8 servings

- -

1¼ cups fresh strawberries
1 cup sugar
1 egg white
sponge cake (optional)
whipped topping (optional)

1. Place **berries, sugar**, and **egg
   white** in a bowl and beat with
   an electric mixer until stiff
   enough to hold its shape, about
   10 minutes.
2. Serve on **cake** or mounded in
   sherbet glasses.
3. Garnish with **whipped topping**,
   if desired.

Note:
Can be served frozen.

❖ *Strawberry-Rhubarb Fool*

Dairy • 6 servings

Chilling Time: 1 hour
6 parfait glasses

. . . .

2 cups chopped fresh rhubarb
½ cup plus 2 tablespoons sugar
  (divided)
2 tablespoons water
2 cups sliced fresh strawberries
2 tablespoons orange-flavored
  liqueur
1⅓ cups heavy cream, chilled
fresh strawberries for garnish

1. Combine **rhubarb**, ½ cup **sugar**, and **water** in saucepan. Bring to a boil. Stir until sugar dissolves. Simmer about 10 minutes or until rhubarb is tender. Transfer to a bowl and cool.
2. Purée **strawberries** and 2 tablespoons sugar in a food processor. Mix with rhubarb. Add **liqueur**.
3. Whip **heavy cream** until stiff. Fold into fruit mixture.
4. Spoon into glasses and chill. Garnish with strawberries.

Hints for carefree baking:

1. First **read** the entire recipe to avoid surprises, eg., do I have all the ingredients and the proper size pan?

2. **Measure,** chop, slice and dice ingredients **in advance,** eg., before pouring in pan **check recipe** to ensure all ingredients have been used, even the ones you prepared earlier in the day.

3. **Avoid distractions,** eg., let your answering machine do its job. Turn off the TV.

4. Remember that **temperatures vary** from oven to oven, therefore, baking times will vary too. Know your oven!

5. **Be creative,** salvage your mistakes, eg., overcooked or crumbled cake can be cubed and tossed with strawberries, or any juicy fruit, and whipped cream or pudding. Serve in pretty cups.

❖ Cold Pumpkin Soufflé

Dairy • 4 servings

Chilling Time: 2 hours
6-cup serving bowl or parfait
  glasses

. . . .

1 envelope unflavored gelatin
¼ cup rum
4 eggs
⅔ cup sugar
1 cup canned pumpkin
½ teaspoon cinnamon
½ teaspoon ginger
¼ teaspoon mace
¼ teaspoon ground cloves
1 cup heavy cream, chilled

1. In an oven proof bowl, sprinkle
   gelatin over **rum** to soften.
   Stand the bowl in a pan of
   simmering water and heat. Shake
   occasionally until very thick.
2. In a separate bowl, beat **eggs**
   thoroughly. Gradually add **sugar**
   and continue to beat mixture
   until smooth and very thick.
3. Stir in **pumpkin** and **spices**.
4. Mix in gelatin. Blend well.
5. Whip **cream** until it holds firm
   peaks. Fold into gelatin mixture.
6. Place in serving bowl. Chill until
   set.

Note:
This recipe contains uncooked eggs.

Apple Country Crisp

Parve • 8 servings

Preheat oven to 350°
Cooking Time: 30 minutes
8 x 8 x 2-inch pan, greased

. . . .

3 cups cored, peeled, thinly
  sliced apples
½ cup flour
¾ cup rolled oats
1 tablespoon wheat germ
¼ cup chopped walnuts
½ cup brown sugar
1 teaspoon cinnamon
1 stick margarine

1. Place **apples** into prepared pan.
2. In a small bowl, combine **flour**
   with **oats, wheat germ, walnuts, sugar**, and **cinnamon**.
3. Cut in **margarine** until topping
   is crumbly.
4. Spoon topping over apples.
5. Bake until apples are soft and
   topping is browned.

Fresh Peach Cobbler

Dairy • 9 servings

Preheat oven to 350°
Cooking Time: 30 minutes
9 x 9 x 2-inch pan, ungreased

FILLING

4½ cups peeled, sliced peaches
1 cup sugar
3 tablespoons flour
¾ teaspoon cinnamon

1. Combine **peaches** with **sugar, flour**, and **cinnamon**. Arrange evenly in prepared pan.
2. Spoon topping over fruit to create 9 sections.
3. Bake until topping starts to brown and filling is bubbly.

BATTER TOPPING

1½ cups flour
3 tablespoons sugar
2¼ teaspoons baking powder
¾ teaspoon salt
½ cup oil
4 tablespoons milk
1 egg

1. Combine **flour** with **sugar, baking powder**, and **salt**.
2. Mix **oil** with **milk** and **egg**. Add to dry ingredients and mix until just blended.

Variation:
Any fresh fruit in season may be used.

Peach Blueberry Cobbler

Dairy • 6 to 8 servings

Preheat oven to 350°
Cooking Time: 40 to 45 minutes
8-inch square pan, greased

FRUIT MIXTURE

¼ cup sugar
¼ cup brown sugar
1 tablespoon cornstarch
½ cup water
1 tablespoon lemon juice
29 ounces sliced peaches, drained
10 ounce package frozen blueberries, defrosted, and drained

1. In a saucepan, combine **sugars** and **cornstarch**. Add **water**. Cook over medium heat, stirring constantly, until thick.
2. Add **lemon juice** to **fruit**, then add fruit to thickened sauce.
3. Pour into prepared pan and keep in oven until topping is made.

TOPPING

½ cup plus 2 tablespoons sugar (divided)
1 cup flour
1½ teaspoons baking powder
½ cup milk
¼ cup soft butter
¼ teaspoon nutmeg

1. Sift ½ cup **sugar** with **flour** and **baking powder**.
2. Add **milk** and **butter**. Beat until smooth. Spoon over fruit.
3. Mix remaining 2 tablespoons sugar and **nutmeg** together. Sprinkle over topping.
4. Raise oven temperature to 375°. Bake until topping is lightly browned.

Almond Baked Apples

Dairy • 12 servings

Preheat oven to 425°
Cooking Time: 15 to 20 minutes
13 x 9 x 2-inch greased pan

4 tablespoons butter
¼ cup sugar
1 tablespoon flour
1 tablespoon milk
1 cup sliced almonds
1 teaspoon vanilla
6 large apples
heavy cream, chilled (optional)

1. Over medium heat, melt **butter** with **sugar, flour**, and **milk**.
2. Remove from heat. Stir in **almonds** and **vanilla**.
3. Peel, core and cut **apples** in half.
4. Place apples, rounded sides up, close together in prepared pan.
5. Top with almond mixture.
6. Bake until apples are soft.
7. Pour **cream** over warm apples and serve.

Tipsy Pears

Parve • 8 servings

Preheat oven 375°
Cooking Time: 50 to 60 minutes
13 x 9 x 2-inch pan

SYRUP

1½ cups dry white wine
1¼ cups sugar
shredded zest of two oranges
2 cinnamon sticks
⅓ cup orange liqueur
2 cups cold water

1. Combine **wine, sugar, orange zest, cinnamon sticks, liqueur**, and cold **water** in sauce pan.
2. Boil until sugar is dissolved. Simmer 5 minutes.

PEARS

8 Bosc pears
1 lemon, halved

1. Peel **pears**. Leave stems intact. Cover with cold water, containing **lemon**, until ready to bake.
2. Drain pears and arrange in baking dish. Pour syrup over pears. Cover tightly with foil. Bake 30 minutes.
3. Remove foil and gently turn pears. Replace foil and bake 20 to 30 minutes, or until pears are fork tender.
4. Cool and place pears on serving dish. Pour syrup over pears.

Note:
Can be served warm or chilled.

❖ *Pears Hélène*

Dairy • 6 servings

Large covered saucepan

PEARS

. . . .

3 pears
2 cups water
⅔ cup sugar
1 teaspoon vanilla
6 slices sponge cake (optional)
1 quart vanilla ice cream
hot fudge sauce
crystallized violets (optional)

1. Peel, halve, and core **pears**. Combine **water** and **sugar** and bring to a boil. Add pears, reduce heat. Simmer, covered, 5 minutes, or until pears are pierced easily with a paring knife. Turn pears once while simmering.
2. Add **vanilla**. Let pears cool in syrup.
3. Serve **sponge cake** topped with **ice cream** and drained pear half. Serve with fudge sauce over the top or on the side. Garnish with a **violet**.

HOT FUDGE SAUCE

. . . .

½ cup cocoa
1 cup sugar
1 cup light corn syrup
½ cup light cream or evaporated milk
¼ teaspoon salt
3 tablespoons butter
1 teaspoon vanilla

1. In a saucepan combine **cocoa** with **sugar, syrup, cream, salt**, and **butter**. Cook over medium heat, stirring constantly, until mixture comes to a full rolling boil. Boil briskly 3 minutes, stirring occasionally.
2. Remove from heat and add **vanilla**. Serve warm.

Note:
Sauce can be made ahead and stored in the refrigerator. To reheat, place in a pan of hot, not boiling, water until sauce has thinned to pouring consistency.

❖ Fresh Fruit Trifle with Rum Syrup

Dairy • 12 to 14 servings

Chilling Time: 2 hours
Trifle bowl or 14 cup glass bowl

CUSTARD FILLING

1 cup sugar
5 egg yolks
⅔ cup flour
2 cups boiling milk
1 tablespoon butter
2 teaspoons vanilla
3 tablespoons rum

1. Gradually beat **sugar** into **egg yolks** until mixture is pale yellow, 2 to 3 minutes.
2. Beat in **flour**.
3. Gradually add **milk**, beating continuously.
4. Heat mixture over moderate high heat. Stir. Lumps will smooth out as it is beaten. Boil 1 minute.
5. Remove from heat and add **butter, vanilla**, and **rum**. Refrigerate, covered.

DARK RUM SYRUP

¾ cup water
⅓ cup sugar
3 tablespoons dark rum

1. Combine **water** and **sugar** in a saucepan. Heat until sugar dissolves.
2. Remove from heat and add **rum**. Set aside.

CAKE

1 pound cake
5 cups fresh blueberries, raspberries, dark cherries, or blackberries
1 banana, thinly sliced
½ pint heavy cream, chilled
1 kiwi for garnish

1. Cut **pound cake** into small cubes. Pour rum sauce on top.
2. In a bowl, layer custard, cake, then assorted **fruit** and **banana**. Make 4 to 5 layers.
4. Top with **heavy cream** whipped until stiff. Garnish with **kiwi**.

Substitution:
Frozen, unsweetened fruit, defrosted and drained, can be used.

Note:
Custard filling can be made one day ahead.

Hint:
To keep **cut fruit** from turning brown, toss with citrus juice, or dip in one quart of cold water mixed with three tablespoons of lemon juice.

Festive Fruit Trifle

Dairy • 8 to 12 servings

Chilling Time: 2 hours
Deep bowl or trifle dish

. . . .

1 pound cake
8 ounces sour cream
4 ounces vanilla instant pudding
1 cup milk
½ pint whipping cream, chilled
2 cups sliced fresh strawberries
2 large bananas, sliced and
 brushed with lemon juice
8 ounces pineapple chunks,
 drained
1 ounce semi-sweet chocolate

1. Cut **pound cake** into 2 inch
 cubes and divide into 3 parts.
2. Combine **sour cream**, **pudding**,
 and **milk**.
3. Whip **cream** until stiff.
4. Layer ingredients as follows:
 cake cubes, **strawberries**,
 pudding, cake cubes,
 bananas, **pineapple**, pudding,
 cake cubes.
5. Frost with whipped cream,
 garnish with shaved **chocolate**.

Easy Chocolate Mousse

Dairy • 6 to 8 servings

Chilling Time: Overnight
Individual dessert glasses

. . . .

4 tablespoons butter, unsalted
4 ounces semi-sweet chocolate
4 eggs, separated

1. Melt **butter** and **chocolate**
 together in a double-boiler.
 Let cool.
2. Separate **eggs**.
3. Beat **egg whites** until stiff.
4. Add **yolks**, one at a time, to
 melted chocolate mixture.
5. Gradually, fold egg whites into
 chocolate mixture.
6. Spoon into individual glasses,
 or a 4 cup soufflé dish.
 Refrigerate overnight.

Note:
This recipe contains uncooked egg
yolks and whites.

Rum Chocolate Mousse

Dairy • 6 servings

Chilling Time: 2 hours

- -

4 eggs, separated
1 cup chocolate chips
5 tablespoons boiling water
2 tablespoons dark rum
whipped topping for garnish

1. In a small bowl, beat **egg whites** until stiff.
2. In a blender, process **chocolate chips** for 6 seconds. Scrape down sides of blender.
3. Add boiling **water** and blend for 10 seconds.
4. Add **egg yolks** and **rum**. Blend for 3 seconds. Transfer to a large bowl.
5. Gradually, fold egg whites into chocolate mixture.
6. Spoon into dessert cups. Garnish with **whipped topping**. Refrigerate at least 2 hours.

Note:
This recipe contains uncooked egg yolks and whites.

❖ Maple Pecan Parfait

Dairy • 6 servings

Freezing Time: 2 hours
6 individual dessert glasses

- -

¾ cup maple syrup
2 stiffly beaten egg whites
1 teaspoon vanilla
1 cup heavy cream, whipped
¾ cup chopped pecans (divided)

1. Bring **maple syrup** to a boil. Maple syrup comes to a boil quickly. Cook until it spins a light thread (228°) on a candy thermometer.
2. Fold syrup, gradually, into the beaten **egg whites**. Continue to beat until meringue is very thick, about 8 minutes.
3. Stir in **vanilla**.
4. Fold in **whipped cream** and ½ cup **pecans**.
5. Spoon into 6 serving cups. Sprinkle with remaining pecans.
6. Freeze for at least 2 hours.

Note:
This recipe contains uncooked egg whites.

No Cook Fudge

Parve • 64 pieces

Chilling Time: 20 minutes
8 x 8-inch pan, ungreased

. . . .

2 sticks margarine, melted
1 teaspoon vanilla
3 tablespoons cocoa
1 pound powdered sugar
1 cup peanut butter
walnuts (optional)

1. With an electric mixer, beat **margarine, vanilla, cocoa, powdered sugar**, and **peanut butter** together until well blended.
2. Pour into pan. Garnish with **walnuts**. Place in refrigerator until set.
3. Cut into 1-inch squares.

Hot Fudge Sauce

Dairy • 1½ cups

1-quart pot

. . . .

6 ounces chocolate chips
5 ounces evaporated milk
⅓ cup light corn syrup

1. Place **chips, milk**, and **syrup** in top of a double boiler.
2. Heat over hot water, not boiling, until chips are melted.

Note:
This keeps for up to 1 month in a refrigerator. It can be reheated in a microwave oven.

The Jewish Home Auxiliary of Rochester, New York, thanks the members, families and friends who have contributed to this book. We sincerely hope that no one has been inadvertently overlooked. We regret that we were unable to include many quality recipes which were submitted due to similarity or availability of space.

Jackie Aab
Judy Abelman
Helen Abelson
D. Abrams
Judy Ackerman
Barbara Adams
Devra Adelstein
Rose Adelstein
Elaine Adler
Miriam Ahitow
Cheryl Albanese
Annabelle Albaranes
Sue Albert
Lee Alderman
Judith K. Alderman
Anna Alent
Miriam Altman
Betty Alva
Yetta Ambush
Arlie Anderson
Janet Anderson
Lani Anderson
P.R. Anderson
Sharon Andolina
Anonymous
Geraldine Appelbaum
Caroline Arditi
Sandra Arnold
Julia Aroeste
Gail Aroeste
Ann Astarita
Etta Atkin
Yvonne Attie
Margie Axelrod
Joyce Axelrod
Jan Bachofer
Irene Baechtold
Sharon Baechtold
Edna Bailey
Margery Baittle

Becky Baker
James Baker
Janis Baker
Lee Baker
Sandra Baker
Michele Barbero
Sarah Barbero
Susan Barclay
Molley Barnett
Bea Baron
Elaine Baskin
Anita Bauman
Linda Bean
Zelda Becker
Hazel Beckerman
Arlene Belicove
David Belicove
Lorie Ben-Ezra
Marlene Bender
Carol Bennett
Violet Bennett
Kimberly Berge
Fraida Berger
Marcy Berger
Nancy Berk
Millie Berman
Sally Berman
Maureen Bermas
Irma Bernstein
Merle Bernstein
Pamela Martel
   Bernstein
Elia Bianchetto
Pat Bianchi
Pat Bielawa
Jean Billington
Bonnie Birkhan
Janice Birnbaum
Joel Bloom
Lee Bloom

Ruth Bloom
Elaine Blum
Terri Bobry
Betsy Bobry
Deborah Bohli
Nannette Bordenstein
Joan Bouthillier
Richard Braiman
Shirley Braiman
Josephine Braitman
Nancy Brandriss
Joanne Brandt
Elaine Brauer
Lillian Braveman
Ruth Braverman
Barbara Braverman
Sandy Brenner
Neil Brenner
Sue Brent
Rose Bresloff
Carol Brickman
Henra Briskin
Sarah Brodsky
Marcia Bronsther
Betsy Brugg
Beth Bruner
John Buhr
Sarah Bullard
Sonya Burgher
Janet Neff Bush
Sally Calderon
Emily Camhi
Ruth Capell
Patricia Capellazzi
Charlene Caplan
Molla Carr
Sharon Cerasoli
John Chacchia
Rivka Chatman
Pamela Cheek

Annabeth Chickering
Tricia Christensen
Nancy Cianciotto
Valerie Ciufo
Joan Clar
Cyndie Clark
Holly Clark
Marty Clayton
Harriet Clifton
Ellen Cody-Wrobel
Norma Coblenz
Ada Cohen
Bruce Cohen
Charlotte Cohen
Doris E. Cohen
Dorothy Cohen
Elyse Cohen
Eric Cohen
Fran London Cohen
Gloria Cohen
Harry Cohen
Heather Cohen
Helen Cohen
Ilene Cohen
Pincus Cohen
Rose Shechet Cohen
S. Nelson Cohen
Suzanne Cohen
Sally Coilan
Ethel Coleman
Mary Joe Colligan
Ludmilla Condello
Lori Conway
Helen Cooper
Lillian Courtheoux
Cornelia Cowles
Leslie Crane
Agatha Crumb
Eleanor Cushing
Denise Mann Cyrkin

Elizabeth Daniel
Eileen Daniel
Liz Daniel
Jackie Davidson
Maureen Davies
Deborah Davis
Diane Davis
Marcia Davis
Mariam Davis
Peg Davis
Joan Dempsey
Johanna Gitlin DePuyt
Sarah Derman
Sheryl Diana
Marge DiLiddo
Judy Dixon
Maureen Dobies
Ann Dorfman
Kay Dorr
Rhea Drexler
Sandy Dreyfuss
Lee Dubickas
Kala Dunsky
Anita Dushay
Lorraine Dvorin
Rhana Greenberg
    Dyme
Ilene Steron Eddy
Marcia Eisenberg
Virginia Eisenhart
Ben Eisenstein
Lee Eldredge
Barbara Elkind
Marcia Elwitt
Judy Engerman
Constance English
Florence Eppstein
Louise Epstein
Nadine Erdle
Tiffany Erdle
Marvin Erlichman
Faith Ertischek
Shirley Fagenbaum
Lillian Fain
Dotty Feinberg
Ethel Feldman
Judy Feller
Bess Fenster
Remy Fenster
Howard Fernandez
Karen Fernandez
Barbara Fine
Shelly Fine
Janet Fink
Janet Fisher
Sultana Fisher

Heidi Fishman
Michele FitzSimmons
Alex Flessig
Danielle Flessig
Kevin Flessig
Pam Fox
Marilyn Frank
Judith Frankel
Beth Freedman
Lee Friedman
Ilene Fund
Carol Fybush
Jan Ryan Gan
Annette Garver
Donna Karen Genier
Essie Germanow
Shoshana Germanow
Claudia Giffen
Gail Gilberg
Juliene Gilbert
Joan Gilels
Leona Ginsberg
Mary Jane Gissin
Shelly Gitlin
Jill Glazer
Rachel Glazer
Jessica Glidden
Ann Carol Goldberg
Eva Goldberg
Jill Goldberg
Julia Goldberg
SoraLee Goldberg
Donna Golden
Ruth Goldenberg
Barbara Goldman
Caroline Goldman
Eileen Goldman
Eleanor Goldman
Gussie Goldman
Joyce Goldman
Ruth R. Goldman
Doreen Goldstein
Inga Goldstein
Ruth Goldstein
David Gordon
Ginnie Gordon
Lil Gordon
Rachel Gordon
Miriam Gotesman
Fay Gottfried
Mim Greenberg
Ellen Greenfield
Maxine Greenfield
Roger Greiten
Roz Griesbach
Bev Groden

Bernard Gross
Diane Gross
Paula Gross
Rabbi Marc Gruber
Harold Gupp
Helene Gupp
Cynthia Gurell
Sandy Gurev
Paula Gutkin
Carol Sue Hai
Sharon Hall
Sherry Hall
Edith Halpern
Noreen Halpern
Sherrie Handelman
Susan Harf
Felice Harris
Beth Anne Hawn
Carm Heidt
June Helberg
Shirley Helderman
Shoshana Herman
Virginia Herraro
Lisa Hersh
Barbara Higgins
Judy Hirschberg
Carol Nobel Hirsh
Ronnie Hirst
Sally Hirst
Penni Hirtenstein
Laurie Hoffend
Polly Hoffend
Elaine Hoffman
Nancy Yanes Hoffman
Sheryl Hogan
Barbara Hollander
Connie Hoover
Shirley Horowitch
Beth Hurwitz
Lucy Hutchinson
Norma Hyman
Marilyn Rosen Hymes
Liz Iman
Chana Isaacs
Susan Itkin
Eileen Jachles
Mercelle Jackson
Phyllis Jackson
Sarah Jackson
David Jacobs
Joan Jacobs
Dr. Florence Jacoby
Paula Greenberg
    Jarnicki
Debbie Jaun
Nancy Ann Jeffreys

Pat Johns
Marybeth Julian
Ruth Kahn
Nina Kalen
Thelma Kandell
Maggie Kane
Cookie Kaplan
Gloria Kaplan
Judy Kaplan
Phyllis Kaplan
Deborah Karlin
Florence Kasanov
Karen Kasanov
Kathy Kasanov
Mariam Katiatz
Michelle Katon
Muriel Katz
Ruth Katz
Betty Katzen
Fran Kaufman
Heidi Kaufman
Laura Kaufman
Naomi Kaufman
Phyllis Kaukeinen
Gail Kayson
Kay Keogh
Belle Kessler
Debbie Kinel
Bob Kinney
Charlotte Kinney
Pearl Kissel
Linda F. Klafter
Beverly Klass
Alysia Kleeberg
Eileen Kleeberg
Maureen Klein
Rheva Kleinberg
Marla Kleinman
Marty Kleinman
Penelope Kleinman
Michelle Klepper
Lois Klonick
Patti Kluge
Jacob Kluger
Lois Kluger
Leslie Knapp
Marian Kobrin
Dvorah Kolko
Mona Friedman Kolko
Deborah Korus
Shirley Kosaw
Laura Kosmerl
Beth Kosoff
Ann Kraska
Nancy Kraus
Gail Kravitz

Arthur D. Kuh
Edward S. Kuh
Lawrence H. Kuh
Lisa Porter Kuh
Jack Kunz
Susan Kur
Harriet Kurz
Jack Kurz
Myrna LaBaer
Kelly LaBocca
Nancy Lampe
Terry LaPaglia
Phyllis Lasky
Kathy Lasser
Micki Lasser
Rita Laws
Larry Lays
Martha Lays
Suzanne Cunningham
   Lays
Mildred Lazarus
Ruth Lazarus
Sylvia Lazeroff
Bonnie Lebowitz
Donna Lederman
Annette Lee
Lenore Lesser
Elise Lestin
Rose Levin
Jacqueline Levine
Val Levine
Arlean Levinson
Florence Levinson
Gordon Levinson
Tillie Levinson
Wendy Levinson
Susan Levintir
Lee Levy
Bess Lewinson
Bess Lewis
Rabbi Judith Lewis
Marilyn Lewis
Sylvia Lewis
Suzanne Ley
Olive Liberman
Sanford Liebschutz
Sarah F. Liebschutz
Denise Lippa
Susan Lippman
Linda Lipson
Jane Littwitz
Barbara Lovenheim
John Lovenheim
June Lovenheim
Karen Lustig
Audrey Luxemberg

Lisa Luxemberg
Chris Maas
Len Maas
Linda MacDuffie
Mildred Mammano
Maureen Mandwelle
Honey Manson
Judy Mark
Ruth Markin
Dina Markowitz
Sheila Markowitz
Mary Marone
Myra Marsey
Judy Marshall
Lisa Marvald
Camille Marzouk
Carol Maskiell
Sherri McArdle
Marie McGuigan
Pamela McNelly
Bob Meisel
Susan Meisel
Anne Mellen
Cindy Merrill
Sidney Metzger
Lauren C. Meyer
Paula Meyers
Cindy Michl-
   Welchman
Alana Miller
Andrea Miller
Carol Miller
Caroline Miller
Gail Miller
Hinda Miller
Mona Miller
Ruth Gordon Miller
Ruth Miller
Phyllis Mills
Hyla Mink
Sandra Missal
Betty Mock
Shannon Mock
Pam Morgan
Randy Morganstern
Arlene Morris
Brenda Moss
Irma Moss
Gail B. Katz Mount
Patty Mummert
Martin Nacman
Shirley Naimark
Bruce Newman
Grace Newman
Helene Newman
Iris Newman

Karen Newman
Maxine Newman
Rona Newman
Helen Gartner Nobel
Shirley Nobel
Kathleen Nojay
Linda Novak
Louise Novros
Joan Nusbaum
Susan Nusbaum
Ricko Ogaki
Beth Olenski
Betty Oppenheimer
Margaret
   Oppenheimer
Denise O'Reilly
Ann Osterwinter
Molly Panner
Jonathan Papkin
Karen Pariser
Carol Patagonia
Heidi Payment
Shula Pearlman
Ruth Peck
Helen Perry
Maxine Peters
Alyne Phillips
Beth Phillips
Debbie Phillips
Florence Phillips
Dorothy Pies
Penny Pinsky
Judy Pitlick
Janette Porretti
Virginia Posner
Mary Prevost
Nancy Price
Grace Priceman
Joanne Prives
Jean Quigley
Jeffrey Quigley
Nancy Quigley
Janice Rachfal
Mary Ellen Rakiewicz
Rosalie Rapkin
Bea Rapowitz
Abbey Rasnick
Marilyn Reich
Janet Remizowski
Janice Resnick
Amy Ressel
Margarita Reyzelman
Candice Richardson
Jane Richardson
Rochelle Richter
Dr. Malvin Ring

Beverly Robbins
Bill Robert
Beverly Robinson
Cheryl Robinson
Gary Robinson
Stuart Robinson
Diane Rock
Carrie Rogers
Beverly Gold Rose
Sharon Rose
Ellen Rosen
Irene Rosen
Maxine Rosen
Mildred Rosenbaum
Renee Rosenbaum
Shirley Rosenbaum
Sunny Rosenberg
Hannah Rosenblatt
Karen Rosenbloom
Susan Rosenbloom
Shirley Rosenthal
Alice Rosenzweig
Rachel Rosner
Amy Roth
Ann Rotit
Ray Roveda
Bea Roxin
Helen Rubens
Jane Rubens
Linda Rubens
Linda Ruda
Marilyn Rudin
Sandra Rulnick
Jane Rushefsky
Margie Sabath
Fred Saburro
Marlene Salamone
Ruth Salesin
Florine Sands
Elaine Sanzel
Wendy Sax
Cheryl Scalera
Sandy Schiffman
Dorothy Schiller
Beth Schlabach
Deborah A. Schluter
Robert C. Schluter
John Schoonmaker
Carol Schott
Eloise Schrag
Libby Schreiber
Mildred Schrier
Dorothy Schuller
Jacquie Schuster
Caroline Schwartz
Edith Tobe Schwartz

Elaine Schwarz
Howard Schecter
Joan Segal
Esther Seidberg
Shirlee Seidberg
Arlene Seideman
Edna Seidmann
Harriet Seigal
Helen Senzel
Amy Shaffer
Deborah Silverman
    Shames
Ellen Shapiro
Linda Glass Shapiro
Irene Shapiro
Anita Shaw
Rhoda Sherman
Lotte Shimberg
Dawn Shulman
Debby Shulman
Devorah Shulman
Mynne Shulman
Nancy Silberstein
Bert Silver
Naomi Silver
Carol Silverman
Lisa Silverman
Norma Silverman
Toby Silverman
Norma Silverstein
Elaine Simon
Marion Simon
Susan Simon
Dr. Phyllis Skolnick
Barbara Slater
Theda Sloan

Dr. Judi Smetana
Emma Smith
Esther Solomon
Susan Spector
Sally Spencer
Lois Spero
Glenna Spindelman
Louise Spivack
Florence Sporn
Nancy Sprenkle
Edith Stein
Marcia Stein
Beth Sterman
Sandy Stern
Elaine Stirk
Patricia Stocker
Adele Stoler
Evalyn Stoler
Jackie Stoler
Rosemarie Stout
J. Strep
Fran Studley
Lillian Sukert
Yola Sukr
Barbara Sullivan
Caroline Sundell
Carol Swallow
Jackie Swift
Margy Taylor
Marilyn Teel
Sandy Temkin
Virginia Tierney
Angela Terry
Dorothy Testa
Eileen Testa
Sharon Thaler

Harriet "Bing" Thayer
Alison Thayer
Doris Toal
Mollie Traub
Sherry Treviso
Lorraine Tyra
Rita Underberg
Carol Vallese
Joan VandenBrul
Nancy VanHooydonk
Joanne Viener
Louise Vigdor
Abe Vigoda
Dorise Vigoda
Elaine Vigoda
Brenda Viola
Blossom Voldman
Dorothy Wallace
Enid Wallack
Trudy Wandtke
Janie Warshaw
Liz Webb
Florence Wecksler
Karyn Weeks
Nancy Weinreb
Beverly Weinstein
Linda Shapiro
    Weinstein
Myrna Weinstein
Sherri Weinstein
Ann D. Weintraub
Mary Jane Wenner
Judy Wertheimer
Kevin Wexler
Sydelle Wexler
Joan Wheeler

Lois Whitcomb
Jean Whitney
Diane E. M. Wiant
Rachel Wicks
Barbara Wickstrom
Leona Willey
Marion Wilmont
Ann Gilbert
    Winterman
Carol Winterman
Julie Winterman
Margie Wiseman
Dawn Wisset
Rose Witrack
Eileen Wolff
Florence Wollen
Anna Wolitsky
Sharon Wong
Pat Woods
Pearl Wostl
Ellen Cody Wrobel
Janet Wurl
Rose Yosovitz
Carol Yunker
Jessica Yunker
Kirsten Zaborny
Ruth Zax
Joyce Zinkin
Sybil Zitrin
Alice Zloth
Susan Zloth
Sarisa Zoghlin
Harriet Zweig

Glossary Of Jewish Food Terms

Blintz
A crepe-like pancake with a filling

Challah
An egg bread, often baked in braided or twisted form.

Gefilte Fish
A mixture of ground fish, crumbs, eggs, and seasonings, usually shaped into balls, and simmered in a fish stock

Hamantashen
Triangular-shaped, filled cookies

Kneidlach
Soup dumplings made with matzoh meal

Knish
A round of rich dough with a meat, cheese, or potato filling that is baked

Kosher/Kashrut
A system of Jewish dietary laws

Kreplach
Triangular pockets of noodle dough filled with ground meat or cheese, usually served in soup

Kugel
Pudding made from noodles, potatoes, or raw vegetables

Latke
Pancake usually made from grated raw potatoes

Matzoh
Unleavened bread

Parve
A neutral food product containing neither meat, milk, nor their by-products

Passover
Jewish festival of freedom, celebrating the exodus from Egypt

Tzimmes
Sweetened, baked combination of yams, carrots, and dried fruits with or without meat.

E Q U I V A L E N T S

Some desserts made with dairy ingredients can be made Parve, or neutral, by substituting a non-dairy liquid creamer for milk or cream, Parve margarine for butter, and non-dairy whipped topping for whipped cream. Substitute vegetable broth for chicken broth to make some dishes Parve.

Kosher substitute for milk or cream: *Mix ½ cup chicken stock with 1 egg yolk and 1 teaspoon of cornstarch for each ½ cup of milk or cream.*

EQUIVALENTS

¼ cup egg substitute = *1 egg*
1 stick butter or margarine = *½ cup*
¼ pound cheddar cheese = *1 cup grated*
1 teaspoon dried, crumbled herbs = *1 tablespoon fresh*
2 medium carrots = *1 cup diced*
1 large onion = *1 cup chopped*
1 medium bell pepper = *¾ cup diced*
6 ounces chocolate chips = *1 cup*
1 medium lemon yields *2 to 3 tablespoons juice*
1 medium lemon yields *1 tablespoon grated zest*
1 medium orange yields *6 to 8 tablespoons juice*
1 medium orange yields *about 2 tablespoons zest*
1 cup heavy cream = *2 cups whipped*
14 graham cracker squares = *1 cup crumbs*
1 cup whole almonds = *8 ounces*
1 cup whole walnuts = *6 ounces*
1 cup raisins = *6 ounces*
3 teaspoons = *1 tablespoon*
2 tablespoons = *1 fluid ounce*
4 tablespoons = *¼ cup*
5⅓ tablespoons = *⅓ cup*
1 cup = *8 fluid ounces*
1 cup cottage cheese = *8 ounces*
⅛ teaspoon garlic powder = *1 small clove*
1 cup raw rice = *3 cups cooked*
2¼ cups packed brown sugar = *1 pound*
2 cups granulated sugar = *1 pound*
3½ cups powdered sugar = *1 pound*

For Passover
1 cup flour = *½ cup matzoh cake meal or ¾ cup potato starch*
½ cup flour = *2 tablespoons matzoh cake meal or 6 tablespoons potato starch*
1 cup powdered sugar: *1 cup sugar minus 2 tablespoons sugar*
Pulverize sugar in a blender. Sift with 1½ teaspoons potato starch.

(See page 280 for other substitutes)

I N D E X

D – *Dairy*   *P* – *Pareve*   *M* – *Meat*   ✿ – *Holiday*

D – *Dairy*   *P* – *Pareve*   *M* – *Meat*   ✡ – *Holiday*

D – *Dairy*   **P** – *Pareve*   **M** – *Meat*   ✿ – *Holiday*

D – Dairy   *P* – Pareve   *M* – Meat   ✡ – Holiday

D – *Dairy*   **P** – *Pareve*   **M** – *Meat*   ✡ – *Holiday*

D – Dairy   **P** – Pareve   **M** – Meat   ✡ – Holiday

D – Dairy   P – Pareve   M – Meat   ✡ – Holiday

D – *Dairy*   ***P*** – *Pareve*   ***M*** – *Meat*   ✡ – *Holiday*

D – *Dairy*   **P** – *Pareve*   **M** – *Meat*   ✿ – *Holiday*

D – Dairy   *P* – Pareve   *M* – Meat   ✡ – Holiday

D – *Dairy*   **P** – *Pareve*   **M** – *Meat*   ✿ – *Holiday*

D – *Dairy*   **P** – *Pareve*   **M** – *Meat*   ✿ – *Holiday*

Order Form

Mail to:
BEYOND CHICKEN SOUP
JEWISH HOME OF ROCHESTER
2021 WINTON ROAD SOUTH
ROCHESTER, NY 14618

NAME _____

ADDRESS _____ APT. _____

CITY _____ STATE _____ ZIP_____

PHONE NUMBER   (_____)_____

BEST TIME TO CALL _____

Please send me the following order	QUANTITY	X	PRICE	=	AMOUNT
Beyond Chicken Soup			$19.95		
Make checks payable to: **BEYOND CHICKEN SOUP** Please do not send cash. Sorry, no COD orders. All orders shipped to a NYS address must include New York State sales tax (at the appropriate rate) on the total of books plus shipping costs. Payment by MasterCard or Visa acceptable. Please PRINT legibly.	SHIPPING & HANDLING $3.00 *First copy to address above*				
	ADDITIONAL COPIES @ $1.50 *mailed to the same address*				
	SUBTOTAL				
	N.Y.S. SALES TAX *at appropriate rate*				
	TOTAL AMOUNT				

Thank you for your order

METHOD OF PAYMENT

☐ Check enclosed $_____ | Charge to: ☐ MASTERCARD ☐ VISA

ACCOUNT NUMBER

_____

SIGNATURE (as shown on credit card is required for authorization)   EXPIRATION DATE

Gift Shipments. Use spaces on other side. If more space is needed, attach a separate sheet. Your name and address must be on each sheet.

SEE
OTHER
SIDE

SHIPPING INFORMATION
FOR ADDITIONAL BOOKS ORDERED

For each address—$3. for first book. Additional books $1.50 each

NAME _____

ADDRESS _____ APT. # _____

CITY _____ STATE _____ ZIP _____

NAME _____

ADDRESS _____ APT. # _____

CITY _____ STATE _____ ZIP _____

NAME _____

ADDRESS _____ APT. # _____

CITY _____ STATE _____ ZIP _____

NAME _____

ADDRESS _____ APT. # _____

CITY _____ STATE _____ ZIP _____

NAME _____

ADDRESS _____ APT. # _____

CITY _____ STATE _____ ZIP _____

NAME _____

ADDRESS _____ APT. # _____

CITY _____ STATE _____ ZIP _____

. . . .

The proceeds from the sale of BEYOND CHICKEN SOUP will be
used to further enhance the quality of life for the residents of the
Jewish Home. Many of these vital, on-going programs are supported
by the Jewish Home Auxiliary and staffed by our volunteers/members.
For more information about the Auxiliary, check here. ➡ ☐